This text is available in a variety of formats—print and digital. Check your favorite digital provider for your e-text, including **CourseSmart, Kindle, Nook,** and **more**. To learn more about our programs, pricing options, and customization, visit

Reaching Audiences

A Guide to Media Writing

SIXTH EDITION

Jan Johnson Yopp

University of North Carolina at Chapel Hill

Katherine C. McAdams

University of Maryland at College Park

Boston   Columbus   Indianapolis   New York   San Francisco   Upper Saddle River
Amsterdam   CapeTown   Dubai   London   Madrid   Milan   Munich   Paris   Montréal   Toronto
Delhi   Mexico City   São Paulo   Sydney   Hong Kong   Seoul   Singapore   Taipei   Tokyo

Editor in Chief: Ashley Dodge
Senior Acquisitions Editor: Melissa Mashburn
Editorial Assistant: Megan Hermida
Executive Marketing Manager: Kelly May
Marketing Coordinator: Theresa Rotondo
Media Producer: Paul DeLuca
Digital Media Editor: Lisa Dotson
Production Project Manager: Romaine Denis
Project Coordination, Text Design, and
  Electronic Page Makeup: Anandakrishnan Natarajan,
  Integra Software Services Pvt. Ltd.
Creative Director: Jayne Conte
Cover Designer: Suzanne Duda
Printer/Binder: Courier, Inc./Westford
Cover Printer: Courier, Inc./Westford

Credits and acknowledgments borrowed from other sources and reproduced, with permission, in this textbook appear on the appropriate page within text.

Library of Congress Cataloging-in-Publication Data
Yopp, Jan Johnson, author.
  Reaching Audiences : A Guide to Media Writing/Jan Johnson Yopp, University of North Carolina at Chapel Hill; Katherine C. McAdams, University of Maryland at College Park.—6th ed.
    pages cm
  Previous edition: Reaching Audiences/Jan Johnson Yopp, Katherine C. McAdams, Ryan M. Thornburg, 2010, 5th ed.
  Includes bibliographical references and index.
  ISBN-13: 978-0-205-87437-8
  ISBN-10: 0-205-87437-1
  1. Mass media—Authorship.   2. Mass media—Audiences.   I. McAdams, Katherine C., author.   II. Title.
  P96.A86M38 2014
  808.06'6302—dc23
                                                                2012040708

1 2 3 4 5 6 7 8 9 10 —V092— 18 17 16 15 14 13

ISBN-13: 978-0-205-87440-8
ISBN-10:   0-205-87440-1

Contents

PART THREE ▪ *Gathering Information*

Preface

More than 20 years ago, we had a great idea: We wanted to create a book about the core skills needed for all media writing—the skills writers need so they can reach audiences anywhere, in any medium, on any topic. Today our little book is more valuable than ever in a world where media delivery changes almost daily, creating a rich chaos that is challenging for writers and audiences.

The 24/7 information world has changed almost everything we do as professional communicators and has made streamlined messages more important than ever. Now the audience must have simple structures that can be easily understood, updated, re-posted, or revised. Regardless of communications platform—blog or website; social media sites like Twitter; radio, video, or print—core principles of clear writing remain unchanged.

New to the Sixth Edition

In editing the Sixth Edition, we have focused again on teaching writers to reach active audiences in a vibrant, fast-changing world by applying age-old principles of good communication. The 14 chapters in this book stress the basic writing skills essential to any student in any mass communication field. The essentials of good writing apply to all writers, regardless of platform.

Key improvements and additions in this new edition include:

- Full revision of the text that expands the traditional emphasis on print and broadcast media to include all media—new media, mobile media, social media—as they relate to communications fields from news reporting, to marketing, to public relations. New examples have been selected from a broad array of media and other sources. Outdated language and technologies have been checked and edited to ensure that references are inclusive and up to date.

- More than ever, a focus on effective writing for all media writers. In Chapter 5 "Getting to the Point," the section "Writing Leads for Digital Media" also introduces the concept of search engine optimization. The online chapter has been extensively revised to highlight approaches to online writing (Chapter 8). The chapter on various formats for media writing has been moved up to Chapter 7, placing emphasis on nondeadline writing and alternatives to the inverted pyramid style. Effects of new technology and social media are explored in Chapter 14, "Strategic Communication."

- Throughout the book, more attention is paid to effects of the 24/7 news cycle, including the perpetual demand for new information for and from audiences. This constant need affects journalists, public relations practitioners, and social media marketers who must be careful researchers, wordsmiths, and editors. Around-the-clock demands on writers create new requirements: to maintain core values of accuracy, completeness, and relevancy while meeting deadlines that come every hour, or even more frequently. The Sixth Edition reminds writers of increased needs for information for their respective audiences.

- New coverage of legal considerations raised by working online and in social media such as Twitter.

- Standards of performance for today's multiplatform journalists that permeate each chapter, particularly the need for critical thinking in making decisions about content and modes of delivery. A refrain throughout the revised book is that accuracy is a must for every writer every day.

- A renewed and stronger charge to media writers that guides the reader through the Sixth Edition: Writers must adjust to and take advantage of new technology and, at the same time, stay focused on providing content that is well crafted in the style that fits the message.

Messages today are shorter and are sent to pocket-sized devices that our audiences are never without. We clearly embrace technology with all its changes and challenges. Without it, we would not have been able to revise this text efficiently and easily.

Part One of the book presents the basic components of the writing process and the critical role of audiences. Students will learn the need for accuracy and specific ways to improve writing—from word selection and sentence length to grammar and usage. Students also will learn the steps of editing, a crucial part of the writing process for any delivery system.

Part Two shows students how to write leads for different media and how to organize story formats, including those for online and social media.

Part Three discusses how to gather information through three principal methods: research, observation, and interviewing. Students also are introduced to online searches and resources as well as the dangers of libel and unethical conduct in information gathering and how to avoid bias in writing.

Part Four discusses specific kinds of media writing: broadcast and strategic communication, often referred to as public relations and advertising. These types of messages also must be formatted to reach particular audiences within social media and emerging media platforms.

The appendices to the text contain the answer keys to the self-guided grammar and math tests as well as the full text of an article used as an example at several points in the book.

By the time students read this edition, technology will have changed from what exists as we write this sentence. Technology changes. The importance of good writing does not.

What's Ahead for Today's Students

Just as technology allows users to access information faster and more selectively, it also allows communicators to create multiplatform messages efficiently and quickly. Those messages will flow from the point of creation to audiences that will use the information and even resend or repurpose it in ways the writer can't predict. Today's communicators must create messages that have value and integrity, wherever their final destinations might be.

Students in journalism and mass communication programs today already are familiar with video, audio, and social media. Many of their messages are about themselves, so they are aware of techniques that work on a small scale to reach family and friends.

To become the professional communicators of tomorrow, students must extend their present knowledge, learning to see a world of events and ideas as possible subjects for messages and to see a diverse array of groups, organizations, and even populations as potential audiences. The emphasis in this Sixth Edition—on critical thinking, on the 24/7 news cycle, and on new media and their audiences—will help students develop the news sense and critical-thinking skills needed in today's challenging media environment.

Technology allows anyone with information to put it out for public view. But without clear content and style, much published information, however easily accessed, might be difficult for audiences to understand.

Whether the message is a Tweet or a 2,500-word article, students who want to become exceptional communicators must know how to gather

information, sort it, and put it in a format audiences will notice and understand. They must be willing to check for accuracy, including checking for
sources' authenticity. And they must use critical-thinking skills to connect the
message with their audiences.

The sequence of content in the Sixth Edition is designed to take each
student through a set of experiences that will shape the skills and attitudes of a
professional communicator, one who recognizes and manages the communication challenges of today and is equipped for the changes to come.

Jan Johnson Yopp
Katherine C. McAdams
2013

Acknowledgments

Instructor and Student Resources

Key instructor resources include an *Instructor's Manual with Workbook* (ISBN 0205874398). Please contact your Pearson representative regarding options for creating a custom version of our text that includes the workbook exercises. The *Instructor's Manual* is available at www.pearsonhighered.com/irc (access code required).

For a complete listing of the instructor and student resources available with this text, please visit the Reaching Audiences e-Catalog page at www.pearsonhighered.com.

Writing a book is never the work of just the individuals whose names are under the title, and so it is with this book and its Sixth Edition. A number of colleagues and friends have provided invaluable contributions.

The core of the book would not have been done without Kevin Davis of Macmillan, who many years ago saw the potential in our initial concept and encouraged us to write.

We thank Melissa Mashburn, Megan Hermida, and Romaine Denis for their guidance and assistance on the sixth edition as well as Anandakrishnan Natarajan at Integra-PDY and the proofreading staff for their attention to detail in editing the manuscript.

We also thank the University of North Carolina at Chapel Hill: Assistant Professor Daren Brabham, Senior Lecturer David Cupp, Assistant Professor Trevy McDonald, Associate Professor Andy Bechtel, Associate Professor Lois Boynton, Associate Professor Rhonda Gibson, Professor John Sweeney, Professor-Emerita Ruth Walden, librarian Stephanie Brown, and Lecturer-Emerita Val Lauder. At Towson University, we thank Professor Beth Haller. We also thank Kelly Giles and Peter Crysdale. In addition, we gratefully acknowledge the following reviewers of this Sixth Edition: Hazel Cole, McNeese State University; Karen Dunn, Queens University of Charlotte; Jerry Gambell, Ithaca College; and Melanie Wilderman, Northwestern Oklahoma State University.

Beyond our professional colleagues, we also acknowledge the contributions of our families and their support.

—J.J.Y.

—K.C.M.

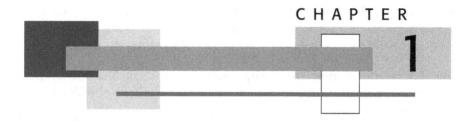

Understanding Today's Audiences

Each morning, Tom Adams rises at 6 a.m. and reaches for his smartphone to check the weather and last night's sports scores. After he showers and dresses, he checks his phone again for any traffic alerts he might have to deal with on his way to work. At 7 a.m., he pours a traveling cup full to the brim and heads for his car, stooping to pick up the *Washington Post* on his doorstep. Today's *Post* rides shotgun for the 15-mile trip to the environmental consulting firm where Adams works.

While driving, Adams plugs in his iPod to listen to a podcast of highlights from his newest music mix created by his daughter. His phone buzzes with a text message from his friend, and he wonders if their softball game for tonight may be cancelled because of rain.

Once in the office, Adams flips open his laptop. He logs in to his account on Facebook to track his friends throughout the day and quickly browses a few blogs that round up the latest news on environmental science and regulation. At lunch, he checks Twitter for the latest on the professional organizations he follows—and on the Washington Nationals baseball team. He scans a few national online news sites and then sorts through the day's postal mail: two brochures on upcoming seminars along with current copies of the *Environmental Reporter* and the *Federal Register*.

It is noon in the Washington, D.C., area, and Adams already has processed hundreds of media messages—and ignored or missed thousands more. By the time he returns home at 6:30 p.m., he will have processed hundreds more before he ever sits down to order an "on-demand" movie or play online games with his brother in Miami.

Several hundred miles away, Lorayne Oglesbee begins her day with a televised morning show, complete with news, weather, and tips for entertainment, cooking, and fashion. As she dresses and packs her briefcase, she pauses to check the local forecast on the Weather Channel. She says goodbye to her two school-aged daughters. Before her three-mile drive to work, she sends a text message to her sister to confirm their lunch date.

As she drives, she listens to National Public Radio before beginning her day as an attorney for a large regional hospital. She spends the morning learning how to use the new tablet that has been provided to all senior staff.

After lunch with her sister, she spends the afternoon with online legal databases to prepare for an upcoming case. By the end of the day, she has drafted a brief that she emails to a colleague for review. She responds to email messages that arrive late in the day to avoid having to work in the evening.

Think about your day so far. How did you get and send information as you moved through your day? You, like Adams and Oglesbee, are bombarded by media messages from news sites, Facebook, Twitter, email, and texting friends. On your digital devices, you face many choices about what to read, view, and access.

You, like the average person, are blocking or tossing out messages judged irrelevant, unclear, or uninteresting. At the same time, you are selecting information sources such as fashion blogs or celebrity tweets.

Ours is a sound byte world, where much information comes in the form of headlines— hundreds of them every minute. The careful writer will offer the audience words and phrases that stand out and link to more in-depth information.

The fate of any message lies in good writing crafted in a style that will capture a busy, active audience. This chapter discusses

- how writers can understand and serve audiences,
- how writers can overcome roadblocks to reaching audiences, and
- why the writing process is important for communicators, even in a time of headlines and shorter messages.

Reaching Audiences

People today have a nearly insatiable desire to be informed about events, such as devastating tornadoes in the Midwest, the deaths of celebrities, or how college teams fare in national tournaments. People in an uncertain and changing world are looking for information that keeps them safe and saves them money.

Today's audiences also seek relief from economic and military tensions around the world and turn to media for entertainment and information about leisure activities. Some people enjoy the analysis and discussion of events found on online independent sites and blogs.

Others turn to Twitter feeds, Facebook fan pages, or text messages from relatives and friends. Overall, audiences want and need information that will help them cope with—or escape from—everyday life.

How do writers get through the clutter of today's lifestyles and the glut of media messages? How do they reach waiting audiences? They do it with good writing. Audiences will not stick with messages that are confusing, incoherent, or unbelievable. Writers today must craft messages that attract and hold people with their content and structure. Messages today must be simple, clear, accurate, and relevant and often are emotionally compelling.

Writing Is the Basic Task

Before they are printed, posted, broadcast, aired, or distributed, messages are written. Communicators have to write first, regardless of what medium or technology they use. Consider these examples:

- A radio reporter types stories before she reads them on the 6 a.m. news show.
- A public relations specialist sends a targeted email to legislators, informing them of the state's natural gas surplus.
- An advertising copywriter creates a direct mail letter for customers of a sporting goods company.
- A television journalist tweets an update on a high-profile murder case.
- The editor of the campus newspaper blogs about her decision to publish a controversial photograph.
- An online journalism student writes the introduction to a multimedia documentary on hog farmers.
- A web site developer maps an animated guide to holiday events.

All communicators must write a message before it is sent to its intended audience. Once writers let go of a message, they have little control over whether the audience pays attention. Although the message might arrive, it might be crowded out, deleted, ignored, or overlooked.

Roadblocks to Reaching Audiences

A variety of obstacles exist between writers and their audiences:

- **Media and information glut.** Each memo, article, text, Tweet, advertisement, or news brief has infinitely more competition for an individual's attention than could have been imagined a decade ago. New information delivery systems become available almost daily.

People use interactive and on-demand media in addition to traditional magazines and newspapers. They are hungry for information of all kinds and can choose from an array of media and electronic devices that are most relevant to their lifestyles.

▪ **Hectic lifestyles.** Audiences today are busier than ever with multiple commitments to work, family, and leisure. People are spending more time online consuming and interacting with media than ever before. The Pew Center reported that in 2012, more than half or 53 percent of adults 65 or older said they go online or use email, a significant number for a group that had been slow to go online. Age, income, and education are the primary predictors of who goes online. Many adults hold more than one job, so going online allows them to accomplish more in less time in activities such as shopping.

▪ **Diversity of audiences.** U.S. society continues to grow increasingly diverse in terms of racial or ethnic makeup, sexual orientation, socio-economic status, family structure, and so on. Media writers constantly must work to keep up with changes in audience as well as in audience needs and interests. No longer is the average media consumer a white, middle-class man or woman.

▪ **Unfriendly messages.** A message that bores audiences or takes them too long to understand can be the greatest roadblock. For audiences to pay attention, messages must be readable, compelling, clear, and simple.

Media Glut

Today's world offers more to read, watch, and listen to than anyone could possibly consume. In the early 1960s, Marshall McLuhan predicted today's trends, suggesting that new media would alter society in dramatic, unanticipated ways:

> *Electronic technology is reshaping and restructuring social patterns of interdependence and every aspect of our personal life. It is forcing us to reconsider and reevaluate practically every thought, every action and every institution formerly taken for granted. Everything is changing— you, your family, your neighborhood, your education, your government, your relation to "the others."*

He was right: Society has changed. McLuhan could hardly have envisioned the information explosion today. No one can possibly read or even see the tiniest fraction of information available today. Media permeate daily life. Technology has overcome the barriers of geography and cost—almost anyone can buy the equipment to be in touch with anyone anywhere in the world. People in remote areas can tune in to events via satellite, grandparents in Atlanta can watch their granddaughter's dance recital in Milwaukee via Skype, and developments at the San Diego Zoo may be watched online 24/7, worldwide, on the zoo's pandacam.

As audiences have moved to new technologies to get entertainment and news instantly, the so-called traditional media have been affected. Since the 1980s, the circulation of daily newspapers has dropped, and hundreds of newspapers have closed. While newspapers have created online versions, these have not been as well received and successful in generating income as have new sites that have taken advantage of online innovation and delivery.

Watching television news is still a daily activity for most Americans. Although television still appears to be the main source of news, it also has dealt with declining ratings and increased competition from other news sources, particularly for entertainment. People have many more options for video content, such as YouTube. ComScore, a company that tracks and analyzes media usage, including social media, reported that more than 180 million U.S. Internet users watched 36.6 billion online content videos in one month in 2012. Apple's iTunes Store has thousands of downloads of TV episodes and movies, among other items, and all subscriptions can be aggregated under iCloud.

Traditional media have seen an explosion of niche creations—such as magazines, cable channels, satellite radio, and television—and all have increased offerings on the media buffet. More specialized media, more diverse media, and more electronic media—in fact, more media of all kinds—are on the market and taking audiences on a roller-coaster ride into an unimagined future of interactive and virtual reality. And all these media, old and new, compete fiercely for audience share and attention.

In the last decade, the advent of social media has further congested the media mix and increased competition for audience time. ComScore reported in 2012 that almost 17 percent of online minutes are spent on social networking sites. With only 24 hours in a day, people's attention to previous media favorites is declining or has even disappeared.

Today's media audiences are filled with people accustomed to fast food, fast travel, fast information—and lots of it. An ever-increasing array of mobile devices and applications can deliver immediate, high-quality information that an expectant audience uses for daily tasks, such as commuting and banking.

Lifestyles and Diversity

Media have proliferated, but no new hours have been added in the day to give audiences more time to use more media. Even though some audience members use new media to search for information, others are more resistant, still relying on old favorites. Some people may not have money to buy smartphones, tablets, or computers. Writers must be aware, therefore, that not all audiences have access to all media.

The makeup of households is changing, and some changes are driven by the economy. The latest U.S. Census data shows that between 2007 and 2010, the number of adult children who resided in their parents' household increased by 1.2 million to a total of 15.8 million. In 2010, there were 22.0 million shared households—where one other adult who is not the householder, spouse, or cohabiting partner lives—in the United States, an 11.4 percent increase from 2007.

Single-occupant, single-parent, and blended families are more common than the so-called typical family household. Neighborhoods and communities that were once homogeneous are now home to many racial and cultural groups.

At the same time people's lifestyles are changing in the United States, another trend is affecting media use: cultural diversity. The latest U.S. Census data show that the non-Hispanic white population is growing at the slowest rate, though it still is the largest single race and ethnic group by headcount and was 64 percent of the U.S. population.

In the first decade of this century, Hispanics accounted for more than half the population growth and made up 16 percent of the population. The black or African-American population comprised 13 percent and Asian-American, 5 percent. Some people of mixed heritage, about 3 percent of the population, do not classify themselves in a single ethnic category; the majority in that group identified two races.

Although ethnic- and gender-specific media have long had a role in this country, the changing complexion of the United States has meant an increase in media that address specific groups and individuals. The changes have meant new topics, new discussions, new themes, and new services.

Changing diversity means media are also working to hire employees who represent different groups so that staff will more accurately reflect the makeup of the population in general. This evolution has not been easy. U.S. diversity is not as well represented in newsrooms, for example, as it is in the population overall.

Knowing Audiences

People who write tend to read more than the average person. They are likely to be more educated, have a larger vocabulary, and exhibit a greater interest in various topics. They may write to please themselves or to satisfy what they think audiences want to know. As lifestyles and diversity change, these writers might be out of touch with their audiences and not know who their audiences truly are.

Such ignorance is dangerous. Writers are at risk if they do not know their audiences. They also cannot assume that all audiences can grasp complicated, technical messages. Successful writers make an effort to know and get in touch with their audiences.

Identifying Audiences

An audience might be few in number (members of Temple Sinai) or huge (Americans interested in better health care). Members of small audiences have much in common. Some typical smaller audiences within the U.S. population are veterans, working mothers, union members, and power company customers. Regardless of size, every audience may be subdivided. For example, members of the congregation at Temple Sinai will include smaller audiences of children, teens, young adults, singles, marrieds, new parents, empty nesters, maintenance staff, grounds workers, and so on. Even a smaller audience in the congregation, such as immigrants from other countries, could be further divided into those from specific countries, such as Poland, Germany, or Israel.

Breaking an audience into its composite groups is an important activity for people who need to communicate essential messages. Each subgroup may have specific needs for information and a particular way of getting it. A university, for example, has many audiences, including students, faculty, staff, alumni, potential students, governing bodies, the media, and potential donors. No single message will effectively reach all of these audiences. Most universities spend a great deal of time and money developing specific messages targeted to their many audiences, such as the online newsletter for alumni, tweets for students, direct mail for potential donors, and emailed news advisories for reporters.

Writers must identify their audiences. A shortcut is to ask the question, "Who cares?" The answer will be a list of groups or individuals who are potential consumers of the message.

Let's try the "Who cares?" method for listing audiences for a message. You are writing an article for your company newsletter on a new policy that provides preventive health care benefits to employees with children. "Who cares?" yields this list:

- married employees with children,
- single employees with children,
- employees thinking about having or adopting children, and
- part-time employees who have no children but wish they had health care benefits.

Listing audiences is important because once writers have listed them, they might change their writing approach. For the employee newsletter, your first sentence might be:

A new company policy will provide health care benefits for preventive medicine.

But after you list audiences, your opening becomes more personal:

> As a single parent, staff geologist John Payne has worried about the extra expense of annual medical exams for his three children and a doctor's visit when the children are only mildly ill.
> But Mega Oil's new health benefits program will ease those worries.
> The plan will reimburse employees with children for preventive health expenses such as well-child checkups.

As audiences are subdivided and defined, so are writing tasks. When writers take time to identify specific audiences, such as single parents, messages can be targeted for those audiences. The approach, structure, and language can be chosen to suit the audience.

The Writing Process Explained

E. B. White, in the introduction to *The Elements of Style*, explains that good writing is a writer's responsibility to the audience. He tells how his professor and coauthor, William "Will" Strunk, disciplined writers out of sympathy for readers:

> *All through* The Elements of Style, *one finds evidences of the author's deep sympathy for the reader. Will felt that the reader was in serious trouble most of the time, a man floundering in a swamp, and that it was the duty of anyone attempting to write English to drain this swamp quickly and get this man up on dry ground or at least throw him a rope.... I have tried to hold steadily in mind this belief of his, this concern for the bewildered reader.*

As a teacher in the early 20th century, Strunk knew that poor type quality in printed works and low levels of literacy hindered readers. Today, writers contend with new distractions Strunk could never have imagined. But the remedy in either era is the same: clear messages that show consideration for audiences.

Many people believe that good, skillful writing springs not from teaching and learning but from inborn talent that eludes most ordinary people.

Nonsense.

Writing a straightforward message requires no more inherent talent than following a road map. Author Joel Saltzman compares learning to write with learning to make salad dressing:

> *This is the only way I know to make a terrific salad dressing: Mix up a batch. Taste it. Mix again.*
> *The secret ingredient is the patience to keep trying—to keep working at it till you get it just right.*
> *Do most people have the talent to make a terrific salad dressing? Absolutely.*
> *Are they willing to make the effort to develop that skill? That's a different question.*

Good writing, like good salad dressing, can make even dry material palatable and can make good subject matter great. Like ingredients in a recipe, each word, sentence, and paragraph is selected carefully with one goal in mind: pleasing the consumer. The first bite will determine whether the diner eats more; good writing will sell a piece beyond the first paragraph. Like cooking, not every writing session will produce a masterpiece, but the end product must be tasty.

Writers today work in the same way that writers have worked throughout time—by following a regimen called the writing process. Once writers have identified their topics, they follow seven stages of the writing process presented here: information gathering, thinking and planning, listing, drafting, rewriting, sharing, and polishing.

All writers—whether producing a dissertation or a birth announcement—follow these steps. Even students writing under deadline pressure in class can go through the process in an abbreviated way: thinking, organizing, writing, and editing.

Stages of the Writing Process

The same sequence of steps outlined here occurs in good writing of all kinds. Once they have a topic, all communicators must gather information, think about and plan the message, list key information, write the message, rewrite the message, share it, and polish it by checking and editing. Together, these separate stages of activity form the writing process: a set of behaviors common to all writers. Writers may vary the order of the stages and repeat some of them, but each stage is essential to producing a good message.

Critical thinking is essential at each stage. In selecting a topic, writers have to assess the value of the idea, whether it will appeal to audiences, whether information is available, and how to approach the research and information gathering. As writing progresses, writers continue to think carefully about how to communicate the information clearly and in such a way that that the audience gets the message.

If readers or listeners cannot understand the message, the writer has failed. For communication to be successful, audiences have to understand the message well enough to act or react. They might form or alter opinions; they might learn new facts; or they might write responses to blog posts. Prior to any of these actions, audiences must have clear, cogent information.

Each stage in the writing process is briefly explained here. Consider the critical thinking skills needed in each stage. Later chapters in this book will explain writing tasks in greater detail. You will be referred to relevant chapters as each stage is discussed.

Stage One: Information Gathering.   Good writers are seekers. Gathering information or reporting on your topic is the first stage of the writing process.

To begin the search for information, you must answer questions that all people are prone to ask: Who? What? When? Where? Why? How? How much?

Basic facts and figures are easy to obtain online, but the Internet is just one tool. Every writer needs to go beyond superficial statistics and consult sources, such as those outlined in Chapter 9.

Never begin to write without talking to other people or reading their work. Good writing requires basic external information or research. Go beyond your own knowledge to find answers. Even if you are an expert on the topic, you must find other reliable authorities as quotable sources.

In writing an announcement of an art exhibit at a local gallery, for example, a writer might begin the questioning by talking with obvious experts—perhaps the curator and an art professor—who can provide answers and lead the writer to additional sources. For the exhibit announcement, aside from the basic *when* and *where* questions, the audience still needs to know the following: What types of artwork will be shown? Will prizes be awarded? Will any special guests appear at a reception? The additional questions will guide the next steps in the information-gathering search:

1. **Interviews.**   Writers must talk in person or by phone or email to authorities or other appropriate sources. (Interviewing is discussed in Chapter 10.)

2. **Library and online research.**   Any kind of writing can require research in libraries, web sites, or databases. For example, if the art on display at the gallery celebrates Impressionism, the writer needs to find out about the Impressionists and their art. (Basic research skills are included in Chapter 9.)

3. **Other sources.**   Brochures, publications, or archives can provide helpful information. For example, an article or brochure about last year's art exhibit could be located through an online archive and made accessible via a link in the finished story. (Chapter 9 explains how to use innovative and traditional reference sources.)

It is important to gather information from a variety of sources. Ideally, a writer compiles more information than actually is needed so that he or she can be selective about which information to use.

A writer takes notes on every source used in the information-gathering stage and takes care to cite that source. He or she never knows when an important fact or statistic will emerge, when a quotable statement will be uttered, or when the source of the information may be questioned. Careful notes enable writers to attribute interesting or unusual information to sources and to be accurate about what they have written. Some writers refer to the information-gathering stage as "immersion" in the topic. Whatever it is called, this first stage of writing turns the writer into an informal expert on the subject matter.

Stage Two: Thinking and Planning. Once information is gathered, the writer studies the notes taken in Stage One for what information seems most important and most interesting and then determines the angle and focus.

A good writer always makes decisions about priorities, keeping in mind the audience that will receive the message. Successful writers actually picture the probable audience, hold that image in mind, and plan the message for that imaginary group. Some writers say they write for a specific person, such as a truck driver in Toledo, a best friend, or Aunt Mary in Hartford. Sometimes the thinking stage will allow the writer to see possibilities for creative approaches to writing.

In this stage of the writing process, the writer might realize that more reporting is needed before listing and writing can begin. Once the writer has gathered enough information, he or she will begin to evaluate and set priorities, asking, "What does my audience need to know first? What next?" and so on. If no further gaps in information become apparent at this stage, the writer moves on to Stage Three.

Stage Three: Listing. This stage requires writers to list the facts and ideas that must be included in the message. Some writers note key words; others write detailed outlines. Initial lists should be made by brainstorming, jotting down each important element, then perhaps deleting, adding, or combining items in each list.

Once lists are complete, the writer reviews them and attempts to rank the information. Imagine, for example, the top three priority items on the list are "student art in the show," "students outside the arts," and "Impressionism is the theme." Isolating these items guides the writer to structure a message that will feature student art, mention Impressionism, and appeal to students in majors other than the arts.

In this stage, the writer imposes order and organization on the information, and the text begins to take shape.

Stage Four: Writing the Message as You Would Tell It. For most people, even experienced writers, writing seems somewhat unnatural. In contrast, conversational speech always seems to flow. So the efficient writer writes a message as he or she might tell it to a friend, thinking about the language that will appeal and resonate.

Checking the lists made in Stage Three, the writer would begin by telling about the first and most important element in the message, perhaps like this:

> A student art show that displays the talents of 27 of the university's young Impressionists will open at 7 p.m. Wednesday in the Parents' Association Gallery in Stamp Student Union.

Once this telling process has begun, it continues easily. The writer will move through interesting aspects of the message to a stopping point after the listed priorities have been included. By the end of this stage, the writer has created a first version of the message, sometimes called a draft. This version differs from a finished, polished message. Think of the draft as a raw lump of clay, in which substance is what counts. The stages that follow will shape the clay, giving form to the finished message. Writing or drafting messages is discussed in Chapters 5, 6, 7, and 8.

Stage Five: Rewriting.   In this stage, conventions of the written language are imposed on the draft. Writers must look at their work with the eye of an editor, critically assessing how to improve the message. Sentences are checked for completeness and coherence, paragraphs are formed and organized, and transitions and stylistic flourishes are added. Here the writer must apply the limitations of specific formats, such as the 140-character limit on tweets or word or character counts on hyperlinks.

Only through rewriting—sometimes repeated rewriting—can a message be streamlined to reach its intended audience. All good writers rewrite; great writers pride themselves on the painstaking reworking of their original phrases. Author E. B. White labored for three years over his slim classic *Charlotte's Web*, and he willingly revised much of his other work as many as 14 times.

Of course, writers on deadline cannot afford the luxury of spending years, or even hours, rewriting a draft. But they can carefully edit the content and check the accuracy of their work even in a few minutes, determining if all facts are included and supported in effectively organized language. At this stage, every writer is a tough editor of his or her work.

Rewriting is separate from polishing (Stage Seven), in which fine points of style, such as capitalization, are debated. If a writer stops in mid-draft to debate a style point, the train of thought is interrupted, and the writing process stops. Small decisions are left for the last stage—a stage that may be conducted by someone other than the writer.

Rewriting is the bulk of the writing process. It is hard, time-consuming work; factors to consider in the process are discussed in Chapters 2 and 3. A rewritten draft is far from a finished work, however. Writers develop shortcuts to rewriting as they become familiar with formats, as described in Chapters 6 and 7. But no good writer ever skips the rewriting stage, even to tweet.

Stage Six: Sharing.   The rewritten message should go to another reader— almost any other reader. By this stage, writers might have lost perspective on the message. They have become knowledgeable about the topic, and they might not be able to judge how an average member of the audience would receive the message.

Sharing your work at this stage gives you a much better idea of how an audience member might react. Outside readers will quickly let you know whether the information is confusing or unclear, or whether any important details are missing.

It is a good idea to share your work with a naive reader—someone who knows far less about your topic than you. Sometimes a colleague at work or a family member is an excellent choice for sharing because of that person's distance from your topic.

In large offices, outside review of your message might be built in. For example, in big companies, writing usually is reviewed by one or more editors and often by top management. Such an editing process is helpful in many ways, and certainly it saves the time and trouble of finding someone with whom to share your writing.

Regardless of who is sharing and commenting on your work, you as a writer must never forget that you did the initial research. You have expertise on your topic that your colleagues, family members, or even top managers might not have. Be sure to get feedback from your outside readers in a setting where you both can talk. You might need to explain why certain parts of your message are written as they are.

Good editing is negotiation; no editor should be a dictator. You as a writer need to work with, and not for, editors and outside reviewers. Together, you can produce clear, correct writing.

Stage Seven: Polishing.   The final stage in the writing process is one that many people ignore or abhor. This stage ensures the mechanical aspects of writing are accurate and clear. A misplaced comma can confuse a reader.

Here's where the writer of the art gallery story would consider: Is there an apostrophe after "Parents"? as Is the word "the" capitalized in "The Parents Association Gallery"? Finding the answers to such polishing questions is an essential part of the writing process, and it is appropriately the last stage. Many young writers feel that all capitalization, punctuation, grammar, usage, and spelling must be perfect, even in an initial draft. Concentrating on perfection in all those areas is unimportant in the early stages of writing. You might spend 10 minutes looking in the dictionary for a word you eventually decide not to use.

Working on word-by-word perfection at the early stages of writing is wasteful and even paralyzing. Writers who worry about every comma will find it difficult to get through the stages of writing. But all writers must know basic grammar, spelling, and punctuation, which are reviewed in Chapter 2, before they spend time polishing with stylebooks, dictionaries, and thesauruses.

All writers should polish their work, even when they pass the message to someone for final editing. An editor or editorial assistant might make the final checks for correctness and consistency and put a message in its final form. Confident writers welcome assistance with these cosmetic touches, knowing that letter-perfect writing will add to the credibility and clarity of their message.

On Your Own

Getting messages across to people in today's society is an unparalleled challenge. Writers have to accept that they cannot do much to change an individual consumer's lifestyle or habits. They cannot reduce the number of media or modify society's diversity.

They can't know which new electronic devices and applications will carry tomorrow's messages or which ones will shape media in the future.

Remember in the Adams and Oglesbee examples that people do not accept or assimilate every message that comes their way. They sift through messages and choose which ones they will hear and read from amid the daily clutter.

But writers can control one aspect of reaching audiences: They can use their critical thinking skills to select topics and the approach to a message. They can apply techniques and structures that best fit their audiences. They can follow the stages of writing to ensure messages are concise, complete, and correct—ready to meet their expectant audience's needs and interests.

Exercises

1. Keep a media log for a 24-hour period between today and the next class. Make a chart showing how you got information, how you communicated information, and which media you used. Indicate how long you viewed or read, a summary of messages, and what else you were doing while using each medium. Indicate whether you had interferences or distractions. Be prepared to compare your media-use patterns with those of others in the class.

2. Interview a relative about his or her media use, formulating questions based on your log. Explore how his or her media use has changed during the last five years, 10 years. Where does the person get most news? Entertainment? Information that is dependable? In-depth information? Does your relative use new media or more traditional media? What is his or her age?

3. Choose a news event that occurred today. Select the articles from different media that reported the event. Compare the way each introduced and developed the article. Look at writing style, language, length of story, anecdotes, and quotations. Does the format for presenting the news fit the medium's audiences? How?

4. Interview a classmate. Follow the stages of writing in producing a 30-line story about the person. Explain what you did in each stage. For example, in listing, you might list the person's accomplishments or extracurricular activities. In sharing, you might have another classmate read your draft.

References

"2010 Census Shows America's Diversity." U.S. Census, March 24, 2011. http://2010
.census.gov/news/releases/operations/cb11-cn125.html. Accessed July 7, 2012.

Apples iTunes homepage. http://www.apple.com/itunes/store/podcasts.html.

Associated Press Managing Editors Home Page. www.apme.com.

"Census Bureau Report Shows Shared Households Increased 11.4 Percent from
2007 to 2010." U.S. Census, June 20, 2012. http://www.census.gov/newsroom/
releases/archives/families_households/cb12-111.html. Accessed July 7, 2012.

"comScore Releases the 2012 U.S. Digital Future in News report." comScore. http://
www.comscore.com/Insights/Press_Releases/2012/2/comScore_Releases_
the_2012_U.S._Digital_Future_in_Focus. Accessed October 25, 2012.

"comScore Releases May 2012 U.S. Online Video Rankings." comScore. http://
www.comscore.com/Press_Events/Press_Releases/2012/6/comScore_Releases_
May_2012_U.S._Online_Video_Rankings. Accessed July 5, 2012.

"Digital Differences: For Some Groups Disparities in Internet Use Remain." Pew
Internet & American Life Project, April 13, 2012. http://www.pewtrusts.org/
our_work_report_detail.aspx?id=85899381395&category=52. Accessed July 5,
2012.

McLuhan, Marshall, and Fiore, Q. *The Medium Is the Message: An Inventory of Effects.*
New York: Bantam Books, 1967.

"Older Adults and Internet Use." Pew Internet & American Life Project, June 6, 2012.
http://www.pewtrusts.org/our_work_report_detail.aspx?id=85899396673&categ
ory=52. Accessed July 5, 2012.

The Poynter Institute Media Diversity Beyond 2000 Project Report. http://www
.poynter.org/wp-content/uploads/2012/01/Models-of-Excellence-Report.pdf.

Saltzman, Joel. *If You Can Talk, You Can Write.* New York: Ballantine Books, 1993.

"The State of the Blogosphere." Sifry's Alerts. April 5, 2007. http://www.sifry.com/
alerts/archives/000493.html.

Strunk, William, Jr., and White, E. B. *The Elements of Style.* New York: Macmillan,
1979.

U.S. Census Bureau Home Page. www.census.gov/population.

CHAPTER

2

Tools for Writers
Spelling, Grammar, and Math

- The announcement of a national meeting of Girl Scouts advises them to meet at the National Maul.

- A Philadelphia headline boasts, "Phillys Put Nats on Notice."

- A company's annual report notes that revenues rose from 80 million to 90 million, or a 10 percent increase.

- A bank newsletter reports a merger, saying, "We have great respect for First Home Savings, and we look forward to working with them."

A close check of all the above statements shows that Girl Scouts actually are headed for the National Mall; that the plural of Philly is Phillies; that revenues actually rose 12 percent; and that First Home Savings, as an institution, must be referred to as "it" rather than as "them."

Writers take great care as they gather information and write. But if they are not careful in checking their grammar, punctuation, spelling, numbers, or facts, they can damage their credibility—as well as their company's credibility. On the Internet, inaccuracies may be forwarded and spread indefinitely. Readers are unlikely to see posted corrections.

Errors need not be dramatic to cause audiences to pause or be dismayed. Large and small errors such as those listed above usually are caused by haste or carelessness, and readers react to them.

Research has shown that when messages are perceived to be error-free, they also are thought to be credible and well written. The perception of quality carries over to the writer and to the medium, be it newspaper, television, or online. In other words, messages free of errors are perceived to be of high quality and produced by professionals.

16

Students often argue that they do not need spelling, grammar, or punctuation skills. They believe an editor will fix any errors or that errors will be caught by spell-checkers or grammar-checkers built into computer software. Wrong. As a writer types a few keystrokes, the system might complete the word but not select the word the writer intended. As a media writer, you must be prepared to be both writer and editor and to find such errors. Spell-checkers also don't always catch the difference between *maul* and *mall*, *principal* and *principle*, or *affect* and *effect*. Any number of synonyms and homonyms can present problems, so it's up to you to know the difference.

Communicators who pay attention to their audiences know they must also pay attention to detail. That means attending to spelling, grammar, punctuation, and style. Most media have style manuals that contain many clear writing guidelines. They follow Associated Press style, or they have developed style guidelines of their own. Adopting a specific style ensures consistency in all articles, regardless of who writes them or where they appear. Even in short text messages, writers follow a certain style of known abbreviations; otherwise, recipients would have difficulty translating the meaning. (Style is covered in Chapter 3.)

Writers today are expected to know basic math and elementary statistics. They need to know how to compute percentages, figure out square footage, determine whether poll data are representative, and analyze budget figures.

In this chapter, you will learn

- typical spelling errors,
- common adult grammar problems, and
- bottom-line math skills.

Spelling in the Computer Age

Writers, beware: Certain spelling skills are essential in the digital era. This warning might sound exaggerated because, as we all know, computers can check spellings of thousands of words in minutes. But take heed.

What Spell-Checkers Will (and Won't) Do

Checking systems embedded in computers are a great invention, virtually eliminating senseless typographical errors, such as "scuh" and "typograpical," as well as common spelling problems such as "seperate" and "mispell." Sometimes, however, spell-checkers merely highlight many potential problems without correcting them. You, the writer, are expected to check the highlighted words or phrases and to approve them or provide correction.

Here's an example: If a computer merely finds a word in its dictionary, it "checks" that word, assuring the writer that the spelling is correct. Say, for example, the computer encounters this sentence: "Robin was going too the fare." The sentence checks the words "too" and "fare." They exist in the dictionary, so they pass muster. And if "Robin" happens to be spelled correctly as "Robyn," that error will go unchecked because "robin" would be found in the computer's dictionary. Or perhaps the typo is an actual word, such as "count" instead of "court." The error would slip by as correct, and the writer would have created an immediate audience-stopper and confusion.

So spell-checkers aid writers in most spelling dilemmas, but not all of them. Some of the most challenging spelling tasks (listed in the next section) are still the writer's responsibility.

A Do-It-Yourself List.   By now, it should be clear that spell-checkers will not do everything. The writer has the hands-on, do-it-yourself responsibility of checking the following problems that spell-checkers do not correct.

Homonyms.   Writers must distinguish among homonyms, or words that sound alike but have different meanings and are spelled differently. Any writer's credibility would drop if his or her readers saw these sentences:

- Mrs. Margolis consulted two professional piers before suspending the student.
  (Readers will see Mrs. Margolis conferring in a lakeside setting.)

- Barnes said he didn't want to altar his plans.
  (Will Barnes offer his plan during religious services?)

- All navel movements will be approved by the commanding officer.
  (Whose belly buttons are moving?)

- Investigators found millions of land mines sewn into the earth.
  (Did someone use a needle and thread?)

Such homonyms as "alter" and "altar," "pier" and "peer," and "sewn" and "sown" sometimes escape highlighting by spell-checkers that recognize each as a word in the dictionary. Writers who are overconfident in the ability of spell-checkers will undoubtedly leave some errors in their writing. A list of words writers should watch for includes the following:

aid, aide	it's, its
no, know	their, they're, there
to, two, too	whose, who's

Some subtle and damaging errors are made when writers confuse other commonly occurring homonyms, such as those listed below. Good writers distinguish between or among homonyms.

a lot (colloquial expression
    substituted for "many" or
    "much")
allot (to distribute)

allude (refer to)
elude (escape)

altar (in a church)
alter (change)

altogether (adverb meaning
    entirely)
all together (adjective meaning
    in a group)

bare (naked, uncovered)
baring (showing)

bear (animal, to support)
bearing (supporting)

bore (to drill, to be dull)
boar (pig)

canvas (cloth)
canvass (to poll)

capitol (building)
capital (city)

complement (fills up or
    completes)
compliment (flattering
    statement)

council (assembly)
counsel (to advise, legal adviser)
consul (diplomatic officer)

dual (two)
duel (combat between two people)

flair (style; panache)
flare (torch)

effect (noun, meaning result,
    verb meaning bring about)
affect (verb, meaning influence
    or cause, noun, meaning
    facial expression)

gorilla (ape)
guerrilla (person who engages in
    warfare)

immigrate (come to a new
    country)
emigrate (leave one's country)

legislator (individual official)
legislature (body)

miner (in a mine)
minor (underage)

naval (of the navy)
navel (belly button)

peer (social equal)
pier (water walkway)

pore (small opening;
    to examine closely)
pour (to cause to flow)

principal (head, first)
principle (lesson, belief)

role (in a play)
roll (list)

stair (step in a staircase)
stare (regard intensely)

stationary (permanent)
stationery (paper)

vain (conceited)
vein (blood vessel)
vane (wind detector)

Similar Words with Different Uses. Spell-checkers will highlight commonly confused pairs of words, such as "border" and "boarder," "conscience" and "conscious," "flout" and "flaunt," "loose" and "lose," "lead" and "led," "populace" and "populous," or "read" and "red." Keeping a good dictionary, stylebook, or grammar guide handy is the best way to make distinctions between similar words. Again, the writer or editor must catch the error, even though his or her computer includes a spell-checker.

Compound Words. Some compound words, such as "bookkeeper," "speedboat," and "stylebook," will pass spell-checkers as two words, even though they are correctly spelled as single words. The reason? The spell-checker recognizes the separate words—"book" "keeper," "speed," "boat," and "style"—as valid dictionary entries, leaving the writer appearing not to know the correct spelling.

Proper Names. As noted earlier, proper names—unlike most units of language—may be spelled any way an individual desires. The infinite variety of name spellings makes it essential to check and double-check all names, regardless of what spell-checking approves. Many names, such as Robin and Lily, are also common nouns listed in computer dictionaries. Often the correct spelling for the proper name is different from that offered by a spell-checker. For example, Robin may be "Robyn," and Lily may spell her name "Lillie." Double-check names in any document.

Both spell-checking and manual, word-by-word editing are essential parts of the writing process. No software can replace the complex decision-making an editor provides. In the digital age, good writers and editors ensure accurate writing.

BOX 2.1   Useful Tools for Writers

Professional writers and editors have their favorite resources. Despite their age, some reference books have timeless value. Others are more modern websites. All will help strengthen your media writing.

Books

Christian, Darrell, Jacobsen, Sally, and Minthorn, David, editors. *The Associated Press and Stylebook and Briefing on Media Law.* New York: The Associated Press, 2012.

Cook, Claire Kehrwald. *Line by Line: How to Improve Your Own Writing.* Boston: Houghton Mifflin, 1985.

Kessler, Lauren, and McDonald, Duncan. *When Words Collide*. Belmont, Calif.: Wadsworth, 2004.

Strunk, William, Jr., and White, E. B. *The Elements of Style*, Third Edition. New York: Macmillan, 1979.

Wickham, Kathleen Woodruff. *Math Tools for Journalists*. Oak Park, Ill.: Marion Street Press, 2002.

Web Sites

Dictionary.com, http://dictionary.reference.com.

Oxford English Dictionary, http://www.oed.com, the definitive record of the English language.

EditTeach.org, www.editteach.org, with resources for language, editing, teaching.

Radford, Tim. "Manifesto for the simple scribe—my 25 commandments for journalists, http://www.guardian.co.uk/science/blog/2011/jan/19/manifesto-simple-scribe-commandments-journalists [posted by former Guardian writer and editor].

Rogers, Tony. "Six tips to improve your newswriting," http://journalism.about.com/od/writing/tp/Newswriting.htm.

News University, www.newsu.org, with access to a range of reporting and writing courses that require user registration.

"The Purdue Online Writing Lab" (OWL), http://owl.english.purdue.edu.

Grammar to the Rescue

Our world is fast-paced and fast-changing—hardly the kind of place you would expect to need something as tedious as a lesson on grammar. But today's communicator cannot afford to slow down audiences, and faulty grammar does just that. Just as writers are cautioned about relying too much on spell-checking systems in computers, they should be aware that grammar-checking programs also have flaws.

Consider the reader who encounters "its" where "it's" should be. For a split second, the reader will pause and wonder about the error, the writer, and the site. Sometimes the musing reader will stop reading entirely because of the slowdown or because of the reduced credibility or appeal of the flawed message.

People do not have to be grammar experts to stop and wonder about correctness. For example, any unusual use of "whom" or "who" might cause a reader to reflect rather than to read on. "Now, what was it I learned about whom?" the reader muses, and the tempo of reading is lost.

Television viewers might cringe when the news announcer says, "The committee will reconvene their meeting tomorrow morning." They know a committee is referred to with an "its," not a "their." As the viewers know pause to correct the sentence, they lose the remainder of the announcer's message.

But My Grammar Is Good...

Most of us who pursue writing as a career consider ourselves to be language experts, and in general, our grammar and language use are far above average. Even educated people have problems, however. Evidence of grammar problems is found in mistakes made daily by adults in business letters, memos, and reports, as well as in newspapers and on the airways. An ad proclaims, "There's no down payment and no service charge!" To be grammatically correct, it should say, "There are no down payment and no service charge." A newsletter states, "Children will be grouped by age, irregardless of grade in school." There is no such word as "irregardless"—it simply is an aberration of "regardless."

Educated people regularly make grammar mistakes that other educated people will recognize. Writers need to identify their most frequent grammar errors and learn how to correct them. A first step in checking your grammar is to know what errors you are most likely to make.

Grammar Problems

Author Katherine C. McAdams developed "The Grammar Slammer," a workshop on grammar problems that identifies five areas in which real-life errors are most likely to occur:

1. Punctuation, especially commas, semicolons, colons, apostrophes, dashes, and hyphens.

2. Subject and verb agreement.

3. Correct pronoun choices that provide agreement and avoid gender bias, such as "Each student has his or her book" rather than the more common and erroneous "Each student has their book."

4. Correct sentence structures, especially when sentences use modifiers or require parallel structure.

5. Word use—that is, using words (such as "regardless") correctly; this area often involves spelling problems and confusing words that sound alike (such as "affect" and "effect," or "vain" and "vein").

This section follows the format of the Grammar Slammer workshop, giving a short lesson on each of the problem areas and following that lesson with some exercises. The approach is designed for writers who are bright, motivated, and capable of learning quickly.

The lessons provide a quick fix rather than an in-depth understanding. They are designed to refresh and renew rather than to re-educate. Going through the grammar lessons will help you identify your grammar deficiencies. You can then be on guard for your particular problems when writing and editing. You might find you have many weaknesses in language skills. If so, you will want to study the books recommended at the end of this chapter or take a grammar course.

Test Yourself

To determine your grammar problem areas, take the following diagnostic quiz. Record your answers on a sheet of paper.

Grammar Slammer Diagnostic Quiz

The following sentences contain errors in grammar and punctuation. No sentence contains more than one error. Read each sentence. Circle the error, and note how the sentence should be written correctly. Sentence 1 is corrected for you as an example.

1. If past performance is any indication, Maryland should be considered a top challenger for the championship; having downed defending regional champion Duke twice in the regular season. (*Correction*: Use a comma in place of the semicolon because the second half of the sentence is not an independent clause.)

2. The list of candidates being considered for the position of university chancellor have been trimmed to approximately 50 names, including four university officials.

3. The computer did not seem to be working today, it kept shutting down when instructed to save any document.

4. The following afternoon, Wednesday, October 25 a Royal Indian Air Force DC-3 landed on the unpaved runway at Srinagar Airport.

5. Traditionally expected to be in control of their surroundings, the insecurity makes students uncomfortable in their new situation.

6. The president's body will lay in state until services are held at the chapel.

7. Each student is expected to purchase their books prior to the first day of class.

8. Among those who attended services for the coach were Ralph Brooks, head football coach at Eastern, Mary Barnes, chancellor; Michael Thomas, former chancellor; and Paul Wells, former athletic director.

9. She predicted that neither the speaker ~~or~~ nor the minority whip would receive the Republican nomination.

10. In its advertising, the Acme Recycling Company claims that they are in business only to do good works for the community.

11. Millie Rosefield, chair of the Cityville Historic Preservation Committee ran fifth in the Nov. 6 race for four council seats.

12. One of every five of the state's residents live in the sort of poverty that drove Erskine Caldwell to write.

13. Three-fourths of the business district in Long Beach, N.C. was destroyed by Hurricane Hugo, which struck the coast in 1989.

14. Many children in the 1950s used to believe that he could acquire practically superhuman strength by eating the right cereal.

15. The mayor said the parade would feature the homecoming queen, the marching band will play, and as many floats as possible.

16. Several people, all of them eager to give their opinions and all of them pressing forward to meet the governor, who was conducting interviews with voters in the area.

17. I like ice cream and cookies; I don't like cakes with icing.

18. Rosalie complained, and she had no heat.

19. Being a weight lifter, his muscles were well developed.

20. The alligator is hunted for ~~their~~ its skin.

Several of the following words are misspelled. Circle the misspelled words and write the correct spelling for each in the space provided.

1. principal (of a school) ———————————————————

2. waiver (permission slip) ———————————————————

3. bore (a wild pig) ———————————————————

4. naval (belly button) ———————————————————

5. stationery (you write on it) ———————————————————

6. role (a list) ———————————————————

7. lead (a heavy metal) ———————————————————

8. canvass (cloth) ———————————————————

9. complement (flattering statement) ———————————————————

10. cite (reference or footnote) ———————————————————

Answers for the diagnostic quiz are included in Appendix A at the end of the book.

Grammar Problems Up Close

Examine the items you missed on the diagnostic quiz. You should have an idea of which grammar problems you need to review. The discussion of each problem is presented here, followed by exercises. Test your proficiency and move on. Record your answers on a sheet of paper. To check your work, look at the answers in Appendix A.

Problem 1: Punctuation

Perhaps no problem looms larger than punctuation. Few people actually know the rules and regulations of punctuation use. Most of us, much of the time, use the "feel good" school of punctuation, saying, "I just feel like I need a comma here" or "A semicolon just felt right."

Professional communicators must give up their "feel good" philosophy of punctuating. The first rule of punctuating professionally is this: **Do not punctuate unless you know a rule.** When you even think of adding a mark of punctuation, stop and decide whether it is justified by the rules in this chapter. If not, you probably do not need to punctuate at all.

If you find you are punctuating excessively—that is, using more than three punctuation marks within any given sentence—it is probably time to rewrite that sentence. Sentences requiring many punctuation marks, even if they are all correct, usually are too long and complex to be easily understood. So another rule of punctuating professionally is this: Less is better. Less punctuation leads to clearer, more readable copy. When in doubt, leave the comma out.

Commas. Literally hundreds of comma rules exist. But the nine listed here, distilled by high school English teacher Mary Penny in the 1940s, have been found over the years to take care of most everyday comma problems.

Rule 1. Use commas in compound sentences when clauses are separated by a conjunction such as "and," "but," "for," "nor," or "yet."

■ She managed the restaurant, but he did the cooking.

Note: In such sentences, leaving out the conjunction leads to an error known as a comma splice, whereby a comma is left to do the work of joining two sentences: "She managed the restaurant, he did the cooking." Like weak splices in a rope, commas are not strong enough for this task. A period or semicolon is needed to make a correct sentence:

■ She managed the restaurant; he did the cooking.
■ She managed the restaurant. He did the cooking.

Rule 2. Use commas to separate elements in a series. Such elements usually are adjectives, verbs, or nouns.

Note: Journalism departs from traditional rules of punctuation by leaving the comma out before a conjunction in a series of elements, following this rule in *The Associated Press Stylebook*. The text in this book follows the comma in a series rule, but the journalism examples do not—as you may have already noticed in reading this text.

English composition version:

- The tall, dark, handsome man hailed, lauded, and applauded Ben, George, Maude, and Rebecca.

Journalism version:

- The tall, dark, handsome man hailed, lauded and applauded Ben, George, Maude and Rebecca.

Rule 3. Use commas when attributing from quoted material. Commas set off words of attribution from the words of a one-sentence quotation unless a question mark or exclamation mark is preferred. Use them also in greetings:

- He said, "Hello."
- "Good-bye," she replied.
- "The fair has been canceled," she said.

Rule 4. Commas follow introductory matter, such as after an introductory adverbial clause:

- When the team was forced to kick, the coach sent in his best players.

Commas also follow two or more introductory prepositional phrases:

- In the spring she returned to College Park. (no comma)
- In the spring of 2012, she returned to College Park. (comma needed because "in" and "of" are two prepositional phrases)

Also use a comma with a phrase that contains a verbal (i.e., a verb form used as a modifier):

- Singing as she worked, Mary answered her phone.
- Kicked by a horse, Don was more than stunned.
- To cure hiccups, drink from the far side of a glass.

Rule 5. Commas follow the salutation of a friendly letter and capitalized elements, such as the complimentary close (e.g., Sincerely, Very truly yours). A colon follows the salutation of a business letter:

- Dear James,
- Dear Dean Smith:
- Sincerely, Dean Smith

Rule 6. Commas follow all items in a date or full address:

- July 16, 1992, is his date of birth.
- She has lived in Lake City, Fla., all her life.

Rule 7. Commas set off nonessential words or phrases:

- Well, we will just have to walk home.

Commas also set off appositives, which are words or phrases that rename a noun. Appositives amplify a subject:

- Betty Brown, his mother-in-law, has been married four times.

Also use commas to set off nonessential modifying clauses and phrases:

- The president-elect, suffering from laryngitis, canceled his speech.

Rule 8. Commas surround words of direct address:

- Maria, please pass the butter.
- I can see, Fred, that you are lazy.

Rule 9. Commas indicate omitted verbs that are expressed in another part of the sentence:

- Talent often is inherited; genius, never.

This rule is an old one and is rarely used today except in headlines. It would be rare to find a comma indicating an omitted verb in contemporary writing, but far from surprising to see such headlines as:

- Pilots Ask for Guns; Airlines, for Marshals
- Coach Smith Has Much to Gain This Season; His Team, Even More

Semicolons and Colons.   Miss Penny added three more rules to her list to take care of another widespread punctuation problem: the correct use of semicolons and colons. Miss Penny's rules 10 and 11 explain the two uses of the semicolon—the only two uses. Rule 12 explains the use of colons.

Rule 10.   Semicolons connect two complete sentences if sentences share a related thought or theme. Use of a semicolon usually creates a sense of drama:

- The brown-eyed, dark-haired, vivacious model, at age 18, seemed destined for quick success; on Sept. 11, 2001, her apparent destiny was altered.

Rule 11.   Semicolons are used in a list separating items that require significant internal punctuation:

- He lived six years in Richmond, Va.; four years in Raleigh, N.C.; one year in Greenville, S.C.; and six months in Baton Rouge, La.

Rule 12.   Colons precede formal lists, illustrations, multisentence quotes, and enumerations:

- The following students received scholarships: Jim Johnson, Juanita Lopez, Martha Taylor, Tiffany Eldridge, and Courtney Sampson.
- He answered her with a parable: "A man once had six sons. Five of them...."
- The senator listed the steps in her economic recovery program: first, to raise interest rates; second, to reduce spending....

Do not use a colon after "include" or forms of "to be," such as "was" or "were." Example: Her best friends were Sally, Marisa, and Claire.

Slammer for Commas, Semicolons, and Colons

Now, using Miss Penny's list of 12 rules as your reference, complete the following exercise. Remember, the most important rule is that you do not punctuate unless you know a rule. Defend each mark of punctuation you use by citing one of the Penny rules on a sheet of paper and listing the rule or rules you used you used next to the sentence.

Rule(s)

_4_**1.** Although we watched the Super Bowl, we don't know who won.

_____**2.** John Blimpo an egocentric man dropped his hat in the fruit salad.

10+9

_**10**_**3.** Guitars have six strings; basses, four.

_____**4.** The tall dark handsome man listed his hobbies as reading fishing painting and writing.

_____**5.** To Whom It May Concern

The spelling and grammar test will be given on March 3 4 and 5 2013 in Room 502 of Knight Hall.

Grammatically yours

Dean Sarah Jones

_**8**_**6.** Dad, go ahead and send the money now.

_____**7.** The women's basketball team was down by four points at halftime however it came back to crush the opponent.

_____**8.** Congress passed the bill but the debate took several months.

_____**9.** Well just be in by daybreak.

_**10**_**10.** Her blind date was a real disappointment; he talked loudly and constantly about his pet snake.

_____**11.** She was elected on Nov. 4 2008 in Baltimore Md. the city of her birth.

_**12**_**12.** She named her courses for the fall semester: journalism, English political science, history, and French.

+2

Check your work by looking at the answers in Appendix A. Then go on to tackle some other troublesome marks of punctuation.

Hyphens and Dashes.   Remember that hyphens and dashes, although often confused, are different. The hyphen differs from a dash in both use and appearance. The hyphen is shorter (- as opposed to —), and it comes, without additional spaces, between two words combined to express some new concept, such as polka-dot and part-time. Hyphens are useful joiners that bring some creativity to language.

Rather than joining, dashes are useful in separating phrases—usually in cases where that separation can be heard. Dashes are sometimes used to replace commas to ensure that a pause is audible and even dramatic (e.g., "Although charming, he was—on the other hand—a thief.").

Here is a list of guidelines for using hyphens and dashes correctly:

1. Never use a hyphen after a word ending in "ly."

   ■ The newly elected president stepped to the podium.

2. Use a hyphen to connect two or more related modifying words that do not function independently.
   - Kim always ordered the blue-plate special.
   - Todd dreaded any face-to-face confrontations.

3. The dash is a punctuation mark one "hears." It is a noticeable pause. Choose a dash instead of a comma so the audience can "hear" the pause.

4. Dashes work where commas would also work. The only difference is the dash adds drama—and an audible break in the text. Because dashes may substitute for commas, they are used to set off nonessential material.
   - The murderer was—if you can believe it—a priest.

5. Too many dashes in any text may be distracting and even irritating to readers. Limit dashes to only the most dramatic of pauses. In most cases, such as this example, commas will suffice.
   - She is—as most of you know—a punctuation expert.

Other marks of punctuation, especially apostrophes, can be troublesome. Correct use may vary from time to time and publication to publication. Always check your stylebook, and keep a current grammar reference book handy.

Problem 2: Subject and Verb Agreement

Few writers make obvious errors in subject and verb agreement, such as "I is interested in cars" or "The class know it's time to go to lunch." But most people struggle with the following subject–verb agreement problems:

1. Collective subjects can be confusing. Some nouns that appear to be plural are treated as singular units:
   - The *Girl Scouts* is a fine organization.
   - *Checkers* is an ancient game.
   - *Economics* is a difficult subject

   Some collective subjects, however, have Latinate endings and remain plural, although spoken language tends to make them singular. In formal writing, these plurals require plural verbs:
   - The *media* have raised the issue of the senator's competency.
   - The *alumni* are funding a new building.

2. The pronouns "each," "either," "neither," "anyone," "everyone," and "anybody" are always singular, regardless of what follows them in a phrase. Take, for example, this sentence:
   - Either of the girls is an excellent choice for president.

The phrase "of the girls" does not change the singular number of the true subject of this sentence: the pronoun "either." Following are some other examples of correct usage:

- Neither has my vote.
- Either is fine with me.
- Each has an excellent option.
- Anyone is capable of helping the homeless.
- Everyone is fond of Jerry.

3. A fraction or percentage of a whole is considered a singular subject.
   - Three-quarters of the pie is gone.
   - Sixty-seven percent of the voters is needed.

4. Compound subjects, in which two or more nouns function as the subject of a sentence, can lead to agreement problems. To solve such problems, substitute a single pronoun, such as "they" or "it," for the sentence's subject or subjects. For example, transform this problem sentence: "The students and the teacher is/are waiting for the bus." By substituting, the subject becomes "they": They are waiting for the bus. The following are some other examples:
   - The opening number and the grand finale thrill the audience. (They thrill)
   - There are no down payment and no service charge. (They are not charged)
   - The Eagles, a classic rock band, is my dad's favorite group. (It is his favorite)

5. When subjects are structured with either/or and neither/nor, use the verb number that corresponds to the subject closest to the verb, as in the following cases:
   - Either the leader or the scouts pitch the tent.
   - Either the scouts or the leader pitches the tent.
   - Neither the parents nor the students win when rules are broken.

Slammer for Subject–Verb Agreement

Check your knowledge of subject–verb agreement by taking the following quiz. Select the verb that agrees.

1. He did say he would look at the sheet of names, which includes/include the owners of two apartment buildings.

2. Their number and influence appears/appear greatest in West Germany.

3. Experience in the backfield and the line gives/give the coach a good feeling on the eve of any opening game.

4. A first offense for having fewer than 25 cartons of untaxed cigarettes results/result in a $500 fine.

5. Before you make a final judgment on this student's story, consider the time and effort that has/have gone into it.

6. Who does the teaching? Full professors. But so does/do associates, assistants, and instructors.

7. She said they would visit Peaks of Otter, which is/are near Lynchburg, Va.

8. The news media is/are calling for a peace treaty that is fair to everyone.

9. The United Mine Workers exhibit/exhibits solidarity during elections.

10. There is/are 10 million bricks in this building.

11. The president said that students today are too job-oriented and neglect the broader areas of study that constitutes/constitute a true education.

12. Five fire companies fought the blaze, which the firefighters said was/were the longest this year.

13. Each of the 100 people believes/believe in God.

14. It is/are the boats, not the swimmers, that stir up the dirt in the lake.

15. The editor told the staff there was a shortage of money for the newsroom, a shortage she said she would explain to the board of directors, which decides/decide all matters on the budget.

16. One of my classmates typifies/typify student apathy.

17. Drinking beer and sleeping is/are the most important things in my life.

18. Dillon said he has insurance for everything except the buildings, which is/are owned by Thomas F. Williams.

19. Approximately 51 percent of the U.S. population is/are female.

20. There is/are only one way to beat taxes.

21. Neither the professor nor her two assistants teaches/teach this course in a style students like.

22. Each student is/are responsible for getting the work done on time.

23. All students considers/consider that an imposition.

24. The General Assembly and the governor disagrees/disagree on the solution.

Check your answers against those in Appendix A.

Problem 3: Correct Use of Pronouns

Pronouns are little words—"he," "she," "you," "they," "I," "it"—that stand for proper nouns. Look at this sentence:

■ International Trucking is hiring 20 new drivers because it is expanding in the Southeast.

In this sentence, the word "it" is used to substitute for International Trucking. Pronouns help avoid needless repetition in language by doing the work of the larger nouns, called antecedents. In the previous example, "International Trucking" is the antecedent for the pronoun "it."

Pronouns must agree with their antecedents, as in the following examples:

■ Marianne said she (Marianne) would never color her (Marianne's) hair.
■ Baltimore became a model city after it (Baltimore) successfully restored the waterfront.
■ Journalism is a popular major, and now it (journalism) prepares students for many careers.

Following are guidelines to ensure correct pronoun choices:

1. Watch for collective subjects—groups treated as single units—and use the correct pronoun.
   ■ The committee gave its report.
   ■ The United Mine Workers gave out a list of its legislative goals.
2. When using singular pronouns, use singular verbs.
   ■ Each of the rose bushes was at its peak.
   ■ Everyone in the audience rose to his or her feet and chanted.
3. Use correct pronouns to handle issues of sexism in language. The generic person is no longer "he."
   ■ Each of the students had his or her book.
   ■ The students had their books.
4. Be attentive to stray phrases or clauses that come between pronouns and antecedents and cause agreement problems.
   ■ He presented the list of candidates being considered for the office and told the committee members to choose from it. (For antecedent agreement; "it" refers to the list)
   ■ He posted the list of candidates for the position and read it aloud. (For antecedent agreement; "it" refers to the list)

5. Use reflexive pronouns, such as himself or herself, only when a subject is doing something to herself or himself or themselves.
   ▪ Jan introduced herself to the new chancellor.
   ▪ Henry never could forgive himself.
   ▪ The relatives had the chalet to themselves.

Slammer for Pronouns

To ensure that you understand agreement of pronoun and antecedent, select the appropriate pronoun for each of the following sentences.

1. Each student had (his or her/their) assignment completed before class.
2. General Foods plans to change (its/their) approach to marketing baked goods.
3. Larry introduced (him/himself) and me to the governor.
4. The jury took (their/its) deliberations seriously.
5. The board of directors set a date for (their/its) annual retreat.
6. The Orioles (is/are) my favorite team.
7. Neither the Terps nor the Crimson Tide (was/were) having a winning season.
8. Neither of the teams (was/were) victorious.
9. The alumni voted to charge $1 an issue for (their/its) magazine.
10. Any of the three finalists (is/are) an excellent choice.
11. The six-member committee voted to reverse (its/their) decision.
12. The librarian's collection fascinated him, and he asked to borrow from (her/it).
13. The media (is/are) ignoring the mayor's speeches.
14. Each of the students could handle the job by (himself or herself/ themselves).
15. Everyone in the audience rose to (his or her/their) feet for the ovation.

Check your work against the answers in Appendix A, and prepare to tackle the biggest pronoun problem of all: the *who/whom* dilemma.

Who and Whom. The word "whom" has all but disappeared from spoken English, so it is little wonder that few of us know how to use it correctly. Even though usage is changing, writers of published materials still need to know the rules that govern the distinction between "who" and "whom":

1. "Who" is a substitute for subjects referring to "he," "we," or "she," or the nominative pronoun.

   ■ Who saw the meteor?

   The statement, "He saw the meteor," as a question becomes, "Who saw the meteor?" "Who" is substituted for the subject "he." Relative clauses work the same way when "who" is substituted for a subject. In the sentence, "He questioned the man who saw the meteor," "who" substitutes for the subject of the clause, "He saw the meteor." The entire clause serves as an object of the verb "questioned." But the function of the clause does not change the role of a pronoun; in this sentence, the role of "who" is as the subject of the verb "saw."

2. "Whom" is a substitute for objective pronouns, such as "him," "her," or "them."

   ■ Whom did he question for hours?

   The statement, "He questioned her for hours," as a question becomes, "Whom did he question for hours?" "Whom" is substituted for "her" as the object of the verb "questioned." Substitution works the same way in relative clauses. In the sentence, "Marcella was the one whom he questioned for hours," "whom" substitutes for the object "her" in the clause, "He questioned her for hours." Again, it is the role of the pronoun within its subject-verb structure that determines whether it is the subject or the object and therefore "who" or "whom."

That and Which.   Another fine distinction between pronouns is the difference between "that" and "which." Again, the spoken language no longer follows strict rules regarding these subordinate conjunctions, but careful writers need to observe the following guidelines:

1. "That" is a restrictive pronoun, indicating that the information it precedes is essential for correct understanding of the sentence.

   ■ Dogs prefer bones that improve their dental health.
   The use of "that" tells us that dogs prefer only this specific kind of bone.

2. "Which" precedes nonessential material; therefore, it typically appears with commas (the ones used to set off nonessential information).

   ■ Dogs prefer bones, which improve their dental health. The use of "which" tells us that all bones benefit dogs' teeth and gums.

3. "That" and "which" are not interchangeable. As you can see in the example sentences, the meaning of the sentence is affected when the comma is added in the second sentence and "that" becomes "which." In the first sentence, dogs like only bones that are good for them; in the second, dogs like bones better than other things, and bones just happen to be good for dental health. The second sentence is far more logical.

Slammer for Who/Whom and That/Which

Select the appropriate pronoun in the following sentences:

1. Alvin, (who/whom) everyone adored, absconded with the family fortune.
2. Betty, (who/whom) was the apple of his eye, followed him to Mexico.
3. The FBI agents (who/whom) Alvin had avoided for several months finally arrested him.
4. Veronica, Alvin's sister, (who/whom) needed the money desperately, refused to post bond.
5. Alvin, (who's/whose) health was delicate, wasted away in prison.

Select the appropriate pronoun, then note the proper punctuation as needed in the following sentences:

1. Betty bought a gun (that/which) was on sale and set out to free Alvin.
2. She headed north from Mexico in a stolen car (that/which) had more than 130,000 miles showing on its odometer.
3. The car (that/which) had New Jersey license plates was quickly spotted by police in Texas.
4. The Texans (that/which/who/whom) spoke in a slow drawl told her she was wanted in New Jersey for conspiring with Alvin.
5. She pulled out the gun (that/which) she had in her glove compartment and started shooting.
6. The police officer (that/which/who/whom) was standing closest to her car died after he was struck by a bullet.
7. Other officers took Betty's gun (that/which) now was empty of bullets.
8. They also arrested Betty and placed her in a local jail (that/which) overlooked the Rio Grande.

Check your answers against those in Appendix A and move on to the next grammar problem.

Problem 4: Sentence Structure

Aside from fragments and run-on sentences, two other categories cause most adults problems with sentence structure: faulty parallelism and modifier placement.

Journalists often struggle with giving sentences parallel structure—that is, making sure that series or lists of phrases are parallel in form. Rather than, "He enjoys reading and to go skiing," use the parallel form, saying, "He enjoys reading and skiing." Writers must always remember to check lists within sentences as well as bulleted lists to see that phrases are stated in parallel form, as shown in these examples:

■ Marvelene listed steps in planning a successful party: sending invitations early, greeting guests personally, and supplying abundant food and drink. (Note the parallel gerunds: "sending," "greeting," "supplying.")

■ A successful host always is sure
  —to send invitations early,
  —to greet guests personally, and
  —to supply abundant food and drink. (These infinitives are parallel.)

Other sentence errors might occur when modifiers are placed incorrectly and give readers an inaccurate, sometimes humorous, picture as, for example, in these sentences:

Wrong:	Swinging from an overhead wire, we saw a kite.
Better:	We saw a kite swinging from an overhead wire.
Wrong:	When wheeled into the operating room, the nurse placed a mask over my face.
Better:	The nurse placed a mask over my face after I was wheeled into the operating room.
Wrong:	The jury found him guilty of killing his wife after deliberating for three days.
Better:	After deliberating for three days, the jury found him guilty of killing his wife.

To solve modifier placement problems, place modifying clauses and phrases closest to what they modify.

Slammer for Modifiers

Rewrite these sentences to correct misplaced modifiers. Some sentences are correct as written.

1. The waiter served ice cream in glass bowls which started melting immediately.

2. The Simpsons gave a toy robot with flashing eyes to one of their sons.

3. We saw a herd of sheep on the way to our hotel.

4. Most people have strawberry shortcake topped with mounds of whipped cream.

5. The house is one of the oldest in Rockville, where Mrs. Rooks taught ballet.

6. Flying at an altitude of several thousand feet, the paratroopers could see for miles.

7. I could not convince the child to stop running into the street without yelling.

8. After the first act of the play, Brooke's performance improves, the critic said.

9. While watching the ball game, Sue's horse ran away.

10. The museum director showed me a spider with the orange diamond on its belly.

11. The bank approves loans to reliable individuals of any size.

12. Running on the beach, the sun rose before my eyes.

13. Riding in a glass-bottom boat, we saw thousands of colorful fish.

14. Aunt Helen asked us before we left to call on her.

15. Do it yourself: Make up a sentence suffering from modifier malady. Then correct it.

Check your work against the answers in Appendix A, then prepare for the final grammar problem: word usage.

Problem 5: Word Usage

English is a language enriched by words borrowed from other languages, resulting in a rich vocabulary—but also, in many cases, in unorthodox spelling and idiosyncratic usage. It makes little sense to have both "affect" and "effect" in the same language, functioning so similarly but not identically. And why do we distinguish between "pore" and "pour," or "flair" and "flare"? Who cares?

Careful writers have to care because subtle usage errors can cause big misunderstandings. Correct usage leads to credibility; readers have confidence in error-free reading.

Slammer for Troublesome Words

Use a dictionary and AP Stylebook to help identify correct usage for each of the following troublesome words.

Hopefully
Affect versus effect
Less versus fewer
Lie versus lay
Sit versus set
Comprise versus compose

Use the references again to change the words used incorrectly in the following sentences:

1. The most affective writing follows good writing principals.
2. The perspective budget for the coming year will include raises for the city's firefighters.
3. An incoming ice storm will effect whether we can drive to work tomorrow.
4. The state historical society will reenact signing the state constitution in the Capital.
5. The country's navel force has been reduced.
6. His desire for money is his principle guiding force in business.
7. The coach said the team ignored his advise to make it a passing game.
8. Jiminy Cricket said Pinocchio should let his conscious be his guide.
9. The engineer eliminated the High Road sight because it sloped to much.
10. Returning the stolen car to it's owner is the best decision.

Math for Writers

All professional communicators must be able to handle routine computations such as adding, subtracting, multiplying, dividing, figuring ratios and percentages, and rounding off numbers. Such simple calculations routinely are used in daily journalism, and any error makes a story inaccurate.

Professor Emeritus Phil Meyer at the University of North Carolina at Chapel Hill always advised mass communication students that if they chose the field because they thought they could escape math, they were wrong. Basic math is necessary.

Here's a typical example of statistical writing that misses the mark: An advertisement tells audiences that computer prices have dropped 200 percent. This news would appeal to someone shopping for a new computer. But what's wrong here? When the price drops 100 percent, the item is free. Below 100 percent means stores are paying customers to take away computers. The writer needs a few quick lessons on math.

Here's another example of a writer in need of math skills: A news story reports that police chased a suspect for 90 minutes from Town X to Town Y, a distance of 300 miles. Possible? Hardly. The cars would be traveling 200 miles per hour to cover that distance in 90 minutes. Something is wrong with the information—unless the cars were literally flying.

Basic Math

Basic math errors show up continually in writing, usually because writers are careless. But a reader somewhere is going to see the error and doubt the writer's and the medium's credibility. Media writers need to know some simple math. At the very least, they need to recognize when data are misrepresented and find someone who can do correct calculations.

Percent. A news report says that the president's popularity dropped from 65 to 55 percent, a decrease of 10 percent. Correct? No. The decrease is 10 percentage points, but not 10 percent. That's the first lesson to learn in writing about percent. If you subtract 55 percent from 65 percent, you get a 10-point difference. To calculate the percent difference, you need to find the difference and divide that by the base or original figure: % = d/b (i.e., percent = difference/ base). Here, that would be 10/65, a change of 15 percent. It works the same way with increases. If the popularity goes up from 55 percent to 65 percent, the difference is 10 percentage points, which yields 10/55, or an 18 percent increase.

For another example, let's look at a financial story on company revenues. Suppose Midland Trucking Company had revenues last fiscal year of $535,000 and revenues this year of $635,000. The difference is $100,000. If you follow the formula d/b = percent difference, you would divide $100,000 by $535,000. The percent change is 18.6 percent or, rounded off, 19 percent.

If you made an error and divided the difference by the new amount of $635,000, you would get an increase of 16 percent, a significant difference from 19 percent—and one that could affect stockholders' perception of company management. The writer for the company's annual report must be careful in calculating numbers that could influence investments or stockholder confidence.

Rates. Often, writers will state numbers as a rate—1 in 10 or 3 in 100—so that complicated figures are easier to understand. For example, a writer finds a health department report saying that 0.0021 percent of teens aged 13 to 19 in the county became pregnant last year. The writer decides to translate the percentage into a figure that people can visualize.

One way to calculate the rate is to multiply the percent figure by 100 or 1,000 so that decimals no longer appear. In this case, multiplying 0.0021 by 1,000 gives a rate of 2.1 per 1,000. Rates can be stated by hundreds, thousands, tens of thousands, and on up. More clearly stated, the rate of teen pregnancy is

2.1 per 1,000, or about two teens out of every 1,000 teens aged 13 to 19 living in the county got pregnant last year.

Probability. Writers need to have an appreciation for probability theory and an understanding of the likelihood that a predicted event will actually occur. If there is a 40 percent chance of rain, how likely is it that we will get wet? Should we write or broadcast the news that rain is on the way? We hear probability each time we listen to a weather report. But if the probability of rain is 40 percent, it's important to remember there's also a 60 percent probability that the weather will be clear.

Writers often make errors when they combine one probability with another, such as "The football coach predicts a 50 percent chance of thunderstorms and a 50 percent chance the game could be delayed." Does that mean a 100 percent chance the game will be delayed? No. To calculate the probability in this case, you must multiply one probability with another. The probability of thunderstorms and a game postponement is .5 × .5 or a 25 percent chance both will occur.

Reporting Poll Data

Many numbers are reported in poll stories every day in the media. An article notes that the president has a 63 percent approval rating. What does 63 percent mean to the average reader or listener? Translated, the 63 percent means more than six out of 10 people (remember your percentage calculations from earlier in this section) approve of his performance—and four of every 10 do not. You can break that down even further to say simply that three out of five (divide 6 and 10 by 2 to bring to their lowest common denominator) people approve of the president.

When reporting poll data, it is important to make the statistics as clear and understandable as possible. Readers need to grasp what the numbers mean. To report poll numbers correctly, writers must be able to read the charts to determine what the poll figures mean. The following table presents poll results, divided into categories by income. These responses came from people queried at a local mall about whether they support Proposition Y, a proposal for a new city entertainment tax:

	Yes	*No*	*Total*
Earn $50,000 or less a year			
Count	148	152	300
Percent	49.3%	50.7%	100%
Percent of total	26%	27%	
Earn $50,001 or more a year			
Count	159	109	268
Percent	59.2%	40.8%	100%
Percent of total	28%	19%	

A writer notes that almost 50 percent of respondents who earn under $50,000 a year support Proposition Y on the ballot. He or she can even translate that 49.3 number to one out of two people interviewed in that income bracket and still be fairly accurate.

But then the writer notes that 59 percent of respondents earn more than $50,000 and support Proposition Y. Is the writer correct? No. The 59 percent figure represents what percentage of those people who earn that amount of money favor the proposition. The total number of people who earn $50,001 a year or more is 159 plus 109 (268). Of the 268 people in that income bracket, 59 percent favor the proposition.

To find out the percentage who actually earn more than $50,000 a year, go back to the actual counts and recalculate from there. If you add all the counts in each box, you will find 568 respondents to the survey. To find out how many earn more than $50,000 a year, divide difference by base, or 268 divided by 568, or 47 percent of those surveyed earn more money—much less than 59 percent.

It is extremely important when reading poll results to read the information correctly and calculate differences correctly. Also, be sure to translate your information into tangible language.

Margin of Error

A necessary part of poll reporting is reporting margin of error. In a poll on the safety of the nation, 87 percent report feeling safe, "plus or minus 3 percent." That "plus or minus" figure is the margin of error.

In simple terms, the error figure, usually from 1 to 5 percent, represents the accuracy of the poll results. Researchers know that in any survey they must allow room for error. Common sense and statistics tell us that the more respondents polled, the more accurately the poll results reflect the opinions of the public at large. Statistically, once the number of people polled reaches a certain level, the margin of error doesn't change or improve much. With several hundred respondents, the margin of error stays around plus or minus 4 to 5 percent. If careful sampling methods are used, poll results will allow researchers to interview 1,200 U.S. residents and then estimate what 280 million people believe. Most pollsters strive for a margin of error around 3 percent. Let's see how that works.

A poll says 45 percent of Americans believe the tax burden is too great on middle-income people. Another 42 percent believe it is just about right, and 13 percent have no opinion. The pollster reports a plus or minus 3 percent margin of error. Here's how the results look in chart form:

Reported results (with error +/– 3%)	
Too great	45%
Just about right	42%
No opinion	13%

The margin of error indicates the 45 percent who believe the tax burden is too great may, in reality, be 42 percent (minus 3 percent). Or it may be as high as 48 percent (plus 3 percent). Likewise, for those who think the tax burden is just about right, the range in reality could be as much as 45 percent to as little as 39 percent. So it's likely neither group can claim a clear majority. With such close percentages, a writer cannot say, "Most Americans said they think the tax burden on the middle class is too great." It would be more accurate to report that many Americans believe the tax burden is fairly distributed.

The Associated Press Stylebook has a separate entry for polls and surveys and lists items that should be included in any poll story. This entry discusses margin of error and urges writers to take care, especially when reporting that one candidate is leading another. According to the stylebook, only when the difference between the candidates is more than twice the margin of error can you say one candidate is ahead. The same rule applies to the tax burden survey results presented here: The difference between the two groups is 3 percentage points, not the 6 required to be twice the margin of error of plus or minus 3 percent. So it's clear that in the case of individual opinions about tax burdens—and in many political poll results—a writer would have to say that opinion is just about even.

Tips

Many schools and departments of journalism and mass communication require their students to have basic competencies in math. At the University of Maryland, College Park, faculty members in the College of Journalism require a score of B or better on a math competency test for all journalism and mass communication majors.

Students who want to test their skills can take a math test online at www .unc.edu/~pmeyer/carstat/. Professor Emeritus Phil Meyer and Associate Professor Bill Cloud at UNC-Chapel Hill produced the test, along with partner *USA Today*.

When writing about numbers, refer to *The Associated Press Stylebook*, which suggests rounding numbers to no more than two decimal places. Readers have little use for numbers such as $1,463,729. In this case, the writer needs to round the number to $1.46 million. Rounding numbers makes it easier for readers to digest numbers and helps avoid misreading.

The Associated Press Stylebook has other entries that relate to numbers, such as those on decimals, fractions, percentages, median, average, norm, and the metric system. Another section explains business terms. All these entries help writers when numbers are an issue—often the case in communications professions.

Slammer for Math

The following exercises will test your basic math skills. Please use a calculator. Answers are found in Appendix B.

1. The jury has 13 members. There are four members who are women. There are two African American jurors, and only one of them is a man. There also is one Hispanic American man on the jury. (Round percentages to the nearest tenth.)

   a. What is the ratio of men to women on the jury?
   b. What percentage of the jury is female?
   c. What percentage of Hispanic American men makes up the jury?
   d. What percentage of African American men makes up the jury?

2. The town manager tells the town council that he is proposing that the town build a new recreation center. The center would be 15,000 square feet. He has an estimate that the cost to build would be $85 per square foot plus an additional $25 per square foot for furnishings.

   a. What is the cost to build the center?
   b. What is the cost to furnish the center?
   c. What is the total cost for building and furnishing the center?
   d. Round the total cost to the nearest $100,000.

3. A local advertising company is sponsoring a community-wide yard sale in a local middle school parking lot. Each booth space is equivalent to two parking spaces. Each parking space measures 12 feet by 8 feet. The parking lot has 240 spaces.

   a. What is the square footage of one booth?
   b. How many booths can the advertising company rent?
   c. At $30 a booth, how much revenue will the company earn?
   d. You decide to rent two booths to get rid of your old furniture. How much space do you get?

4. Sarah Lamb owns a condominium valued for tax purposes at $175,000. The town's tax rate is 85 cents per $100 valuation, but the City Council is proposing to raise the tax rate by 3 cents for next year.

   a. How much in taxes did Sarah pay this year?
   b. How much will she pay under the proposed tax rate?
   c. What percentage increase will that be in her tax bill?
   d. If her property increases in value 5 percent by next year, how much will her tax bill be under the proposed tax rate?

5. Look at the following chart about support for three candidates for mayor.

	Small	*Small*	*Tucker*
Female			
Count	107	137	31
Percentage	38.9%	49.7%	11.4%
Male			
Count	192	137	23
Percentage	54.4%	39.0%	6.5%

   a. How many respondents were women?
   b. What percentage of the total respondents were women?
   c. What percentage of the total respondents favored Tucker?
   d. What percentage of the total respondents favored Small?

6. Christine wants to go to the state fair Friday night. Her mother said there is a 50 percent probability that she will be able to take Christine to the fair. But Christine's band director said there is a 75 percent chance that he will schedule band practice on Friday night. What is the probability that Christine will actually get to the fair?

7. Jonathan works 40 hours a week at a local hardware store. He earns $7.50 an hour. The manager said he will give Jonathan a 25-cent per hour pay raise. How much will Jonathan earn a week with the raise?

   a. $340
   b. $10
   c. $310
   d. $260

8. Mr. Tennyson is teaching his class how to convert to the metric system. If the average weight for the class members is 135 pounds, what is that in kilograms? (Note: 0.454 kilograms is equal to one pound.)

   a. 61.29
   b. 50.3
   c. 792
   d. 297
   e. 74.2

References _____

Christian, Darrell, Jacobsen, Sally, and Minthorn, David, editors. *The Associated Press Stylebook and Briefing on Media Law*. New York: The Associated Press, 2012.s

McAdams, Katherine C. *The Grammar Slammer*. College of Journalism, University of Maryland, 1991.

Meyer, Philip, Doig, Stephen, and Hansen, Barbara. "Statistical Tools for Computer-Assisted Reporting." www.unc.edu/~pmeyer/carstat/.

Penny, Mary. "Class handouts." Raleigh, NC: Needham Broughton High School, 1974.

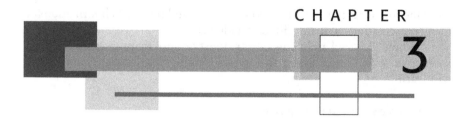

Editing for Audiences

Good writing depends on good editing. Many students or beginning writers assume a writing job is finished once they get a message written. But that's exactly when editing must begin, even in a short text message or microblog. With your final reading of any draft, ideas for improving the message should begin to flow: How can the message be more focused? Streamlined? Intriguing? What kinds of fine-tuning can send the message on its way, with clarity and accuracy, to intended audiences?

While some people choose editing as their job, every writer must be an editor. Self-editing has become even more critical as more content is posted online without being edited first. While an editor might read a story before it is printed in a newspaper or magazine, a story posted online might not be reviewed. A blogger might be both writer and editor for his or her own work. The burden for editing increasingly falls more squarely on the writer.

You already have learned some ways to improve your writing through strategic planning and correct use of language and numbers. These same techniques are applied in the editing process, along with many other guidelines. Hundreds of books have been written about editing (Amazon.com lists more than 1,500), all filled with advice and rules on style and correctness. No one can remember all the rules while writing a first or even a second or third draft.

Remember from the stages of writing in Chapter 1: Between the first draft and the finished product come polishing and editing. The first draft should be as good as possible; then, self-editing and the editing of others will refine and improve it. An accomplished novelist and teacher, the late Doris Betts told her students: "Handing in your first draft is like passing around your spittle." In other words, an unedited message is unprofessional and offensive.

Editing is more than just a courtesy to readers. It is a necessity because a single set of facts may be edited to produce several messages. For example, a print article on car maintenance might also be edited to appear in the "Living" section of a website or in an automotive blog. Editing is more than just checking for correctness: Today's editor sculpts and reformats information for many presentations to many different audiences.

When all is said and done, editors must be sure that messages conform to correct style before going to intended audiences. In this chapter, you will learn

- basic style and editing rules,
- how media sometimes require different kinds of editing, and
- steps to guide the editing process.

Watching Style

Part of good editing is ensuring consistency throughout writing. Using a consistent style guarantees that a certain pattern persists in word usage, titles, punctuation, abbreviations, grammar, and spelling. If "Dr." means doctor in the first paragraph of an online story, it will not mean "Drive" as part of someone's address later in the piece. Consistent usage builds credibility and reduces chances of audience confusion.

Media organizations follow a style that guarantees consistency. Most newspapers and public relations firms follow the style in *The Associated Press Stylebook and Briefing on Media Law*, updated annually as usage evolves. Other publications, including *The Washington Post* and *The New York Times*, have their own style manuals. Many universities and publishing houses use *The Chicago Manual of Style* or the style manual of the Modern Language Association. Online news sites don't share a common industry standard for style on things such as verb tenses, link text, and site navigation.

Media professionals also have to learn the "folk styles" that exist more as tradition than anything else and that vary from newsroom to newsroom. They also have to learn new styles, such as those developed with microblogging. Even in a world in which the rules are changing or not yet set, editors will be well served if they remember the reason that style rules exist in the first place: to help the audience more easily understand the message.

This book uses a style that differs from the Associated Press style, so you will notice discrepancies between usage in the text and in examples and exercises. The text follows the style established by the publishing house.

No one is ever expected to memorize stylebooks. Writers and editors must be familiar with the content of style guides so they know where to find the answer whenever a question arises. Writers learn certain rules used so often that they become second nature. For example, most writers become familiar with the capitalization rule for titles: Professional titles are capitalized before a person's name but never after a name. Here's an example, "University President Bill Sandler said classes would end early Tuesday because of the threat of a blizzard." After his name, the title would read, "Bill Sandler, university president, said...."

Basic Style Rules

The most broadly accepted style rules for professional media writers are those set out by *The Associated Press Stylebook*, which covers subjects as diverse as correct abbreviations for military titles, to spellings for Hanukkah and Santa Claus, to capitalization of Kleenex. Several categories in the stylebook are indispensable to media writers. Summaries of those entries that apply to news and online writing are included here. Because the general style rules differ for broadcast writing, they are included in Chapter 13.

Titles.   Long titles should go after an individual's name. William McCorkle's name is not lost if a short title is used before it, such as "University President William McCorkle." But his name would be hard to find if his title were "University Associate Vice Chancellor for Student Affairs and Services." When an individual has a long title, put the title after the name: "William McCorkle, university associate vice chancellor for student affairs and services."

When titles precede names, the titles generally are capitalized. After names, they are not.

Most titles are written out. The only time some are abbreviated is when they precede a name. *The Associated Press Stylebook* indicates which titles can be abbreviated. For example, "governor" may be shortened when used before a name, such as "Gov. Sheila Aycock" and "lieutenant governor" as "Lt. Gov. James Ramsey." Titles that are never abbreviated include "president," "attorney general," "professor," and "superintendent." Most military titles can be abbreviated, and those abbreviations are listed in *The Associated Press Stylebook*.

Stand-alone titles, those not followed by a name, are always written out, and they are never abbreviated or capitalized. Examples are "The vice president said he would turn over the files to the Justice Department" and "The Pakistani general will visit the United States in May." Note that "vice president" is not hyphenated.

Capitalization.   The general rule is to capitalize proper nouns that refer to a person, place, or thing. Examples include "Sacramento is the capital of California" and "Mayor Harmon Bowles agreed to lead the town's Independence Day parade."

Abbreviations.   Abbreviate only what your style manual permits. Abbreviate states' names when they are used with the name of a town or city; otherwise, write them out. Note that the Associated Press does not use postal abbreviations in text, except when the complete address is used with a zip code, as in "124 E. Main St., Lakeland, FL 33801." In other instances, the Associated Press uses the following abbreviations: Ala., Ariz., Ark., Calif., Colo., Conn., Del., Fla., Ga., Ill., Ind., Kan., Ky., La., Md., Mass., Mich.,

Minn., Miss., Mo., Mont., Neb., Nev., N.H., N.J., N.M., N.Y., N.C., N.D., Okla., Ore., Pa., R.I., S.C., S.D., Tenn., Vt., Va., Wash., W.Va., Wis., and Wyo. Eight states' names are never abbreviated: Alaska, Hawaii, Idaho, Iowa, Maine, Ohio, Texas, and Utah.

Months may be abbreviated when they are used with a specific date: "Nov. 12, 1948." Write out "November 1948," however. Never abbreviate March, April, May, June, or July.

Don't abbreviate the days of the week or the words "assistant" and "association."

The Associated Press allows some abbreviations on first reference because people are familiar with them, such as FBI, CIA, UFO, and IBM. But that does not mean writers should use only the abbreviation. The context of the story might require that the full title be used somewhere in the text. On second reference, writers may use the abbreviation or substitute words such as "the bureau," "the agency," "the object," or "the company."

Acronyms.   Acronyms are abbreviations that can be pronounced as words, such as "AIDS" for "acquired immune deficiency syndrome" or "UNESCO" for "United Nations Educational, Scientific and Cultural Organization." See style manuals for the correct first and second references for acronyms, just as with other abbreviations.

Numbers.   The general rule according to AP style is to write out numbers zero through nine and use numerals for numbers 10 and higher. Always spell out numbers at the beginning of a sentence, however. In writing numbers above 999,999, write out the words "million" and "billion" rather than using all those zeroes. For example: "To clear the site, the construction crew moved 1.2 million cubic yards of soil" and "Congressional aides discovered the budget would require an additional $1.4 billion in revenues."

AP style lists two dozen or so exceptions to the rule, but the main ones are these:

Age.   Always use a numeral for age: "She has a 3-year-old daughter and an 85-year-old mother."

Percent.   Always use a numeral: "He estimated 9 percent of employees are truly satisfied with their jobs."

Time.   Always use a numeral: "The guests will arrive at 9 p.m."

Dates.   Again, use numerals: "He was born Jan. 3, 1926."

Temperatures.   Use numerals for all temperatures except zero: "The weather service predicted the coldest weather in 15 years for the weekend, noting that temperatures would drop to 2 to 3 degrees below zero."

Dimensions. Always write height and weight as numerals: "The average height of the team's basketball players is 6 feet 4 inches." "The record-breaking carrot weighed 5 pounds."

Money. Write dollars and cents as numerals: "The price of an egg is about 18 cents." "Hemming the dress will cost $9."

Editing Responsibilities

As a writer, you are responsible for editing and revising your own work, even if you work in a newsroom with a separate copy desk or in a large corporate communications office where others ultimately will edit your work. You are the originator, the one who must shape and streamline the initial draft of the message. Your copy must be clear, fair, accurate, complete, and in correct style when it leaves your hands.

Many resources are available to help develop your editing skills, such as those listed in Box 2.1 in Chapter 2. One easily accessible guide is EditTeach .org (www.editteach.org), launched under a grant from the John S. and James L. Knight Foundation. Its website is geared "for editing professors, students and working professionals to help strengthen the craft of editing and support the work of editors."

As you gain experience as a writer, you also will be asked to revise the work of others. You might be promoted to an editing position or asked for help by others who know less than you do about good writing skills. When you edit others' work, you must apply both editorial and personal skills, coaching and negotiating respectfully with writers. Editing is hard work, and it is time consuming. It can be creative and satisfying. But in any case, it has to be done. Editing is a crucial part of all writing. And like other writing tasks, it proceeds in steps.

The Steps of Editing

Writers should consider editing as a process. Specific steps in editing allow writers-turned-editors to be focused and thorough in the editing process. Of course, writer-editors approach a news brief differently from a long feature. Sometimes, on first reading, an editor will decide the story needs substantial revisions; other times, only minor changes will be needed. That decision is made in the first step of the editing process and will determine how much time needs to be devoted to editing and rewriting.

Today's writers learn to edit at the computer. They might not have time to print out a draft and edit on paper. Editing on-screen saves time and allows the writer to use computer tools, such as the grammar-checker and Web resources for fact-checking, to help in the editing process.

Editing follows basic steps focusing on these elements in this order: content, completeness, accuracy, language, and final read-through.

Reading the Copy for Content.   The first step is to check for content. Read the written piece from start to finish to get a sense of what has been written. You may fix any minor errors, but at this point, determine whether substantial changes are needed. Note sections that need attention.

When editing your own copy, the ideal scenario is to put away a piece of writing for a few days and come back to it. Then you can look at it with a fresh eye—with the eye of an editor rather than the eye of the writer. But you might not have that luxury. If you are pressed for time, get up, walk around, have a snack, and get some fresh air. Then return to your writing. You will see it from a new perspective.

Read aloud to slow down and "hear" what you have actually written—not what you think is there. The most common errors detected by reading aloud are awkward language, inadequate explanations that confuse the meaning, and too much prose on a particular topic.

As you read and detect weaknesses, you can make simple notes, such as "fix," "delete," or "explain." If your piece needs substantial revisions, you might need to consider the audience again and ask yourself: "Does the message attract audience attention and meet audience needs? Does the introduction adequately set up the article? Are all the questions raised answered in subsequent paragraphs? Are opening sentences interesting and written to attract an audience to the message?"

To engage and hold the audience, a writer must look at the overall organization and ask the following questions:

- Is the message developed logically? Do facts follow in a clear sequence?
- Is the transition from one point to another effective? Each paragraph should be tied to the previous one.
- Are paragraphs organized so that each contains one thought or idea? Readers will be confused if too many thoughts are packaged in one paragraph. Start a new paragraph—basically a unit of organization—with a new quote or a new idea.
- Are there statements or sentences that interfere with understanding because they are out of context?
- Do all the quotes add to the message? Would it be better to paraphrase or omit some?

The answers to these questions may require rewriting prior to moving ahead with editing and considering the next step.

Checking for Completeness.   To determine if you need more information, ask the following questions:

- Is the message current? Are the latest statistics used? For example, a television news story on accidental deaths attributed to alcohol must have this year's figures on reported cases, not figures from two years ago, or even last year. Your audience wants to know how serious the situation is today. If those numbers aren't available, you need to say so, and explain why.

■ Are any questions raised left unanswered? Are all essential elements of the message present, including meaningful context? Each message must be complete. A news release that says a company is privately held must define what privately held means.

This step will show how much more reporting must be done so that copy is complete. If more research and subsequent rewriting are needed, you need to return to the first step, checking for content that flows smoothly and logically.

Checking for Accuracy.   Once the content and completeness are okay, writers and editors must check for accuracy—an intense, time-consuming job. No aspect of writing is more important than accuracy. Employees might ridicule an executive who includes inaccurate information in a newsletter. Readers turn away from publications and advertisements where they repeatedly find errors. Students lose faith in textbooks when they uncover incorrect data.

The bottom line is trust: If your audience doesn't trust the validity of any part of your message, it will question the accuracy of the entire message. Once it loses trust, the audience will be less willing to believe in future communications from you and might move to other media, never to return.

Research has shown that even one error in a newspaper can cause readers to doubt the rest of the paper and to have less faith in the reporter's abilities. Accuracy, therefore, can build or break your reputation, not just the reputation of the medium that carries the message. For example, if your online site relies on advertising to support content, the site might not be successful if information is not reliable. Use the following steps to check for accuracy:

■ Check name spellings. Review your notes. Double-check with a researcher or another writer. Use anywho.com or another online reference. Correct names are essential to avoid confusion—and even legal trouble—when people have the same or similar names. For example, in writing about a nightclub singer named Delsie Harper, a reporter inadvertently left off the D, and the newspaper immediately got a call from a church deacon named Elsie Harper.

■ Use reputable sources to confirm information. For example, the city budget director will have more knowledge on the next fiscal year's budget than will an anonymous city employee who calls a newspaper to complain.

■ Make sure quotes that contain opinion or outrageous claims are attributed. Here's an example: "Abused women get what they deserve," a self-proclaimed antifeminist said today. The quote has some credibility with the attribution but would have more if the antifeminist were named.

- If quotes are libelous—that is, damaging to a person's reputation—either make sure they can be defended or cut them. A person's barroom allegation about his next-door neighbor's drug use is not protected by law and should never be published. You could quote a witness's remark in a trial, however, because what occurs in court proceedings is protected. See more about libel in Chapter 12.

- Question statistics. For example, a story reports the president received positive approval from "more than half" of the nation. The actual statistic was 53 percent. The margin of error, or accuracy of the poll, was plus or minus 3 percent. Adding 3 percent to 53 percent means up to 56 percent of the country support the president. But subtracting 3 percent from 53 percent also means that as little as 50 percent of the nation approves of him. And 50 percent is not more than half. More about math is discussed in Chapter 2.

- Recalculate percentages. Your boss might tell you the company CEO will get only a 7.6 percent pay increase for a newsletter story on executive compensation. Check it. A raise from $150,000 to $172,500 is a 15 percent pay increase, not 7.6 percent. The inaccuracy would hardly make other employees confident in the department and its leadership.

- Rely on sources. On technical subjects, when there is doubt about an explanation, call an expert source, and read your material to that person for comment.

- Check links. Where links are imbedded or URLs are included for reference, check to be sure they are live and up to date.

Getting information right is also important because inaccuracies are audience-stoppers. When radio listeners hear statistics that they question, they puzzle over the error and no longer hear what you have to say. The best-constructed message framed in the finest form means nothing if your information is wrong or even confusing.

What if you cannot check a fact? Enlist someone else, such as a reference librarian, to verify what is in question. If you cannot verify information and you are working on a deadline, leave it out. If the information is vital to the message and it can't be checked, the message will have to wait. Never publish information if you have doubts about its accuracy. In a professional office, writers have help from editors or fact-checkers. But regardless of who helps, writers ultimately are responsible for the accuracy of their work.

Using Clear Language.   In this step, you are looking at word usage that will improve your writing. Consider these questions:

- Is the copy clear and easy to read?
- Are words simple, direct, and easy to understand?

- Are jargon and institutional language eliminated?
- Is redundancy eliminated?
- Are sentences short and to the point?

This step includes spelling, grammar, and punctuation. In the digital era, many writers use computers with spelling and grammar checking systems. Few spell-checkers adequately check troublesome homonyms, such as "affect" and "effect," "red" and "read," "naval" and "navel," "stationary" and "stationery," "trustee" and "trusty," "lead" and "led," and so on. Chapter 2 contains a guide to difficult spelling in the computer age.

Just as you have to check spelling, you have to review grammar. Chapter 2 discusses common grammar problems; consult the reference books listed in that chapter for additional help.

Writers must be on the lookout for jargon. Such language should be replaced immediately with clearer terms, so that, for example, "organizational inputs" becomes "suggestions from parent groups" and "facilitation of new methodologies" becomes "trying a new survey."

In this step of editing, you also should pay careful attention to word choice. Do you want to refer to a hit man as "specializing in conflict resolution"? Remember: The right word enhances audience understanding and willingness to pay attention, whether the message is read or heard. "Let your conscious be your guide" might not affect listeners. And some readers might not even notice the confused choice of "conscious" for "conscience." Those who do notice will not be impressed.

If you need to shorten your article, do so by looking at phrases, groups of words, titles, and word usage for shorter ways to state the same idea. For example, the statement "He decided to take part in the debate" could be rewritten "He joined in the debate." Or "The banners that were blue and white fluttered in the breeze" could be changed to "Blue and white banners fluttered in the breeze."

Giving the Piece the Last Once-Over. After revisions are complete, read the entire piece again. At this point, no major reworking should be needed. Check, however, for any editing errors that might have crept in during earlier steps. Check carefully for errors in any sections that have been added or substantially changed. Often, writers make new errors when they revise.

Some writers might question the sequence in editing. But the reasoning is quite simple: It is efficient. If reviewing for language came first, sentences that had been fine-tuned could be deleted during later content editing. It's far better that the sentences go first. More important, the most critical tasks are done first in case the writer-editor runs out of time. For example, it is more important to write a compelling lead than to smooth out a transition. And it is more important for the piece to be complete and accurate than free of style errors.

Note: Editors should be flexible as they edit. If they see a problem that needs to be fixed, regardless of the step, they should address it then. Editors who wait might forget to make the repair.

If you are in an organization or business, you might send your copy to your editor or to a corporate executive for review. If you are an advertising copywriter, the message will go to the account executive and then to the client. In print or online media, the story will go to an editor and in broadcast, to a news director. If you are a high school principal, your newsletter might be reviewed by the school system's superintendent before it is sent to parents. If you are a student, you turn the article in to a professor or instructor. Wherever your readers find your writing, they won't be shy about letting you know about the errors they find.

Never think that turning in your piece ends the editing process. The copy can always come back for another round of editing and changes before republication.

Editing for Online and Other Platforms

Online sites and electronic delivery have presented new opportunities for professional communicators. Microblogs can be posted to alert audiences to a breaking news story and link to an online site. Online news—unlimited by the physical space of a print publication or time constraints of a broadcast—can be more in-depth.

Editors who work online are often required to work quickly to post stories. And they are also required to be more comprehensive as they enhance the story with photos, audio, video, and links to material on other sites.

Online editors sometimes need to tailor the language of the news for the online audience. People who read news online often are more interested in what is happening now, rather than what is delayed or expected. Online readers might spend no more than a few seconds scanning a story before moving on. This perusal places emphasis on brevity and action.

When working online, editors must remember that their headlines, short descriptions, and key phrases might also function as live links. A click takes the reader to the full story or to a photo essay. So in addition to bearing information, these words must move the reader easily to related stories.

Online news also means more than just websites. More and more news is distributed as email, microblogs, or RSS feeds—and much information is shared on social networking sites such as Facebook. Editors should be aware of all the places their words will appear. In some cases, only a small portion of the full text will appear to the audience. Mobile devices such as smartphones present a smaller and shorter view of most messages. Editors need to stay abreast of continuous changes in tools the audience uses and the effect of digital media on writing and style. But regardless of the platform, the same basic editing process outlined earlier in the chapter enhances a writer's ability to craft a relevant and memorable message.

Well-edited websites exploit all the benefits of digital communication: brighter pictures, audio and video, links to original documents or sound, links to their social media networks, and the potential for instant feedback from an active audience. Readers expect to move quickly among media when they are online—from photos to video to sound to social media and back again. Audiences appreciate the extras that come with digital media: more choices, control, interaction, and variety. Writers and editors must deliver these benefits and remember that one story on a given topic could end up being the only story a reader might see. Editors must check to be sure each story is self-sufficient and fully connected to related materials.

When it comes to digital media, editors function as part of teams that could include artists, writers, photographers, videographers, marketers, and others. Even archivists and museum curators get involved when original documents become part of online content. Teams are important because audiences gravitate toward sites that have strong design and are easily navigated. Content is important, but so is the packaging.

Putting the Editing Rules into Practice

With your knowledge of guidelines for good editing in mind, read the following Associated Press story:

> DES MOINES, Iowa – A group of 20 workers at a Quaker Oats plant in Iowa stepped forward Wednesday to claim a $241 million Powerball jackpot.
>
> Lottery spokeswoman Mary Neubauer said the agency verified the winning ticket, which was sold June 13.
>
> One of the workers bought the winning ticket for the group, and the winnings will be split 20 ways, said Dan Morris, a spokesman for the Retail Wholesale and Department Store Union that all the winners belong to in Cedar Rapids, Iowa.
>
> Morris said the winners all are between 35 and 64 years old and work in the Quaker plant's shipping department.
>
> The winners are demanding anonymity following a day of public celebration.
>
> The 20 workers say they'll go to court to get an injunction ensuring their last names aren't released. It's believed to be the first time an Iowa lottery winner has chosen to take legal action to keep a name confidential.
>
> The announcement follows a day of celebration for the group that calls itself the Shipping 20. The group took a chartered bus paid for by their union from Cedar Rapids to Des Moines on Wednesday to present their ticket to lottery officials.
>
> "They're in shock. Still trying to recover," said Joe Day, the group's lawyer.

Day said the group had yet to decide what to do with the winnings, but described the winners as "ecstatic."

"Financial security for a lifetime," he said. "Anybody would want that."

The jackpot is the 15th largest won by Powerball players and, according to Neubauer, would amount to roughly $5.6 million per person after taxes if the group chooses the lump-sum cash option.

The story has compelling interest: magnitude with the size of the jackpot, oddity in the injunction to keep their names confidential, and human interest because 20 fellow employees won. The story follows Associated Press style in using numbers, abbreviations, and titles. Appropriate sources are quotes. This AP story was carried in media across the country along with a photo of the group wearing red, matching t-shirts and validating their tickets at Iowa lottery headquarters—despite the request for an injunction to protect their names.

Exercises

1. Check your ability to apply the rules you have learned so far. On a separate sheet of paper, copyedit the following sentences according to Associated Press style. Also check for any grammar, spelling, or punctuation errors.

   1. Lieutenant Governor Stanley Greene was stripped of his powers by the N.C. Senate.
   2. William Williams, Dean of the Graduate School of Journalism, will speak to students about graduation requirements on Wed. afternoon.
   3. The students are expected to begin the test at 9:00 a.m. Tuesday.
   4. The President lives at 1600 Pennsylvania Avenue, but his mail is delivered to the U.S. Post Office on Twenty-second Street.
   5. The state Senate is expected to enact a bill to require polio vaccinations for children under the age of two.
   6. The airport in Medford, Oregon was closed yesterday after an Alaskan airlines jet made an emergency landing on the runway.
   7. The Atty. Gen. has a B.A. in history from American University.
   8. The then-Soviet block countries sponsored the Friendship Games rather than attend the 1984 olympics in Los Angeles.
   9. The city and county used thirteen busses to transport the children to the July Fourth picnic.
   10. Water freezes at 0 degrees Centigrade.
   11. Three houses on Sims street were destroyed by the fire, which began at 112 Sims Street.

12. Following the Federal Reserve action, three banks announced a one percent increase in the prime rate, putting it at six percent.

13. The late Senator Jesse A. Helms (R-North Carolina) used to be city editor of The Raleigh Times.

14. John L. Harris, 48 years old, of 1632 Winding Way Road was charged Tuesday with cocaine possession.

15. The champion wrestler measured six feet six inches tall and won 4/5 of his fights.

16. Army Sergeant Willie York was charged with misappropriating $1,000,000 dollars in construction equipment.

17. Hurricane Diana, blowing from the East, caused millions of dollars in damages to the east coast of the United States.

18. Colonel Max Shaw, who has served as a national guardsman for more than 20 years, is Ed's commanding officer.

19. Ability with a frisbee is not a valid measure of IQ.

20. We heard the kickoff announced over the radio at the Laundromat.

21. The stockings were hanged by the chimney with care, in hopes that Kirs Kringle soon would be there.

22. Travelling the 48 miles, or 60 kilometers, to Kansas City, we got 32 miles per gallon in our new minivan.

23. The five-year-old boy got on the wrong bus and was missing for two hours.

24. Sarah sold two hundred and two boxes of Girl Scout cookies to her neighbors on Sweetbriar Pkwy. and Pantego Ave.

2. Read the following message. Assume the audience for this information is readers of the campus newspaper. Using only the available information, edit this message according to Associated Press style, and use proper spelling and grammar. Watch out for usage errors and redundancies.

> All of the faculty members from the School of Journalism and Mass Communication will be attending on Thursday of this week a regional meeting of the Association for Education in Journalism and Mass Communication at the Holiday Inn in the state capitol.
>
> The meeting will commence at 10 a.m. in the morning and conclude at 2 p.m. in the afternoon following a noon luncheon.
>
> In the morning, sessions will offer journalism educators the opportunity to have discussions on current issues addressing journalism and mass communication.
>
> At a luncheon program, professor Walter Blayless will be speaking on the topic of increasing online media use and the resulting effect on individual privacy.

> The meeting sponsored by AEJMC is exemplary of the several regional meetings the organization holds across the country each year. The National meeting is always held in August each year at different locations around the country.

As you edit, make a list of questions you would like to ask about information that would improve the message. Also make a list of the steps you followed in editing. Take these two lists and your edited story to your next class, where you can meet with a group of other students to discuss the strengths and weaknesses of various approaches to this editing task.

3. Look at the story you edited in Exercise 2. Now edit it as an online story that will be posted to the campus news website on Thursday morning, the day of the meeting. Which elements of the story are now most important to your audience? Is your lead the same? Or did it change? Also, add three links to related content on the Web and determine which words in the story should be used as links.

References

Christian, Darrell, Jacobsen, Sally, and Minthorn, David, eds. *The Associated Press Stylebook and Briefing on Media Law*. New York: The Associated Press, 2012.

Cook, Clair Kehrwald. *Line by Line: How to Improve Your Own Writing*. Boston: Houghton Mifflin, 1985.

Guidelines for Good Writing

For years, writing coaches have worked to distill a set of qualities in writing that will catch and hold readers. Many people, such as Roy Peter Clark at the Poynter Institute in St. Petersburg, Florida, have spent a great deal of their professional careers analyzing the qualities of good writing. Authors such as William Zinsser, best known for his book *On Writing Well*, offer advice on how to strengthen and improve prose. Even communication researchers, charged with finding out what makes publications sell, have considered which qualities are valued in messages. The research shows the most effective writing is simple and forceful; that is, it says it straight without flourishes and pomp.

In this chapter, you will learn

- four essential qualities in writing: accuracy, clarity, completeness, and fairness,
- five broad rules for writing that will appeal to audiences, and
- specific tips to improve writing.

Watchwords of Writing

No message will succeed if it does not have four essential qualities: accuracy, clarity, completeness, and fairness. We know from the discussion in Chapter 1 that audiences can be fickle; once lost, they might not return. Writing that is accurate, clear, complete, and fair has a better chance of holding audiences, particularly those who might be clicking through websites or leafing through magazines.

Accuracy ensures the credibility of all writing. When an audience catches a misspelled name or an erroneous date, that audience doubts the accuracy of the information that follows. An audience will abandon a communicator or a source it cannot trust.

Clarity means the writer uses language an audience understands. Simple language is preferred over complicated words. Jargon and technical language are avoided. The message comes through.

Completeness anticipates and answers an audience's questions. A complete message satisfies the audience and does so quickly.

Fairness occurs when the writer uses a variety of sources to keep an article balanced, excises any editorial opinion, and strives to be as objective as possible.

Let's look at each element more closely.

Accuracy

Good communication of any kind always contains accurate information. Accuracy is comforting to audiences, who depend on information. Errors can occur at any stage in writing: while gathering information through research and interviewing, transcribing notes, calculating figures, or creating the copy (when typos can occur). To ensure accuracy, writers must use good information-gathering techniques. They must obtain information only from reliable sources, then check and recheck it against other sources. If they find a discrepancy or an error but don't have time to check it, they should follow the adage, "When in doubt, leave it out."

We all are prone to commit errors on occasion. Just because a well-known person recites a fact or the fact is found in a well-known source, such as Wikipedia, doesn't mean it is correct. People might add to a database erroneous information that is not verified, and experts may inadvertently misquote results. Name spellings, middle initials, street numbers, birth dates—seemingly trivial details—become monumentally important once they become part of a message. Such details might be accurate in notes but then could be transcribed erroneously into copy.

Today's information environment constantly tests accuracy. Deadlines, competition, and 24/7 news cycles push reporters and editors to publish, post, or air the news quickly—sometimes too quickly. In their hurry to produce copy, writers run a greater risk of getting information wrong.

Errors have always been a danger to a communicator's credibility, but new technologies have made publishing even more treacherous for writers who don't take the time to get it right. Once incorrect information is online, it is available for others to pick up and repurpose. This incorrect information can then be found and sent forward by other writers who might also fail to double-check for accuracy.

Publishing information online has made it easier to spread inaccurate information, and it has also increased accountability for professional communicators. Some bloggers closely monitor professional news sites, standing ready to criticize inaccuracies. Two of the most prominent sites dedicated to correcting inaccurate information are Snopes.com, a semiprofessional site run by a California couple, and Factcheck.org, funded by the Annenberg Public Policy Center of the University of Pennsylvania.

If messages are wrong, people are misled. Writers and audiences rarely forget the mishap when a name is misspelled or an address is wrong. Inaccuracies in messages lead to distrust among audiences and can lead to libel suits. Once audience members are misled by a source, they have difficulty trusting it again. Even the venerable *New York Times* has struggled with lost credibility because of inaccuracies.

Clarity

A message will have impact if it is clear and straightforward and everyone in its audience can understand it. "Send a check for $75 by February 1 if you want to ski with the Seniors Club in February" makes the requirement clear. The writing is direct and uses simple, to-the-point language.

A message needs to be so clear that no misunderstanding or confusion can possibly result. People rely on media for information on where to vote, get flu shots, take vacations, enroll their children in school, and find cheap gasoline. If the directions to a polling site are unclear, such as "the church on Capitol Square," people will be unhappy when they arrive and discover a church on each corner of Capitol Square.

Style overlaid on a message can also get in the way of comprehension. The length limits of microblogging have created a new shorthand that might not be universally understood. One newcomer to texting thought "LOL" meant "lots of love" instead of "laugh out loud."

Completeness

Useful messages also are complete, giving sufficient information for real understanding and guidance. A news story that omits an important fact can be misleading and even harmful.

When an important highway intersection outside Washington, D.C., was under construction, traffic was rerouted for a 12-hour period. News reports warned drivers about the detour, but some neglected to mention the additional 45 minutes of drive time required to navigate the detour. This problem with completeness caused headaches for the many travelers who missed important appointments.

Again, length constraints of microblogs and texts can interfere with providing enough information. Writers using those platforms often solve the issue by creating tiny URLs that can send followers to a full story.

Fairness

Messages will be more believable if audiences sense that stories are fair. Readers or viewers will turn away from reports they feel are skewed or one-sided unless they are following a blog or writer they know has a specific agenda.

For a story to be fair or balanced, it must have a variety of sources. That doesn't mean that every story must present each side of an issue in the same detail and the same number of words. Such balance is not possible in most writing. A reporter might not be able to get in touch with sources on one side of an issue, but a simple statement that "the opposition party president could not be reached for comment" would let readers know that he or she tried.

Writers must be careful about the language they use so audiences don't ascribe any specific leaning or viewpoint to the story. Language should be neutral. Quotes can be inflammatory or weighty—but such language should be limited to quotes that are attributed to specific sources, rather than ascribed to the writer.

Keys to Good Writing

Researchers, language professionals, and experienced writers agree on five basic tenets of good writing: (1) use short sentences, (2) use short words, (3) eliminate wordiness, (4) avoid jargon, and (5) come to the point quickly. Anyone can apply the rules while writing and editing. These rules have become more important as messages shrink because of digital delivery.

Good Writing Uses Short Sentences

Most readability experts argue that regardless of age, education, or economic status, people prefer and understand writing that uses short sentences. People have little patience with long, complicated sentences that tax brain power. Of course, not all sentences should be short; sentence length should vary. A short sentence can have impact. A long, complex sentence can set up an idea for the audience or create a mood, and a short sentence can follow immediately— almost as a punch line. Get the point?

A study at the American Press Institute showed that reader understanding drops off dramatically if sentences exceed 20 words, and comprehension continues to drop as sentences grow longer. Only about one of 20 people studied could clearly comprehend 50-word sentences, a common length in newspapers and in academic writing.

Short sentences are critical in broadcast writing or links on websites. Tweets are limited to 140 characters and, therefore, demand short sentences as in this Twitter example from Mariah Carey on June 1, 2012: "Today we celebrate the life of the beloved iconic legend Marilyn Monroe who continues to inspire generation after generation." Often tweets are not complete sentences, however, and use abbreviated language.

Professor Fred Fedler of the University of Central Florida said that simplicity makes stories more interesting and forceful. He cites as an example a prize-winning story by World War II journalist Ernie Pyle in which the average sentence length was 10.6 words.

Good Writing Uses Short Words

Perhaps your high school English teacher praised you for using "penurious" rather than "stingy" or "inebriated" rather than "drunk." Then you were expanding your vocabulary, but now your audience will thank you for choosing the simpler word.

Just as with long sentences, readers and listeners become tired and discouraged when faced with too many complex words—usually those exceeding three syllables. To be sure, you can use commonly known, longer words, such as "responsibility," "establishment," "participate," and "governmental." Be sure, however, that the longer words are a better choice than a shorter version, such as "duty," "founding," "join," or "federal" or "state." Mariah Carey's tweet shows a good mix of words that everyone can understand: "celebrate," "beloved," "iconic," "legend," "inspiration," and "generation."

When writing, select the simplest word possible to convey the meaning. For example, in a police story, a writer said, "The contents of the suspicious package were innocuous." Some readers might wonder if the contents were dangerous or not. Use "fight" instead of altercation. Replace "finalize" with a word such as "conclude" or "finish." Rather than "exasperate," use "annoy" or "bother." Instead of "terminating" this paragraph, we will "end" it.

Good Writing Eliminates Wordiness

"You can almost detect a wordy sentence by looking at it—at least if you can recognize weak verbs, ponderous nouns, and strings of prepositional phrases," Claire Kehrwald Cook writes in her book, *Line by Line: How to Improve Your Own Writing*. Her advice gives writers clues about where to find wordiness and where to improve sentence structure.

Author William Zinsser notes that the secret to good writing is to strip every sentence to its basic components. Writers must detach themselves from the information and chisel it to the bare essentials. Writers must throw out extra words and phrases—even extra sentences and paragraphs. Remember this adage: "Two words are never as good as one." Consider the simple word "new." When used in the following sentence, it is unnecessary: "Crews expect the new building to be completed within two months." All buildings under construction are new. Leave the word out.

Audiences can find the facts only when excess is trimmed. Sparse writing is more professional, more informative, more objective, and more likely to be read. In Saltzman's *If You Can Talk, You Can Write*, writer Stanley Elkin describes the process of eliminating excess in writing: "[It's] a kind of whittling, a honing to the bone, until you finally get whatever the hell you're looking for. It's an exercise in sculpture, chipping away at the rock until you find the nose."

Wordy writing is likely to be redundant. No writer needs to say that a fire "completely destroyed" a downtown block; if it was destroyed, the destruction was complete. This classic often appears: "Jones is currently the manager of consumer services." "Is" means "now," and "now" means "currently." Kill the word "currently." Think about other phrases such as "past history," "acres of land," "4 p.m. in the afternoon," "at 12 midnight," "dead body," and "totally incomprehensible."

In seeking wordiness, look specifically for unnecessary adjectives and qualifiers. For example, a project cannot be the "most" unique. "Unique" means one of a kind. Qualifiers such as "very," "truly," and "really" can generally be cut without damage to copy.

Sometimes a statement or entire paragraph that repeats a speaker's direct quotes can be deleted:

> Jones said he was delighted the school would receive $40,000 to use for purchasing audiovisual equipment materials for the library.
> "I am just delighted that we will have the $40,000 to buy audiovisual equipment for the library," Jones said.

Delete the first paragraph. It does more than serve as a transition to the direct quote—it steals it.

As in art, too much embellishment in writing only detracts and distracts. Consider the effectiveness of the following message before and after its extra words are deleted:

> More than 100 years ago, the Tung Wah Dispensary attempted to cure the ailments and afflictions of the San Francisco Chinatown community from its humble outpost at 828 Sacramento Street. When the institution realized that its cramped quarters were counterproductive to the logistics of health care, it expanded its services and relocated to 845 Jackson Street, eventually being renamed the Chinese Hospital.

Simplified, the history looks like this:

> A century ago, the Tung Wah Dispensary treated sickness in San Francisco's Chinatown from its humble outpost at 828 Sacramento Street. Cramped quarters and expanded services led to a new location at 845 Jackson Street, the building that eventually was named the Chinese Hospital.

Without its embellishments—"ailments and afflictions," "institution," and "counterproductive"—this message is much more readable and just as informative.

Good Writing Avoids Jargon or Technical Language

In our high-tech society, so much jargon exists that it is difficult to tell what is jargon and what is plain English. Few people recall that "input" and "output" originated in computer jargon. The same is true of the terms "bottom line,"

"24/7," and "in the red." The Internet has given us "Google" and "blog" as part of common language.

Jargon abounds in everyday life. For example, in listing its objectives for the year, an annual report from an elementary school stated:

> Objective Three: The mean score for the kindergarten program will increase from 5.1 to 5.4 as measured by the FPG Assessment Report. The lead teacher for developmentally appropriate practice coordinated the efforts of our kindergarten teachers to enable our program to meet this objective.

For parents, what does this say? Not much. What is a mean score? What is the FPG Assessment Report? What is developmentally appropriate practice? When people see or hear such words, they stop. Confusion sets in. Parents just want to know how their children are doing in school.

Why Is Jargon Such a No-No? Jargon should be avoided for several reasons. First, it makes too many assumptions about audiences. Technical language serves insiders: those who are familiar with the lingo. "Outsiders" who could benefit from the information might be put off. For example, an art exhibit notice that contains artistic jargon might scare away potential visitors to the gallery. Technical terms might create a feeling that the gallery is reserved for an elite group. As a result, town residents might feel excluded or perceive the message as exclusive. For the same reason, it is also wise to avoid foreign words and phrases in published writing—unless those words are commonly used, such as *voilà*!

Second, jargon has precise meaning only to the insiders who use it. Once again, consider the word "input," which may be anything from telephone conversations to cash contributions. A more specific term is better.

Third, jargon usually is ambiguous. The "bottom line" mentioned in a school newsletter could mean many things: expenditures, income, or both; parent satisfaction; student learning outcomes—or almost anything. Skilled writers avoid vagueness by avoiding jargon.

Whether writers use jargon or technical language depends on their audience. If they are writing for a medical publication whose audience is nurses and doctors, the language can be more specific to that profession.

Too often, though, messages for general audiences or laypeople are filled with educational, legal, economic, or medical jargon. Some technical language has become more understood by the general public, such as "SAT" scores for "Scholastic Assessment Tests" and "AIDS" for "acquired immune deficiency syndrome." But such language too often goes unexplained.

Institutional Language. Another problem related to jargon is the use of institutional language: abstract terms and phrases that might communicate well in a specific workplace or institution but that lose meaning for a general audience. For example, medical professionals use the term "treatment modalities." That terminology is nonspecific and lacks meaning and interest, even to a well-educated general audience. Treatment modalities should be named in terms an audience can understand: a series of shots, an antibiotic for 10 days, physical therapy for several months, and so on. It is easy to find words to substitute for institutional terms, and the simpler words are always more specific.

A professor wrote, "Shrinking and unstable sources of funding lead to short-term dislocations." What he meant was that a lack of funding interrupts research. Some terms cannot be avoided such as the nation's "gross domestic product (GDP)." Writers must explain such words adequately when they use them. As *The Associated Press Stylebook* explains GDP, "The sum of all the goods and services produced within a nation's borders. In the U.S., it is calculated quarterly by the Commerce Department."

Although institutional language might be the conversational standard at work, it rarely works in writing. When you are talking, you can be sure how much your audience knows about your topic. You can supplement messages with hand gestures, facial expressions, and other visual aids. You can clarify or define confusing terms if your audience looks puzzled or asks questions.

When you are writing, your text stands alone and must be absolutely clear. Your goal as a writer is to eliminate misunderstanding; omitting jargon and technical language is a giant step toward that goal.

Good Writing Comes to the Point Quickly

Chapter 5 will focus on the need for writers to come to the point quickly, perhaps the most problematic of writing challenges. A writer might not want to come to the point because the point is unpleasant: A company has lost money or laid off employees, or a popular program has been discontinued. But audiences see through attempts to delay bad news and interpret them as sneaky ways to hide information. However unwelcome the message, direct communication conveys a feeling of openness and honesty.

Some writers fail to come to the point because they are in "writer's mode," self-indulgently crafting a long introduction to the main points rather than getting to those points. Readers of media writing want information rather than art, and they consider the most direct messages to be the greatest masterpieces.

Still other writers have trouble coming to the point because they do not know what the point is. Critical thinking—deciding on the main goal in communicating—precedes every writing task. To come to the point, writers must know their audiences and analyze information carefully enough to know the point audiences will want to know.

The late writer and filmmaker Nora Ephron told a story about her high school journalism teacher. In one lesson, he taught his class to recognize main points by telling them their faculty members would be attending a major conference the next day. He asked them to write a news story about it.

In the students' articles, the introductory paragraphs summarized the facts: All teachers would travel to a nearby city and hear famous speakers. After collecting the papers, the teacher threw them away and told the students, "The point is that there will be no school tomorrow." Ephron said she never forgot the point of that exercise:

> *It was an electrifying moment. So that's it, I realized. It's about the point. The classic newspaper lead of who-what-when-where-how and why is utterly meaningless if you haven't figured out the significance of the facts. What is the point? What does it mean? He planted those questions in my head. And for the first year he taught me journalism, every day was like the first; every set of facts had a point buried in it if we looked hard enough. He turned the class into a gorgeous intellectual exercise, and he gave me enthusiasm for the profession I never lost. Also, of course, he taught me something that works just as well in life as it does in journalism.*

Words

Three of the five keys to good writing just given—using short words, avoiding wordiness, and eliminating jargon—focus on words, the basic unit of any oral or written message. A good writer also needs knowledge of language, a good vocabulary, and the sense to know when a word is inappropriate or unnecessary.

The Power of Little Words

Most of the little words in our language come from the original language spoken in England before Roman and French invaders added their vocabulary to the mix. The English common folk retained their own words for everyday things, and they borrowed from Latin and French only when they had to.

As a result, the things nearest and dearest to us still are called by their original English names—home, fire, food, and mother, for example. And it is these words to which English-speaking people still respond emotionally. The word "home" has much stronger emotional appeal than the cooler, more technical word "domicile," which is borrowed from Latin. Likewise, "food" sounds good; "nutrients," a Latin-based word, is another matter.

How Little Words Are Successful

Professor and writing coach Carl Sessions Stepp says people respond to small words because they usually are "first-degree" words, or words that are immediately understood. Everyone has a single, readily available mental picture of "home," along with a host of meanings and feelings associated with that mental picture. But few people can respond so completely to "domicile."

Using "home" instead taps the audience's rich reserves of emotion and information.

Stepp points out that larger, multisyllabic words, many of which have origins in other languages, are "second-degree" words. Such words are abstract rather than concrete. They produce no immediate images in the minds of readers or listeners and are often ambiguous when other information is given. Take, for example, the word "nutrition." Does it mean food substances or measures of vitamins and minerals? It is a second-degree word because the audience needs more information for full understanding.

Consider other second-degree words, such as "facility" and "output." Compare them with these first-degree words: "school" and "grades."

Stepp argues that writers are more likely to appeal to audiences if they choose first-degree words and avoid second-degree words. In writing, we deal with many second-degree words that are part of science, technology, education, and almost every other field. Writers need to remember to define such words in first-degree terms whenever possible, as in this sentence:

> Nutrition—the kinds of foods patients eat every day—is the topic of a workshop for nurses at Sibley Hospital on Saturday.

Little words are more heart-warming and more easily understood. They also save space, time, and the reader's energy. They are more readable. In a story from the *Gillette* (Wyo.) *News-Record*, the language could not be much simpler in describing one man's journey and his goal to help others on their own paths (see Box 4.1). Most fifth graders could read the story with very little trouble.

BOX 4.1   A Gillette Teacher Finds His American Dream

BY NATHAN PAYNE
City/Living Editor

Bertine Bahige leaned back against the wall outside his classroom and looked at the ceiling as he tried to regain his composure.

It was his second class of the day and he already had been in a conversation with a student, trying to keep her in school long enough to graduate in a few weeks.

"I try to give them hope," he said, looking upward.

He wouldn't turn to face his class until he could regain his normal smiling demeanor.

Only minutes before, the 32-year-old math teacher had been greeting each of his students, as he does before every class. He asked them about their most recent performances in track or soccer or sometimes he ribs them about not keeping their grades up in English class.

"I don't understand that because I thought you all spoke English," said the teacher, whose native language is French.

Then came along the one he'd been looking for, the one whose future could hinge on his effort.

He knows she's looking ahead at life hoping to survive, not considering the idea of thriving. It's a fate he once faced himself, a fate he wants to help her overcome.

The countdown

Bahige caught her as she approached his classroom a few minutes before the bell rang.

Like an elementary school pupil might, the high school senior scuffed her feet a little on the polished terrazzo floors as she stepped to within a couple of feet of her teacher. The girl, a precalculus student, looked down and kicked at a line with the toe of her retro sneakers while the last few of her classmates walked past and took their seats.

They both knew what was coming. She is a good student, but she had missed several classes.

"Where have you been?" Bahige asked with concern in his voice.

She looked up with the forced smile of someone who has given up, the kind of smile that is betrayed by the pain in her eyes.

"My dad has been in jail, Mr. B," she said. "We're about to lose our house. I have to work."

She quietly told Bahige that her mother wasn't around, her uncle was moving across the state and she had nowhere to live. She had been working as many hours as possible to simply feed herself, and told him that by the end of the week, she could be sleeping in her car.

"I think I'm going to have to drop," she said, shaking her head.

"It's only 15 days," he pleaded with the senior, hoping she wouldn't lose the past 13 years of hard work, hoping she would see the value in a high school diploma.

She explained that administrators told her that they had limited options for a student like her who has missed so many days of school. How could she worry about coming to the last weeks of school, taking her last exams and wearing a cap and gown if she were homeless?

"I'll talk to some people," he said. "We will figure something out. Just come back to class Wednesday."

She uttered a less-than-reassuring "I'll try," and took her seat between a pair of classmates.

Bahige gazed at the ceiling as though he might find answers there.

He had only a few moments to compose himself before going into his classroom to try to make vectors, parametric equations and matrices relevant to his students' lives.

"I would let her stay in the spare bedroom in my house if it was appropriate," he said, trying to suppress his frustration with the system in which he works.

As he walked through the doorway, he smiled, said "good morning" and pointed to the chalkboard on the west side of his classroom.

On it was a calendar with a white "X" through each of the days past—a countdown to graduation.

(Continued)

(Continued)

"You only have 30 days left until graduation, that's only 15 days in each class," he said. "Make sure you get your work done. You're almost there."

As Bahige began to diagram a math equation for his students, he was as far from his past as he could be.

....

All it takes is hope

Two days after pleading with his student to stay in school, Bahige got what he had hoped for. When class began that Wednesday in April, she was there, in her chair, waiting to learn math.

Each day as Bahige crossed off another box on his countdown to graduation, she was there.

In a week when she and a few hundred of her classmates walk across the graduation stage, it doesn't matter that no one else in the Wyoming Center knows the significance of her accomplishment. Bahige will clap a little louder. She will smile a little wider.

They both know what it took to get there.

Hope.

COMPLETE STORY IN APPENDIX C.

Reprinted with permission of *The Gillette News-Record.*

The Right Word

Wordsmiths such as the late Theodore Bernstein and the late John Bremner long ago decried the lack of precision in language. Bremner lamented what he called "the surge of literary barbarism" in English usage. Both stressed the importance of knowing language and definitions. To language lovers like Bremner, writing is a love affair with language. In his book, *Words on Words,* Bremner wrote,

> To love words, you must first know what they are. Yes, words are symbols of ideas. But many words have lives of their own. They have their own historical and etymological associations, their own romantic and environmental dalliances, their own sonic and visual delights.

A careless writer describes a basketball player as "an intricate part of the team." Perhaps his footwork is intricate, but what the writer really meant to say was "an integral part of the team."

A morning news anchor said people were "respective" of the First Lady when she appeared at the fundraiser. She meant to say "respectful."

A letter from a university provost to a newspaper columnist thanked her for "the prospective" she gave to a local issue. The provost meant "perspective."

In a news story, a student quoted a speaker as saying the decision "reaped haddock" on the school's admissions procedures—a fishy use of "wreaked havoc." Language needs to be specific and correct. When writers misuse or misspell words, such as "brew ha-ha" for "brouhaha," we laugh. As writers, we do not want our audiences laughing at us—unless we mean for them to chuckle with us. The pleas of Bremner and other wordsmiths retain their significance for writers today.

Similar Words

Words that sound alike are troublesome for writers. Among the most common homonyms are "principal" and "principle," "affect" and "effect," and "its" and "it's." Such words are particularly troublesome today when writers depend heavily on computer spell-checkers. Few programs will know the difference between "naval" and "navel" or "stationary" and "stationery," as we discussed in Chapters 2 and 3. The resulting confusion can be misleading and embarrassing. Writers must be comfortable going to dictionary.com or another handy reference book to check correct spelling and usage. Other references, such as those listed at the end of this chapter, are valuable for writers. Refer to Chapter 2 for spelling tips.

Writers should pay careful attention to synonyms. Many writers haul out the thesaurus when they are weary of using a word too often. But a synonym might not be specific. One editing teacher advises against using a thesaurus and prefers a dictionary. Remember that repetition of a word or words throughout a message is acceptable. Repetition can unify a message. For instance, the word "site" might be used throughout a story about the launch of a nonprofit organization's website. It unifies the story and is more specific than other references to online presence.

Word Choice

While taking care with word usage, writers should strive to choose words that are universally accepted and understood. When writers are unsure about a word or its use, they should reach for a stylebook or a dictionary. *The Associated Press Stylebook*, for example, adds cautionary notes about how specific words should be used. The note might warn that the word is offensive or should be used sparingly. Dictionaries will include in the definition whether the word is below the normal standard for literate writing. Dictionaries also will indicate spellings of words and examples of correct usage, as in the case of homonyms. For example, "principal" would be used for the top administrator of a school, not "principle," which is a rule or belief that someone follows.

If a dictionary or a stylebook warns against usage of a word, writers should use it only if they have a compelling reason. They might also have to explain in a note at the beginning of the article or the broadcast that the message contains offensive language. Using profanities and vulgarities is discussed more fully in Chapter 10 on quotes and attribution.

Sentences

Sentences should be complete. Each must have a subject and a verb and must state one complete idea, thought, or meaning. Granted, some writers use short but incomplete sentences for emphasis, such as "The day he left was cold and in the dead of winter. January 22, to be exact." Sentence fragments or stray phrases generally have little place in most media writing, and beginning writers should avoid using them. Such writing does appear in microblogging, however.

This is a fragment: "January 22, to be exact."
This is a sentence: "The day he left was cold and in the dead of winter."
This is a sentence: "That day was January 22, to be exact."

Sentence Types

Grammarians define different types of sentences on the basis of structure.

- A simple sentence is one independent or main clause. It can have more than one subject and verb, object, and modifying phrase.

    The tanker ran aground, spilling 11 million gallons of crude oil into the bay.

    Six seniors and two juniors are on the university's debate team.

- A compound sentence has two or more simple sentences that may be joined by a conjunction such as "and" or "but" or by punctuation such as a semicolon.

    Homer used his share of the settlement to buy a fishing boat, but within two years his business was bankrupt.

    Many people have changed their diets to cut out high-fat foods; others have ignored warnings that a high-fat diet might cause heart disease.

- A complex sentence has at least one independent or main clause and other clauses dependent on the main clause.

    Postings on a social networking site might open your private information to third parties, despite your belief that those details are locked away from everyone but family and friends.

- A compound-complex sentence is a compound sentence with at least two independent clauses and one or more dependent clauses.

    When the stock sale occurred in May, investors expected it to do well; but it lost value immediately, crushing all their hopes.

Vary Sentence Types

Good writers use a variety of sentence types, but they prefer the simple sentence. A good guideline is to use many simple sentences and to use compound sentences formed from short simple sentences.

Writers use complex sentences because of the need for attribution, elaboration, and identification. But they work hard to avoid compound-complex sentences, saving them to express ideas difficult to state any other way.

Studies show that people of all ages and levels of education prefer simple sentences, in which subjects come before verbs and verbs before the remainder of the sentence. A series of simple sentences relaxes readers or listeners and prepares them to encounter something more complex in your text.

Look at the sentence variety in Box 4.2 in Tim Sullivan's story on Tibetan monks learning science. He begins with a mix of complex sentences and simple sentences in the first paragraph.

BOX 4.2   Tibetan Monks Tackle Science in the Indian Hills

BY TIM SULLIVAN
The Associated Press

SARAH, India — The shouts of more than a dozen Tibetan monks echo through the small classroom. Fingers are pointed. Voices collide. When an important point is made, the men smack their hands together and stomp the floor, their robes billowing around them.

It's the way Tibetan Buddhist scholars have traded ideas for centuries. Among them, the debate-as-shouting match is a discipline and a joy.

But this is something different.

Evolutionary theory is mentioned—loudly. One monk invokes Heisenberg's Uncertainty Principle. Another shouts about the subatomic nature of neutrinos.

In an educational complex perched on the edge of a small river valley, in a place where the Himalayan foothills descend into the Indian plains, a group of about 65 Tibetan monks and nuns are working with American scientists to tie their ancient culture to the modern world.

"I'd like to go back to my monastery...to pass on my knowledge to other monks so that they might bring the (scientific) process to others," said Tenzin Choegyal, a 29-year-old monk born in exile in India.

If that seems a modest goal, it reflects an immense change in Tibetan culture, where change has traditionally come at a glacial pace.

(Continued)

(Continued)

Isolated for centuries atop the high Himalayan plateau, and refusing entry to nearly all outsiders, Tibet long saw little of value in modernity.

Education was almost completely limited to monastic schools. Magic and mysticism were—and are—important parts of life to many people. New technologies were something to be feared: Eyeglasses were largely forbidden until well into the 20th century.

No longer. Pushed by the Dalai Lama, a fierce proponent of modern schooling, a series of programs were created in exile to teach scientific education to monks, the traditional core of Tibetan culture.

At the forefront is an intensive summer program, stretched over five years, that brings professors from Emory University in Atlanta. For six days a week, six hours a day, the professors teach everything from basic math to advanced neuroscience.

"The Buddhist religion has a deep concept of the mind that goes back thousands of years," said Larry Young, an Emory psychiatry professor and prominent neuroscientist. "Now they're learning something different about the mind: the mind-body interface, how the brain controls the body."

...The monks and nuns in the Emory program are...brought to the Sarah complex "the best and the brightest," Worthman said, brought to the Sarah complex from monasteries and convents across India and Nepal. While most are in their 20s or 30s, some are far older and long ago earned high-level degrees in Buddhist philosophy.

Still, few learned anything but basic math before the Emory program. Because of the way they study—focusing on debates and the memorization of long written passages, but doing comparatively little writing—few are able to take notes during classroom lectures. Many were raised to see magic as an integral part of the world around them.

To watch them in class, though, is astonishing.

No one yawns. No one dozes. Since almost no one takes notes, it's easy to think they're not paying attention.

But then a monk or a nun in a red robe calls out a question about brain chemistry—or cell biology, or logic—that can leave their teachers stunned.

"They really understand how neurocircuits work at a level that's comparable to what we see at a senior (undergraduate) neuroscience classroom in the United States," said Young.

Common Sentence Errors

In constructing sentences, some writers forget the rule of parallel structure, noted as a grammar problem in Chapter 2. In writing, all parts of any list or series must be parallel—that is, if the first element in the list starts with a noun, all others must be nouns as well. For example, the structure of this sentence is not parallel:

> Plaintiffs reacted to the court's decision with sorrow, rage, surprise, and vowing to appeal the ruling.

Nouns in the list, "sorrow, "rage" and "surprise," are not parallel with the verb form "vowing." The sentence should be rewritten to read:

> Plaintiffs reacted to the court's decision with sorrow, rage, surprise, and vows to appeal the ruling.

When writers start with a specific verb form, such as an infinitive with "to," they must keep the same format. The structure of the following sentence is not parallel:

> In the new budget, the county will have funds to expand social services, to hire five police officers, and for adding bike lanes to Main Street.

It should be rewritten to read:

> In the new budget, the county will have funds to expand social services, to hire five police officers, and to add bike lanes to Main Street.

Another common sentence error is the incorrect placement of modifying phrases or clauses. Such misplaced elements can lead to humorous and misleading sentences, such as the following:

> After wheeling me into the operating room, a mask was placed over my face.

> The bank makes low-interest loans to individuals of any size.

> Mrs. Rogers was arrested shortly after 3 p.m. at the home where the couple lived without incident.

Once spotted, modifier problems are easy to repair. Good writers train themselves to check modifier placement: Did the mask really wheel me into the operating room? Does the bank make loans based on height and weight? Did the couple really live in the house without incident? The questions can be cleared up by quick rewriting:

> After I was wheeled into the operating room, a mask was placed over my face.

> The bank makes low-interest loans of any size to individuals.

> Mrs. Rogers was arrested without incident shortly after 3 p.m. at the home where the couple lived.

A good sentence can never be interpreted to mean more than one thing. Linguists say it has a "single reading"—meaning the reader never needs to go back and read it again to understand it. If the reader goes back, it should be to savor the quality of the writing. Good writing aims for a single reading, so readers move unobstructed through messages to meaning. Once they understand the message, then readers can act or react—and communication is complete.

Paragraphs—Short Paragraphs

Words become sentences, and sentences become paragraphs. English composition books devote entire chapters to the topic of writing good paragraphs. When writers are concerned with transmitting information quickly, their ideas about paragraphing change. A paragraph is a whole presentation or argument on a topic for an English composition or literature class, whereas in mass communication, a paragraph is a single fact, thought, or "sound byte." That single thought or idea might take several sentences to explain. In newswriting, paragraphs often are kept short to break up blocks of gray copy. Journalists talk about "graphs," a shortened version of "paragraphs." One thought or idea is in a graph, and graphs are one sentence on occasion.

Effective use of four graphs of varying lengths is shown in the opening of this story written by *St. Pete Times* reporter Michael Kruse to describe damage from Hurricane Katrina:

> WAVELAND, Miss.—City Hall is gone.
>
> The post office is gone.
>
> The restaurants, the condos, the houses. Gone, gone, gone.
>
> In this coastal town of about 7,000 people, on a wide swath of land that stretches about a mile up from the Gulf of Mexico, almost everything south of the railroad tracks is gone.

Newspaper and magazine writers start a new graph to signal a new fact or a change of speaker—and sometimes just to give the reader a break. Readers appreciate white space in a publication, and frequent paragraph breaks give visual relief by making space—literal and figurative—between ideas.

New Speaker Equals New Paragraph

One of the most useful functions of a frequent paragraph break is that it effectively signals a change, particularly in the case of a direct quote or a change of speakers when several people are quoted. In Nathan Payne's story referenced earlier in this chapter, he uses new paragraphs to separate quotes from actions. Consider this excerpt found in the full story in Appendix C as he describes Bertine Bahige's escape from the rebels:

> With silent steps, he crept away, tiptoeing through the jungle. The snap of a twig or the rustling of leaves could have meant the end of his life.
>
> "I knew I didn't have a choice for failure," he said. "Death was not an issue. There was no prison. You have to overcome fear."

Or the change in speakers in this section of Payne's story:

> "I think I'm going to have to drop," she said, shaking her head.
>
> "It's only 15 days," he pleaded with the senior, hoping she wouldn't lose the past 13 years of hard work, hoping she would see the value in a high school diploma.

With quotes, the short graph adds a conversational tone to newswriting and holds the audience's attention. "New speaker, new graph" is a writer's rule that can add clarity to all writing.

Most writing can benefit from shorter paragraphs. Bite-sized paragraphs may not be appropriate in all settings, but leaner paragraphs tend to streamline messages of all kinds, saving time and space—the most precious resources in any medium.

The Way to Clearer Writing

Writing often moves from the general to the specific, and this chapter is following such a path. At the outset of the chapter, we discussed broad principles of accuracy, clarity, completeness, and fairness. We then looked at the basic tenets of good writing and the components of any piece of writing—words, sentences, and paragraphs—as summarized in Box 4.3. When listed, the rules seem more manageable.

BOX 4.3   Good Writing Rules

1. Good writing uses short sentences.
2. Good writing uses short words.
3. Good writing eliminates wordiness.
4. Good writing clears away redundancy, jargon, and institutional language.
5. Good writing comes to the point quickly.
6. Good writing has a mix of sentence types.
7. Good writing has short paragraphs.

Write the First Draft as You Would Say It

Writing coach Robert Gunning said writers should write the way they talk. He argued that all writing would improve if people simply talked and wrote down what they said. Gunning was onto a great idea: First drafts are most effective when a writer puts down on paper what he or she would tell someone about a topic. Most people talk in subject–verb–object order that is easy to understand. The result is text that is conversational, uses simple language, and is easy to revise into a well-organized written message.

Colorful Description

Author Tom Wolfe made his mark among fiction writers by writing the way he talks—frankly, and with rich description. In his bestseller, *The Bonfire of the Vanities*, Wolfe describes Maria, the girlfriend of his antihero, Sherman McCoy:

> *Now Maria pushed the door all the way open, but instead of ushering him inside, she leaned up against the doorjamb and crossed her legs and folded her arms underneath her breasts and kept staring at him and chuckling. She was wearing high-heeled pumps with a black-and-white checkerboard pattern worked into the leather. Sherman knew little about shoe designs, but it registered on him that this one was of the moment. She wore a tailored white gabardine skirt, very short, a good four inches above the knees, revealing her legs, which to Sherman's eyes were like a dancer's, and emphasizing her tiny waist. She wore a white silk blouse, open down to the top of her breasts. The light in the tiny entryway was such that it threw her entire ensemble into high relief: her dark hair, those cheekbones, the fine features of her face, the swollen curve of her lips, her creamy blouse, those creamy flan breasts, her shimmering shanks, so insouciantly crossed.*

In this passage, all parts of speech become part of the description. The verbs are active: pushed, leaned, folded, worked, and threw. The nouns—doorjamb, pumps, flan, shanks—are concrete and tangible, and the adjectives appeal to the senses: high-heeled, black-and-white, checkerboard, tailored, fine, swollen, creamy, and shimmering. All writers can learn from Wolfe's gift for conversational, dense description that leaves readers with strong sensory images.

Description can be less literary and still paint a picture, as in this excerpt describing a lighthouse that is being restored into a bed and breakfast:

> Rust is what visitors first see when they enter the 140-foot-high Frying Pan Tower. Plus corrosion. Peeling paint. Missing ceiling tiles. The tower has been deteriorating in the wind-and-wave-swept environment since Coast Guard crews left 33 years ago.

The living quarters can best be described as utilitarian. Peeling beige paint hangs from the walls of the rec room. Chairs, table, faded dartboard and pool table are legacies of Coast Guarders. Their cats, Bacon and Eggs, once played here.

Kitchen appliances work when the generator fires up. An elderly refrigerator huffs air that's more cool than cold.

Don't Begin at the Beginning

After seeing a four-car collision, the typical observer arrives home and blurts out: "I saw an incredible wreck on Highway 501. Four cars collided; all the drivers were injured, and one car burned." Only then will the observer back up and give background: "I was in the left lane, coming home from the mall," and so on.

Like urgent conversation, writing needs to jump straight to the point, then fill the reader in—just as we will discuss in Chapter 5 on writing leads. This technique gives writing a conversational tone and at the same time gets to the ever-so-important point of the message.

Starting with salient facts is a natural way to tell about important information. Unfortunately, it is a form that most people forget after years of reading stories and writing essays, both of which usually start with formal introductions. Your goal is to get to your main point as soon as possible in your message. Suspenseful beginnings work best in drama.

Writing and Editing: Two Compatible Tasks

When you spill out your conversational first draft, write it without stopping to edit. Mixing writing and editing wastes time and effort. If you edit as you go (and most amateurs do), you might fuss over a sentence you eventually cut. At the very least, you will interrupt your own thought processes and conversational flow. So write first. If you pause to ponder sentence structure or information, that's okay. But do not wander or stray from writing.

Some beginning writers lack the confidence to sit down and write. But author Joel Saltzman points out that we all are more competent wordsmiths than we think:

> *When you're talking, odds are that 98 percent of the time you don't even think about grammar. You're doing fine and it's just not an issue.... I am suggesting that you don't worry about it right now; because the more you worry about grammar, the less you're going to write.*

Stick with Subject–Verb Order

Most human languages prefer to place subjects before verbs, and English is no exception. Curious people want to know who did something, then what they did (and to whom or what). Keep these audience interests and preferences in mind when you write. Subject–verb–object order generally gives the sentence action.

> Soldiers cleared rocks the size of houses from blocked roads.

> A massive earthquake registering 8.2 on the Richter scale rocked Japan early Friday.

Readers get confused if subjects and verbs are scrambled, regardless of how artistic the result may be:

> Came he swiftly to her bower?

Not in the information age.

Choose Active Verbs

Verbs are action words, but not all verbs are active. Some show no action at all, such as the verb "to be" in all its forms (is, am, are, was, were, be, being). Such verbs are less interesting and harder to picture than active verbs.

Writers prefer active verbs because they contain more information and sensory detail. "He was president" is vague compared with "He dominated the country as president." "Lightner whacked the ball with such force that it sailed over the right outfield wall" simulates the sound of the bat striking the ball. Good writing is filled with active verbs that evoke images in the mind of the reader or listener. In the following lead, the writer uses active verbs in a weather story:

> MOSCOW, Ind. (AP)—Tornadoes ripped through this central Indiana community and skipped over National Guard barracks full of sleeping soldiers as thunderstorms battered the Ohio Valley, authorities said Wednesday.

Choose the Active Voice

When writers use active verbs, they write in active voice.

"Lightner whacked the ball." The subject, Lightner, performs the action. The object, the ball, receives action. This sentence format is called *active voice*, and it is the natural order of English. "A man wearing a stocking mask robbed the university dining hall" carries more action than "the university dining hall was robbed by a man."

Every now and then, a sentence has no obvious subject and must be written in another format, called the *passive voice*. Take, for example, this sentence: "The law was changed several years ago." It is in passive voice. The recipient of the action, the law, has been moved into the subject position— probably because a long legislative process kept the writer from isolating a single person or session responsible for changing the law.

Research shows that people prefer active sentences over passive ones. The sentence "Congress passed the bill" is easier to read and comprehend than its passive equivalent, "The bill was passed by Congress." Skilled writers prefer the active voice and use passive sentences only when necessary. In our example about Lightner, a passive structure would hardly have the same effect: "The ball was whacked by Lightner."

Sometimes writers use passive sentences for emphasis: "The anticrime bill that will give police departments more powers was passed by Congress." Here the writer wants to focus on the provisions of the bill rather than on congressional action and writes the lead accordingly.

Generally Put Time Elements after the Verb

Because verbs are stimulating to readers, they should come before less interesting elements. Audiences need to know when something happened, but they can wait to find out. The time element, a necessary but often dull part of a message, can be relegated to a place after the verb. Some writers prefer to put it immediately after the verb. Here are a few examples:

> The second annual Wiener Festival, featuring dachshunds of all sizes and breeds, will be held Saturday in Laurel.

> Grant applications requesting up to $100,000 for research on learning disabilities may be submitted through June 15 to the National Institutes of Health.

Sometimes, however, the time element carries importance and needs to go elsewhere—even first in the sentence:

> On Wednesday, a 14-year-old youth collected $125,000 he found in a paper bag a year ago. No one claimed the money.

In the above example, the beginning and end of the sentence set up the time span: On Wednesday, the youth cashed in after waiting a year.

> Beginning July 1, North Carolina residents will need to show their Social Security cards or verify their numbers when getting new or replacement driver's licenses.

Right away, people know the laws will change.

Be Specific

Always give the most specific information you can. Significant details enlighten and delight readers and pack information into a few words. Instead of saying actress Mischa Barton went shopping, tell what she bought: toys for her dog.

What kind? Inquiring minds want to know! Instead of saying a reporter had a messy desk, try this:

> On his desk, Howard had a can of unsharpened pencils and two potted ferns, both of them dead.

Watch out for words that have almost a generic quality, such as "facility." Be specific: bank, gymnasium, recreation center, high school. Use the specific noun.

Author Tom Wolfe has a marvelous talent for combining simple words into colorful, entertaining description. In *The Bonfire of the Vanities* excerpt we discussed earlier in the chapter, Wolfe creates pictures with his prose. Like other excellent writers, he uses language to appeal to the senses. Wolfe gives specific details, such as the skirt riding "a good four inches above the knees" and the "checkerboard pattern worked into the leather." His technique is one that all good writers use, regardless of the medium.

Appeal to the Senses

Whether reading or listening, audience members still can use the full range of senses as they absorb information. That means writers must pay attention to their senses when gathering information. Writers can report the facts or describe the scene without being subjective—a fear that keeps many beginning writers from using descriptive writing.

Consider this description of a rower as she launches her boat for a post-dawn row:

> A slight fog clouded the surface of the water, creating an eerie stage to the backdrop of oranges, yellows, browns, and greens of the trees' fall foliage on the far shore. As she carried the scull to the dock, she caught the familiar odor of rotting wood and scum that accumulated along the lake's edge. She eased the boat into the water, and the bow made a gentle plop as it cut the surface and sent a ripple outward. She loved this time of the morning, the lake silent except for nature's noises.

Writing that creates mental pictures, aromas, and sensations is more memorable and more appealing because it transports the audience to the scene of the message. Once captured, the audience is likely to remain in the writer's world long enough to get the message.

You don't need to be a feature writer to use sensory appeal. It works well in everyday forms of communication, such as directions to the company picnic. Instead of "turn right two blocks after the fork in the road and proceed to 1511," how about:

> Look for a grove of tall pines two blocks after the fork in the road; turn right and go to the red mailbox marked 1511. You'll smell pungent smoke from Marvin's famous barbecued ribs.

With such sensory appeal, it is doubtful anyone will get lost.

Use Statistics Sparingly and Powerfully

We live in an era where numbers make powerful messages: A basketball arena will cost $221 million. A pharmaceutical company will lay off 1,600 workers.

Audiences become desensitized if bombarded by alarming numbers, regardless of how striking those numbers may be. Statistics of any kind should be delivered one at a time. Never let two numbers touch in written copy; avoid putting numbers close to one another except in direct comparisons:

> The report assumes oil prices ranging from a low of $113 a barrel to as high as $186 a barrel by 2030; a barrel was trading above $133 on Wednesday.

Another rule of thumb is to limit yourself to no more than three numbers in any paragraph to avoid overwhelming your reader or listener. In a business story, for example, numbers can be confusing, so spread them out and keep them simple. Consider improving the following lead packed with numbers:

> Dr. Marcy LePique, a Flagstaff obstetrician and gynecologist since 2003, has delivered more than 10,000 babies and about 20 litters of puppies in her 25-year career as a physician and 30-year career as a breeder of golden retrievers.

Professor Emeritus Philip Meyer, a former consultant at *USA Today*, suggests that in any statistical report one or two numbers stand out as crucial. The important numbers should appear early in your message, and others may be summarized in lists or tables outside the written text.

Translate Statistics into Everyday, Tangible Terms

People have little intuitive understanding of large numbers. The citizen who learns that a sports arena will cost $221 million is left with many questions: Is that a good price for an arena? How many new schools would that buy? How much will my county taxes increase?

Good writers provide an understanding of big numbers in several ways. One way is to compare one number with another:

> The $221 million price tag compares with the $58.2 million cost of an arena built in 1989 in Springfield.

Another way to present numbers is to give them in terms the average person deals with each day. Few of us can visualize $221 million, but many people can understand a 3.5 percent tax increase to fund the stadium.

The clearest way to present costs is to use an individual citizen as an example:

> A person owning a home with a tax value of $254,000 will pay about $320 more each year in taxes to finance the arena.

Such writing allows the audience to understand personal gains or losses that may be obscured in reports of large numbers.

Double-Check Your Math

Many writers jokingly say they went into communications because they could not do math. But any writer needs to use numbers and must be sure they are correct. Errors can be embarrassing.

In a news story about salary increases at city hall, a reporter looked at the current year's salary for the city attorney: $130,000. The proposed salary for the next fiscal year was $138,000. The city attorney would get a 5 percent pay increase, she wrote. The actual increase was 6 percent. The reporter erroneously divided the difference of $8,000 by the new salary rather than the current salary. Other city employees were upset that the city attorney was getting 5 percent compared with their 2 percent. When the real difference eventually was published, the unhappiness grew. (And the city attorney expressed his anger that the figures were published at all, forgetting that the salaries of public officials are public record.)

When in Doubt, Leave It Out

Unless you check the accuracy of a number, spelling, or surprising fact, leave it out or hold publication until you can verify it. Accuracy is linked, in the minds of audience members, with quality—with media quality and writer quality. Your reputation is riding on what you write.

Some errors are painful to people in the community. A university magazine noted offhandedly that a famous scientist had discovered a new kind of plant. His research assistant, who in fact had made the discovery and received credit for it in scientific journals, called the reporter to correct the error. Few people will ever see a small correction notice, but people such as the offended research assistant will remember the slight for years.

Mistakes, no matter where they appear, also may lead to legal problems. Chapter 12 discusses libel.

Rewrite Long Introductory Phrases

Audiences are eager to get to the point, and long introductory phrases slow them down. Long phrases also interrupt the subject–verb–object pattern that readers and listeners prefer.

Avoid:

Because the Cardinals had been waiting all season for a victory and had received what they considered to be negative media attention, several players refused to be interviewed.

Prefer:

> Several Cardinals players refused to be interviewed after a winless season amid negative media coverage.

Eliminate Long Strings of Prepositional Phrases

Any group of two or more prepositional phrases makes a sentence meander rather than flow. Too many prepositional phrases strung together within a sentence are undesirable but easy to fix. Prepositional phrases are among the movable parts of any sentence; they also can be placed in new (short) sentences.

Avoid:

> The school's marching band will appear in a series of performances on three consecutive Tuesday afternoons on the athletic field near the gymnasium on the school campus beginning this Tuesday.

Prefer:

> The school's marching band will present a series of Tuesday afternoon performances beginning this week. The band will play on the athletic field near the gymnasium.

Look for unnecessary prepositional phrases everywhere in writing. Take

> Marilyn Jacobs, one of the writers of the letter, said the group wants action immediately.

and edit it to read

> Marilyn Jacobs, who helped write the letter, said the group wants action immediately.

Avoid Making Everything Look IMPORTANT

Some writers like to add emphasis by underlining text or using capital letters, exclamation marks, bold type, and even quotation marks. Frequent use of such elements detracts from professional polish. Once in a while, everyone needs to add emphasis. Save it for when it really counts. In some messages, such emphasis can be interpreted as anger, exasperation, and even sarcasm.

Avoid a message that looks like this sentence:

> If you don't get your information sheet in today, you WON'T be in the new directory AT ALL.

Try:

> If you don't get your information sheet in today, you won't be in the new directory.

Clear Out Euphemisms

Most of us were taught to use euphemisms in polite conversation—to say "expecting" rather than "pregnant," "plump" rather than "fat," and "passed away" rather than "died." Most euphemisms are designed to be imprecise—to mislead or give false comfort. In fact, we like euphemisms because they are handy substitutes for embarrassing words. In media writing, straight talk is preferred.

Avoid:

> The guard said two residents of the correctional facility had gone to "their just reward."

Prefer:

> The guard said that two prisoners had died.

Using the straightforward "prisoners" and "died" instead of the longer euphemisms keeps the sentence short and the reading easy. Once euphemisms are removed, the meaning is clear and timeless.

Watch Out for Language Trends

Writers should avoid popular trends in writing that substitute a myriad of words and phrases for ones that had been part of common language. In many cases, the new language is wordy and less precise.

The use of such "pop" language excludes segments of the audience that might not be cued to the lingo. Certainly language evolves. Each time a new edition of *Webster's Dictionary* comes out, new words are included. Many of us can remember when "ain't" was not in the dictionary. Dictionaries list and define words common in the English language, but a dictionary is just one of many sources writers use.

One trend that has pained language experts is the conversion of nouns to verbs. Host has become "to host," and conference has become "to conference." An advertising director notified clients: "We will deadline ad copy for Friday's paper on Wednesday." An anchor said the state was considering "tolling roads," or charging tolls to pay for construction. Many computer terms already are accepted usage, but some writers still cringe when they hear nouns used in verb forms such as "texting," friending," or "googling."

Another trend that offends many writers is the addition of "-ize" to create new words: "prioritize," "finalize," "maximize," "accessorize." Again, although the words have found their way into everyday usage, language professionals try to find better and more accurate verbs.

Keep Writing Readable

Readability is defined most simply as the level of difficulty of a given message. Readable, or high-readability, writing is easy to understand. Several ways to measure readability have been found, most of which are based on (1) sentence length and (2) concentration or number of multisyllable words.

One common readability measure is the Fog Index, developed in the 1940s by Robert Gunning for United Press International wire service. Despite its age, the Fog Index is still used as a measure of readability. To compute a Fog Index, (1) calculate the average number of words per sentence in a given message and (2) count the number of difficult words, or those with three syllables or more, in a 100-word sample from the message. Add these two figures together and multiply by 0.4.

The resulting number—the Fog Index—corresponds to the number of years of education a reader would need to read and understand the copy. For example, a publication with an average of 22 words per sentence and 15 difficult words in the 100-word sample would have a Fog Index of 14.8. That means its readers would require some college education to read the piece comfortably.

Most readability experts agree that clear writing should be at or below the 11th- and 12th-grade levels. Even people with a great deal more education seem most comfortable reading at this level. Many grammar-check software packages have readability measures that automatically tell writers the readability of any piece. The *Wall Street Journal's* Fog Index routinely falls into the 11th- to 12th-grade range, despite the complicated nature of financial reporting. A clever marketing strategy is operating here: Dow Jones knows that to make business reports palatable, they must be readable.

Enough Guidelines!

So many guidelines and rules may seem overwhelming. Fortunately, writers should write without thinking about all these maxims at one time.

Guidelines explained throughout this chapter can help with direct writing. Keep the guidelines in mind as you write, but do not be so tied to them that you stop after every sentence to analyze whether it meets the standards of good writing. Go ahead and write and then go back and apply the guidelines.

Exercises _____

1. Edit the following sentences to make them shorter and to the point:

   ▪ In order to expedite the delivery, the company will add a third delivery truck for its routes on Monday.

   ▪ We will have pizza for dinner whether or not you choose to come.

   ▪ She is presently employed as the assistant to the president, but she expects to make a decision whether or not to change jobs by the end of the year.

   ▪ If they are willing to pay the difference between the economy pack and the family pack, customers will learn that the family pack will save them more money in the long run.

   ▪ Students voted Thursday to conduct a poll to determine the status of living conditions in dormitories.

   ▪ Clarendon Park residents will march Saturday to protest the city council's decision to annex the neighborhood over residents' objections.

   ▪ If the school maintains lines of communication and makes the alumni feel as if they are still a part of the school even though they have already graduated, the school should have no problem reaching its fund-raising goal.

   ▪ The residents of the neighborhood said they would petition the city council to reconsider again the decision to allow beer sales before 11 a.m. on Sunday morning, which would be against the wishes of many church-going citizens.

   ▪ Fifteen scholarship winners, who were chosen because of their high academic achievement, will be given $15,000 in scholarship money to use at the college of their choice after they graduate from high school.

2. Edit the following to eliminate redundancy:

   ▪ Susan is currently director of marketing sales.

   ▪ He served as past president of the Rotary club.

   ▪ The elementary school will need twenty-five acres of land for a multipurpose building, playground, and ball fields.

   ▪ Fire completely destroyed the town hall in the month of June.

   ▪ The future outlook for the economy indicates interest rates may rise slightly.

   ▪ The circus will be at 3 p.m. Sunday afternoon and 7 p.m. Sunday night.

   ▪ Due to the fact that more than two-thirds of the people did not respond, the picnic will be canceled.

   ▪ She climbed up the tree in order to get a better look at the defendant.

   ▪ John went on to say that any student's effort should be recognized.

   ▪ The Broadway show will close down six months after it first began.

3. Look through newspapers, magazines, and websites and select an article or blog that shows five or more of the characteristics of good writing mentioned in this chapter. Clip or print the piece you selected and write a short paper, listing the guidelines for good writing that are followed. For each guideline you mention, quote a passage or paragraph that shows how the writer used the good writing rules or techniques.

4. Calculate the Fog index for (a) a newspaper article, (b) a celebrity tweet, (c) a story on EPSN.com, and (d) the opening paragraph in one of your textbooks. How does readability compare across these publications? What conclusions can you draw from this comparison?

References

Beard Henry, and Cerf, Christopher. *The Official Politically Correct Dictionary and Handbook*. New York: Villard Books, 1992.

Bernstein, Theodore M. *Dos, Don'ts and Maybes of the English Language*. New York: The Times Book Co., 1977.

Bremner, John. *Words on Words*. New York: Columbia University Press, 1980.

Christian, Darrell, Jacobsen, Sally, and Minthorn, David. Editors. *The Associated Press Stylebook and Briefing on Media Law*. New York: The Associated Press: 2012.

Ephron, Nora. "Writers' Workshop," video series produced by South Carolina Educational Television, 1982.

Gunning, Robert. *The Technique of Clear Writing*. New York: McGraw-Hill, 1954.

Pyle, Ernie. *Here Is Your War*. New York: Pocket Books, 1945.

Saltzman, Joel. *If You Can Talk, You Can Write*. New York: Ballantine Books, 1993.

Stepp, Carl Sessions. Excerpt from videotape, "Taking Charge of Your Local Paper." Washington, D.C.: National Rural Electric Cooperatives Association, March 1993.

Strunk, William, Jr., and White, E. B. *The Elements of Style*, Third Edition. New York: Macmillan, 1979.

Wolfe, Tom. *The Bonfire of the Vanities*. New York: Farrar, Straus & Giroux, 1987.

Zinsser, William. *On Writing Well*. New York: Harper & Row, 1976.

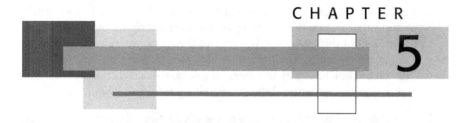

Getting to the Point

When the president of a university spoke at her installation ceremony, she discussed the broad issue of improving undergraduate education and specific ways to achieve that goal. Media began their respective stories from different angles. The student newspaper focused on greater rigor in classroom teaching. A television station with a broad viewing audience began its 6 p.m. report with her call for accountability to state legislators, then posted video and the text of her speech on its website. The university's alumni publication looked at the outcome: the continued strength of the university's reputation and the value of its degree.

Because audiences are information-seeking, writers have to let them know right away what is in the message. Writers familiar with their audiences know which information will be relevant and appealing. Writers must alert audiences to important messages. They know what will attract the attention of the individual who juggles time for job, home, spouse, children, hobbies, and friends.

Messages must therefore hook the audience, whether a 140-character Microblog or a 2,500-word feature. The hook must be set in the first few words, sentences, or paragraphs. The opening sentences are known as the *lead* of the message. In the lead, writers must show the relevance of the message and attract, entertain, and inform audiences or drive them to a website for more information. The lead helps readers or listeners decide whether the message is compelling, entertaining, or informative enough to warrant their full attention.

Leads must fit media styles and formats. While a longer descriptive lead might work in the print edition of a newspaper, a shorter version with important elements that can also help index the story's content would appear on the online site. Even with microblogs, such as Twitter, the entire message serves as a lead to send readers to the entire story. Writers today need to know how to write all types of leads.

This chapter will discuss lead writing, specifically,

■ the role of leads in capturing audiences,
■ elements in lead writing,
■ news values, and
■ types of leads.

What's the Point?

To hook a particular audience, writers must know why they are writing. It sounds simple enough. But many people regard writing as an artistic endeavor, not as a craft. They avoid thinking about the substance of what they are going to say. Their copy might ramble because they have not figured out the main point of the message, an essential first step in hooking the active audience.

Determining the point requires critical thinking. Writers must look at the components of the message and weigh each one according to its importance and relevance. These steps are part of the stages of writing discussed in Chapter 1.

What does an agricultural community need to know about issues in a state legislative session? What do other state residents need to know in general? These audiences will need different hooks when a bill is introduced in the state legislature. While the agricultural community needs to know about potential changes to exemptions for farmland, residents in general want to learn about proposals to increase their state income tax. As writers consider information and audiences, they get closer to the point of the message, establishing where they want to start.

Getting to the point is like opening a package: As you open the carton, you get closer to the real heart of your search. You might toss out Styrofoam popcorn, then layers of tissue paper. Finally, you uncover the gift—the point of your search.

Finding the point of your story is essential to writing. Along the way, writers will discover facts and pieces that relate to the main point, surrounding and supporting it like the tissue paper. Other pieces could be discarded later. But the discovery process must be completed first.

Consider the advertising copywriter who says, "I want to write an ad that will get more business for my client." He or she is still handling the whole package—a big and unworkable problem. Thinking and planning—a stage of writing—will help in moving from the broad idea of producing an ad to the task of communicating the benefit of the service or product.

If the client makes hand lotion, the advertiser's point might be beautiful hands or healthier skin or convenient packaging. If the client owns a tax service, the point might be customer peace of mind and the accountant's knowledge of tax laws. Once that key benefit—the point—has been identified, the writer's job is to select precise words that will emphasize that point and grab a consumer's attention. And once writers have established where to start, they will know where to go next.

In crafting messages, writers focus on the point, the hook, the lead, and the copy.

- The *point* is crucial information that justifies creating a message in the first place: A bill is passed. Middle-income residents will get a break on state income tax rates.
- The *hook* is an enticing opening phrase or sentence that draws audiences into a message. You might soon see more money in your paycheck.
- The *lead* is the opening few sentences of a media message. Typically, it contains the hook and the point. State residents who earn less than $75,000 a year will take home more in their paychecks starting in January, thanks to a new law that dramatically changes the state income tax rate applied to middle-income earners.
- The *copy* is the entire body of a media message, including a lead and all supporting information, such as new facts, background, quotes, and statistics.

In the Beginning Comes the Lead

The lead has a heavy responsibility. By educating, entertaining, or enlightening, it stimulates the reader to pay attention. The lead is relevant to the audience. It also entraps. A publisher once wrote that a lead must be provocative, vigorous, and even at times startling to the reader.

Every piece of writing has a beginning or opening statement; every piece of writing has a lead. Long-time syndicated columnist James J. Kilpatrick once wrote:

> *The lead is vital to any writing, whether one is writing a novel, a short story, a book review, a term paper, a newspaper editorial, or a homily to be read in church on Sunday morning.*

A lead needs to establish relevance for readers, such as college students:

> If you plan to have a summer internship next year, be aware that managers often begin their searches in October and November and make offers in December.

Writing a lead is a crucial assignment for any writer. It ensures that readers get the point quickly so that they can stick with the story or move to other messages.

The lead must also set up the story. After reading or hearing the lead, audiences should know the main points of the message that follows. If not, the lead has misled them, and the writer's credibility is damaged. How does a writer know whether the lead sets up the story? When the story is complete, a writer must consider the key information in the body of the message and ensure it is noted in the lead.

For example, a story reports a robbery at the campus dining hall and includes details about the robber locking the dining hall manager in a closet. That fact should be noted in the lead, along with the information about how the robbery occurred and how much money was taken. The chronological details of the robbery appear later in the body of the story.

Leads and Audience

Different audiences will react differently to leads. That makes sense. The audience of a local newspaper expects writing that differs from what readers of a campus newspaper will want. In a campus newspaper, leads will be focused for a university audience and its interests. The local newspaper has to attract an audience that includes students and university staff as well as people with no connection to the campus. The local newspaper might consider the leads in a campus newspaper inappropriate for its audience.

Writers, whether for newspapers, websites, television stations, blogs, or magazines, have to structure their leads to suit their audiences.

When the U.S. Supreme Court upheld part of an Arizona law to allow police to check the immigration status of people stopped, detained, or arrested, media wrote leads that would be relevant to their readers. National media wrote leads that were focused on the implications for all states, while Arizona media had more local leads. Compare the first lead from *The Washington Post* to the second lead from the *Arizona Daily Star*:

> The Supreme Court on Monday said states may play a limited role in enforcing laws on illegal immigration, upholding part of Arizona's controversial law but striking other portions it said intruded on the federal government's powers.

And:

> The nation's high court ruled this morning that Arizona can require state and local police to check the immigration status of those they have stopped.

In each lead, the writer focused on the Supreme Court decision. The Arizona paper, however, brought the story closer to home by stating specifically what the decision will permit police to do.

How to Get Started

Before constructing a lead, writers must know their information thoroughly. They must look at information collected via research or interviewing, then evaluate it, using judgment and experience to determine what is most relevant to their audiences. As a prewriting activity, some writers go through their notes and add priority numbers next to particular facts.

For example, before writing the lead that tells student readers they should plan in the fall for the next summer's internship, a writer should list information to be included: Students want internships; editors plan eight to 10 months ahead; offers are made in December; don't wait. Next to each fact, the writer should put a number corresponding to its importance to the audience.

In writing the lead, the writer determines that the audience does not need to know the specific date that editors begin to interview or how many editors interview in the fall. Priority number 1 is that editors will start looking soon and readers can avoid missing out on an internship if they plan ahead. The writer sets out the main part of the story—getting ready to seek internships—and then the relevance—students can miss the opportunity to apply if they wait until spring.

Writers can try another prewriting approach to evaluating information. They can simply ask, "What must my audience know?" and then list three to five things in order of importance. In the case of internships, the list would look something like this:

1. It is almost time to start planning for next summer's internship.
2. If students want to have an internship, they need to be prepared now.
3. Editors make hires in December for next year's interns.

The main point would become the lead. Other points would be fashioned into the rest of the copy. Writers then would have followed the format that many journalists use—the inverted pyramid, which ranks information in descending order of importance. That format is discussed in Chapter 6.

Writers who struggle with ranking information and its relevance should remember that most people want to know the personal angle first. It all comes down to the audience's automatic question, "How does this message affect me?" The audience immediately looks for the explanation.

Sometimes stories or messages don't have that simple, personal component. Then writers must look beyond the "what about me?" question to other factors that make some pieces of information more important than others. Such factors are also guides to selecting information for the lead. Those elements are called *news elements* and *news values* and are discussed next in this chapter.

News Elements

Certain elements are of interest in all writing. Journalists over the years have spelled out the elements that must appear in news stories: who, what, when, where, how, and why. While those elements have been critical in news, the list is a basic starting point for any writer in determining what will go first.

These news components can form a question: "Who did what to whom, how, when, where, and why?" Every letter, news story, news release, and most microblogs or advertisements will answer this question.

Why are these elements so important? Because people are most interested in other people, who they are, what they say and do, where they live and work, what happens to them, why they make certain choices, and how they deal with those choices. People also want to know about events that pertain to their interests or celebrities who have captured their attention. They are interested in conflict, competition, and achievements. People want to know about other people who overcome adversity, who are defeated, and who do the unusual. Look at this example:

> A Hollywood, Fla., man and woman exchanged wedding vows at 1,300 feet as they plummeted to earth hand-in-hand under silver parachutes five miles west of here Wednesday afternoon.
>
> Grace Mason and John Kempner met while skydiving at a local club and decided it would be the most significant way to start their married life together.

The elements are there:

Who: Grace and John
What: Got married
When: Wednesday
Where: Near Hollywood, Fla.
How: By parachutes
Why: Because they wanted to start married life in a manner meaningful to their courtship and to them

The two-paragraph lead summarizes what happened. Readers can decide whether they want to read further to learn more about Grace and John. The author has also set it up so that after two paragraphs, the reader knows the most important information and can turn to another message.

Where to Put *Who* and *What*

Putting all the elements in the first sentence can result in a long, convoluted sentence. Consider the following lead and its clearer rewrite:

> Sam Atwood, an associate professor of political science at the university, told students in a speech Thursday in MacPherson Hall that they should be more concerned about world events that more and more directly affect their lives and their future.

Rewritten:

> Students should be concerned about world events that more and more directly affect their lives and their future, an associate professor of political science at the university said Thursday.

In the rewrite, students get the content first. Rather than the professor's complete name, the writer uses a descriptive phrase or identifying label to describe him. The location of the speech and why he was giving it can be included in a subsequent paragraph.

Writers must decide which elements deserve emphasis and are most relevant before they write a lead. All elements will be included somewhere in the story. As a general rule, who and what will be included in the first sentence. Where and when will also appear here because they take up little space. This formula also follows the natural order of the English language: subject, verb, object. Focusing on who, what, when, and where automatically sets up an active structure: "A masked man robbed the university dining hall of $3,000 Wednesday night and locked the dining hall manager in a closet." How and why can be included in the first sentence if they are unusual. A full explanation usually will require several sentences or paragraphs.

Consider this tweet from comedienne Joan Rivers on June 1, 2012:

> *Madonna launched her world tour in Tel Aviv and she looks great...for a woman only 10 years younger than the State of Israel.*

Consider this lead that focuses on *who*, *what*, *when*, and *where*:

> A 14-year-old girl from San Diego correctly spelled "guetapens" and claimed the Scripps National Spelling Bee title on Thursday at National Harbor in Maryland.

Again, the elements are there:

Who:	A 14-year-old girl
What:	Won the National Spelling Bee
When:	Thursday
Where:	National Harbor, Maryland

A Closer Look at the Elements

Let's define the lead elements and what role they play in the copy.

Who defines the person carrying out the action or affected by the story. *Who* may not be a specific name, such as Grace or John, but rather an identification or label. For example, a news release might say in the first sentence that two marketing employees have been promoted and in the second sentence give their names and titles. But if the president is retiring, his name will be given first because it has recognition among company employees and in the community, as in the following:

> Charles Southwick, chief executive officer of Englewood Mills who began his career sweeping floors, will retire April 1 after 42 years with the company.

The *who* is Charles Southwick, specifically named because of the role he plays in the local business community. *What* represents the action: He will retire. Usually, *what* can be simply stated in a verb. Consider this news lead:

> University students will pay $250 more per semester in tuition starting in the fall semester to generate enough funds to restore library collections drastically affected by previous budget cuts.

The phrase "will pay $250 more per semester in tuition" tells *what*. Similarly, in a newsletter to parents, the verb "donate" tells *what*:

> Southeast High School's PTA is asking parents to donate money by July 31 to put at least two computers in every classroom.

What in the example is asking parents for money.

When tells the audience the timeliness of the event or the time frame of specific actions. Often it is one word. In most writing, *when* will go after the verb because the time element rarely is the most interesting information. Few leads begin with *when*. In the tuition example above, "the fall semester" tells when the increase will occur. In the lead on the PTA letter, the time frame is more specific, asking parents to give by July 31.

When can also be used to set up a longer time frame, as in this lead from *The Atlanta Journal-Constitution*:

> ATLANTA—The ghosts of Auburn Avenue still haunt the storied Atlanta street where the Rev. Martin Luther King Jr. was born and black wealth thrived for decades.
>
> Today, the street is a shell of its former self, the bustling mix of banks, night clubs, churches, meat markets and funeral homes long gone, replaced with crumbling facades and cracked sidewalks.

The writer sets up the time frame between what happened more than 60 years ago and today.

Where gives the reader the geographic context of the story. In many cases, location will pique audience interest because readers want to know about events around them. The closer the story is to the reader's backyard, the greater the interest will be.

Many stories, such as those filed by wire services, often start with *where* by using a dateline—the name of the city in capital letters—to let readers know immediately where the event occurred.

> CAIRO—Two American men seized by Bedouin tribesmen were released unharmed Thursday, the latest among several other tourists abducted but later freed unharmed.

In stories without a dateline, the exact location would be the first word or words in the lead only when it offers some unusual aspect to the story. Usually, the *where* is tucked elsewhere into the lead.

> A slice of history awaits you at the Tastee Diner in Silver Spring.

How expands on *what*. Look at the following lead from the Associated Press:

> LONGMIRE, Wash—A Mount Rainier ranger slid more than 3,000 feet to his death on Thursday as he helped in efforts to rescue four injured climbers who fell on a glacier, a National Park Service spokesman said.

The lead tells *who*, *what*, and *where* but also talks about *how*: how the ranger died.

Why gives the audience the reason a decision or a change was made or is pending or the cause of an event. In the ranger example above, readers know why he died: because he was helping to rescue stranded climbers.

In the newsletter, parents are asked to give money. Why? So the school can buy computers. *Why* is often oversimplified or overlooked. Writers should go beyond superficial explanations.

Remember: *How* and *why* should appear in the first sentence or lead if there is some unusual aspect or if they are essential to understanding the message. Consider this Associated Press lead:

> DES MOINES, Iowa—An Iowa woman is running barefoot across the United States to raise money to provide shoes for needy children.

This woman is raising money (*why*) to buy shoes for needy children and (*how*) by running barefoot as the attraction for the fund-raiser.

Watch Out for Too Much

Sometimes all elements fit concisely into a lead, as in the example of the barefoot runner (*when* is implied as now because of the verb construction "is running"). But because all elements do not have to appear in every first sentence, a writer can set up the point of the story by using a few elements in the first sentence and explaining the other elements in later paragraphs. Consider this lead:

> Plans for a major housing development that preservationists believed had died last year have been resurrected by developers who say local planning officials are much more receptive to the revised version.

Are *who*, *what*, *when*, *where*, *how*, and *why* all answered in this first sentence? No.

Who:	Developers
What:	Are resurrecting a housing development plan
When:	Implied now, but not stated
Where:	Implied in the county, but not specifically stated
How:	Not stated
Why:	Because planning officials seem more receptive

The lead would have been too complex if the writer had included more elements, such as adding that preservationists will fight the renewed development with a door-to-door campaign before a planning board hearing next month and the exact location of the 300-acre site. With complicated material, the writer should consider a lead that sets out the new information in the first paragraph followed by some context or an explanatory quote in the second graph.

A lead attracts readers to the story because it has other elements—not just *who, what, when, where, how,* and *why*—that must be considered when the writer is structuring the first sentence. These other elements are called *news values*.

News Values

In structuring leads, writers are guided by what journalists traditionally have called *news values*, or aspects of an event that the audience might want to know about. The more writers know about their audience, the easier it is to predict the news values that will interest people or satisfy them in some way. These values or qualities carry over into any type of media writing, ranging from a multimedia package with video, photographs, and text to a 250-word news release on a company website.

The traditional news values taught by journalism professors should become second nature to any writer: *prominence, timeliness, proximity, impact, magnitude, conflict, oddity,* and *emotional impact*. News values are important in media writing because they guide writers in identifying crucial information. Let's look at each of the news values and how each affects lead writing.

Prominence

When the main characters in your story are well known, that is a signal to put those names in the lead. Readers recognize those names and are drawn into the story.

When well-known figures die, their obituaries become front-page news, such as that of singer Whitney Houston. When celebrities end up in divorce court or have custody battles, their lives make headlines, such as reality star Kim Kardashian. When prominent people have a medical issue, their names draw attention to treatments, as in the case of former Vice President John McCain and his heart condition. Even people who are merely related to famous people are lead-worthy, such as Pippa Middleton, sister of Kate Middleton, who became the Duchess of Cambridge when she married Prince William. Prominence extends even to pets, such as President Obama's Portuguese waterdog, Bo.

Timeliness

One adage in journalism is "old news ain't news." People want to know what is happening as soon as it happens. They want to know information they did not know yesterday. They want timely, up-to-date news and depend increasingly on subscriber services through media outlets, tweets, online news sites, and radio news breaks as initial sources of information. Therefore, *when* an event happened is almost always included in the first sentence of a story so that people will have a context for that event.

> The official ceremony for east Montgomery's latest new school took place this morning, which is named in honor of an icon of Montgomery's civil rights movement.

> A smoky haze covered downtown Denver on Tuesday, the castoff from the High Park Fire about 60 miles north of the city.

Proximity

People are most interested about news that happens close to them. Audiences easily identify with stories with a geographic proximity—that is, those in their own community, town, county, or state. They like to read stories about their neighbors' successes and even defeats.

Audiences are also interested in what happens to people from their communities in other locations. For example, people in Cleveland would want to know about an airplane crash in Washington state that kills residents from their city. A Cleveland newspaper might run this lead:

> SEATTLE, Wash.—Two Cleveland businessmen were among 19 people killed early this morning when a jet struck a radio tower just outside Seattle.

The lead emphasizes Cleveland's loss while reporting that the plane crash occurred. Writers call this *localizing a message*, or putting a local angle on a story that originated miles away so that audiences can see how the message relates to them and their community.

News reports might also have an emotional or nonspatial proximity, whereby readers identify with a certain group of people. People who have suffered heart attacks are interested in articles about how other heart-attack victims have coped. People who live in a college town may be more inclined to read about stories originating from other cities with campuses, even if the cities are far away.

Parents anywhere could relate to the following *Las Vegas* (Nevada) *Sun* lead about the school lunch costs:

> Families may pay up to an additional $45 per child next year under a school lunch price increase being considered by the Clark County School Board.

Impact

Audiences always want to know how they will be affected, whether by a road closing while a sewer line is being laid or by a sale at the local supermarket or by higher college tuition. Readers or viewers ask, "What does this have to do with me?" High in any message should be an explanation of how an event affects individuals' daily lives or why they should be concerned.

When possible, the impact should be translated into tangible terms, just as in the tuition example earlier: Starting in the fall, students will pay $250 more per semester in tuition. Or a water and sewer rate increase approved by the Town Council Tuesday night will mean that the average resident will pay $13.52 a month more for service, bringing the average monthly bill to $81.96.

Sometimes impact is harder to detect. In such cases, it might be even more important for the writer to point out effects on ordinary individuals. Many stories will begin with anecdotal leads that give an example of how an event, decision, or medical breakthrough will affect specific individuals. An anecdotal lead increases the impact because readers often can identify how their own family and friends would fit in the scenario.

In natural disasters, the impact might be stated in terms of the ways in which people are affected. When a hurricane, earthquake, wildfire, or tornado occurs, thousands of residents will probably be without electricity and potentially hundreds of houses damaged.

Consider the impact clearly outlined in this lead from the Associated Press:

NEW YORK (AP)—Floods that have inundated the Midwest could reduce world corn supplies and drive food prices higher at a time when Americans are already stretching their grocery budgets and people in poor countries have rioted over rising food costs.

Impact can be positive, such as free bus service:

Residents can ride the town's buses for free, beginning Monday, the first time the transit service has been offered at no charge to riders.

University students, staff, and faculty will also benefit from the free bus service, made possible by a $200,000 grant from the university to the town.

Magnitude

Some people confuse the distinction between impact and magnitude in defining news values. *Magnitude* is defined as the size of the event. Death, injury, or loss of property are all elements of magnitude that attract audience attention. Large amounts of money, such as lottery winnings, as well as disasters, such as earthquakes, carry magnitude and are always big news. When wildfires ravaged the Colorado mountainsides, the acreage burned as well as the speed and intensity of the flames were part of the magnitude.

When Superstorm Sandy devastated parts of the East Coast of the United States, the physical size of the hurricane comprised one aspect of its magnitude, along with the winds and storm surge. The impact on residents changed their lives for months afterward.

Consider this lead, which has magnitude and an understood impact:

Tuesday morning, 54 school buses will drive more than 1,000 miles as they pick up 2,500 school children for the first day of classes this year.

The magnitude is represented in part by the 2,500 students, the 1,000 miles traveled, and the 54 school buses. The understood impact of the first day of school is much broader, affecting any household in the county with school-age children, an employee of the school system, or an early morning commuter.

Conflict

Most stories contain some kind of conflict: contract disputes with striking workers, continuing struggles in African countries and in the Middle East, the battles between neighbors in rezoning issues, or a grievance filed by an employee against a supervisor. People like to read about conflict. The extent of the conflict, either its size or its duration, will determine whether conflict is included in the lead of the message.

Conflict permeates the news. Residents are concerned when a development might affect their quality of life or their property values, as in this *New York Daily News* lead:

> A new East Flatbush hotel is angering neighbors who fear it will draw drugs and prostitution—and are threatening a "shaming campaign" against frequent clients.

Or on the global stage, as shown in this lead in the *Guardian*:

> Husbands, not strangers or men with guns, are now the biggest threat to women in post-conflict west Africa, according to a report by the International Rescue Committee (IRC) released on Tuesday.

Oddity

Editors often encourage writers to look for oddity or some unusual twist to a story, such as a police officer who responds to the accident call and discovers that one of the injured people is his son. When a doctor used a claw hammer to pull a nail out of a 60-year-old man's skull, the man survived—except for some lingering headaches—and kept the nail as a souvenir. Or in this lead:

> Hurricane season started today, but two Atlantic Ocean storms didn't get the message.
> Tropical storms Alberto and Beryl whipped up the East Coast in the last three weeks, though storms usually form in late summer.

The article tells readers that preseason tropical storms or hurricanes are unusual: 2012 was the third time in 160 years that such storms had developed prior to June 1.

Consider this lead from the *Detroit Free Press:*

> Nothing wrong with teaching your kid your trade. But when your line of work is shoplifting, well....

Or this lead from the *Bismarck Tribune:*

> Riding a bike while intoxicated is still considered driving drunk, police say.

Whenever a writer is working on a message that has an element of oddity, care must be taken to ensure that people are not portrayed as freakish or unnatural. For example, a story on the largest baby born in the county in 30 years might not need to be written at all.

Emotional Impact

Writers are recognizing more and more that people like stories that affect them emotionally and that have *emotional impact*. This news value is also called *human interest* and *universal appeal*. It is the quality that draws audiences to children, young people, and pets, as well as stories tied to love and romance. Emotional events are important elements in stories and generally should be included in the first paragraph, as in this MSNBC example:

> Brendan Haas earned a prize any young kid would appreciate—an all-expense-paid trip to Disney World. Instead of going, though, the Massachusetts boy gave the vacation to the family of a soldier killed in Afghanistan.

The story continues, revealing that Brendan drew the name of the winning family on Memorial Day.

Think about your own interests. In looking at a page of a company newsletter, the photo of children and balloons at the company picnic will probably have more appeal than the picture of the president presenting a $5,000 check to the director of a local community organization. Death and injury convey emotional impact. A spousal murder also captures audience attention, from the arrest through the trial.

Remember the Audience

In applying news values, media writers must think about what is important to their audiences. Knowing the audience determines what's in the lead and affects how the writer will rank information. For example, a college community audience hears the mayor speak in a lecture series. What he says looks like this in the college newspaper's lead:

> Students play a vital role in boosting the town's economy when they shop at downtown businesses, Mayor Leo Ryan said Wednesday.

The primary audience for the college newspaper is students. What the mayor said has a different focus for the lead in the town's general-circulation newspaper:

> Town and college administrators need to develop a joint long-range plan that will address growth, particularly along the campus perimeter, during the next 20 years, Mayor Leo Ryan said Wednesday night.

A general-interest audience, primarily made up of town residents, would be more interested in what the mayor said that affected them directly.

News with a local angle will have more appeal to most audiences. Think of interest in concentric circles: People are interested first in what happens to them and their families; then in what happens in their neighborhoods; then their towns; their counties; their states; their countries; and the world. Leads should be written to focus on the local angle, such as this one for readers in eastern Maryland:

If you are planning to drive to Ocean City for the weekend, avoid Maryland Highway 113 near Dagsboro, where highway crews are working and traffic is slowed to one lane.

Television satirist Jon Stewart often makes fun of reporters who introduce news that they say is "the story everyone is talking about." The humor of this phrase, as Stewart points out, is that the audience isn't talking about the story—it's only the reporters and TV anchors. Apparently, "everyone" doesn't include the audience. The serious point that Stewart makes is that writers, if they aren't careful, can easily mistake their own interests with the interests of the audience.

Sorting It Out

At this point, you are educated about the elements of a lead, but you still may be unclear about the sorting process. Let's walk through it.

Suppose you are a business writer for a local newspaper. In three months, a major employer in town will open a fitness center for employees. The center will be in the old YMCA building next door to the bank's corporate headquarters. You have collected the needed information. Your list of elements looks like this:

Who:	Amana Savings and Loan
What:	Will open a fitness center
Where:	In the old YMCA next door to corporate headquarters
When:	In three months
Why:	To improve employee health and to provide a benefit to employees
How:	By renovating the old YMCA

Now make a list of news values as they relate to the story. Ask whether each applies and if so, how:

Prominence:	No
Timeliness:	Yes, within three months
Proximity:	Yes, in downtown
Impact:	Yes, the renovation will mean local jobs and other economic benefits to the town. It will affect the lives of the company's 275 employees and the townspeople who have been wondering what will happen to the old YMCA.

Magnitude:	Yes, the acquisition and renovation will cost the company almost $4 million.
Conflict:	None internally—shareholders approved the expenditure at the annual meeting. None externally—town residents want the building saved.
Emotional impact:	Possibly, for people who remember using the old YMCA.

In a tweet for those who follow you on Twitter, you might alert them to the longer story posted on the newspaper's online site. The Twitter post would focus on new life for a familiar landmark and link to the complete article. In the online story, you could expand on the information in the tweet and add photos, a timeline, and reader comments. To write both the tweet and the story, you had to ask, "What will my audience want to know first?" The answer is the renovation and the time frame. The renovation is new news. A first draft of the online lead might read like this:

Amana Savings and Loan will spend almost $4 million to renovate the vacant YMCA downtown on Sycamore Street to create an employee fitness center that will open within three months.

Here, you have answered *who*, *what*, *when*, and *where*. You also have addressed the *magnitude* of the project. The second paragraph will answer why and how, and the third paragraph will explain *impact:*

The bank will renovate the old YMCA building to provide a convenient way for employees to remain physically fit, said employee manager Kay Barnes. The bank will use the existing layout and install new equipment and furnishings.

The project will mean new jobs during the renovation and later when the center opens, Barnes noted.

The story can continue with information on the actual renovation, such as the construction company that will do the job, types of equipment and furnishings, and how many jobs might be created, among other facts.

General Rules for Leads

No matter what type of lead you choose to write, all leads have common features.

Leads should be short. As a guide, some writers use no more than 30 words. Many wire service stories have leads no longer than 20 words in the first sentence or paragraph. This MSNBC lead sets up in six words the story about the young actor who played a miniature Darth Vader in a Volkswagen ad:

May the Force be with him.

Essential Lead Elements

1. I have looked at the facts and decided which are the most important.
2. My initial sentence is simple and complete.
3. My lead is accurate.
4. My lead is relevant to my audience and includes keywords to use to find the story online.
5. My lead comes to the point, is well edited, and makes sense.
6. I have used understandable, fresh words and strong, active verbs.
7. My lead sets up the story.

Desirable Elements

1. I have emphasized the latest information.
2. I have included unusual aspects of the message.
3. If possible, I have used a local angle to show how the information relates to readers, listeners, or viewers.
4. I have kept my lead short—no longer than 30 words.
5. My lead attracts the audience's attention.
6. My lead summarizes the message.

Readers will recognize the "Force" connection to the *Star Wars* movies. They will want to know what happened and will continue reading to find out.

Or:

ANN ARBOR, Mich—Open an app. See a flash. Get arrested.

The story explains that a laptop owner had installed security software on his computer. The laptop took the thief's photo, leading to his arrest.

Leads should be concise and to the point.   Writers must eliminate unnecessary words. Look at the following lead and see what has been eliminated in the rewrite and how the focus has changed:

A local day-care center was broken into Wednesday night and property vandalized, toys overturned and a pet rabbit, named Ray, killed with a broom.

Rewritten:

Vandals broke into a local day-care center Wednesday night, killed the center's pet rabbit with a broom, overturned toys, and damaged property.

Words in the lead should be precise and in general vocabulary. The words in the following *Associated Press* lead are precise and show the impact:

> LAND O'LAKES, Fla.—When 3-year-old Mikey Spoul took his father's car for a joyride last month and explained "I go zoom," the act grabbed national attention and even became fodder for late-night show monologue jokes.
>
> But nobody's laughing now. Mikey torched his bedroom curtains with a cigarette lighter and burned down his family's home, authorities said.

Leads should use active verbs. Consider the verbs in the preceding lead example: "grabbed," "torched," and "burned down." Note the use of active verbs in this lead:

> A Cityville man smashed the glass door on a Laundromat washing machine and yanked a 3-year-old child from the swirling waters Saturday morning.

Leads should be simple, not rambling, convoluted sentences. No one wants to work too hard at understanding most communication. The writer is lost if the "huh?" factor enters in. That's when a person has to stop and reread a lead to understand what the writer is saying. Compare the simple lead about the Cityville man in the Laundromat with this more convoluted lead:

> Under a handgun-control plan announced by state and county grassroots organizations Monday, a person who sells a handgun to an unlicensed customer would be liable to a victim for three times his losses if that handgun is used to commit a crime.

Apply what you have learned about leads so far to untangle this report on controlling handguns. What's the point? Some grassroots organizations have come up with an idea for making handgun salespeople more responsible for crime. What does the audience have to know? How about this lead:

> If a local citizens group gets its way, people who sell guns will help pay for the lives and property lost in handgun crimes.

Writers base the structure of their leads on the type of story and the audience. Some types of information, such as police reports, lend themselves to summary leads. Other material works better in a descriptive or anecdotal lead. The next section looks at leads and where each works best.

Summary Leads

The most common lead format is a summary lead that tells or summarizes the most important information:

> Four Cityville teens will receive all-expense-paid trips to the U.S. city of their choice, their prize in a local essay contest.

> To reduce employee attrition, Telstar Corp. will build an on-site day-care center that will enroll 125 children of its employees in May.

> Cityville town administrators will visit Durham, N.C., on Thursday to study how that city has rejuvenated its downtown and boosted economic benefits for local businesses.

The summary lead serves the audience members who skim online articles, company newsletters, or handouts from school; who listen with one ear to radio news reports and one ear to the kids in the backseat of the car; or who casually tune into the morning television news while getting dressed. Summary leads are used often to give people information quickly.

Summary leads are useful. They can be the hook of an online story, the beginning of a news release, the headline of a broadcast story, or a complete tweet.

Complete Leads

Although most summary leads consist of one sentence or one graph, they may be longer to provide adequate information and context. Leads must be clear and easy to understand. Look at this lead from the *Cape Cod Times*:

> She won four Senior Olympic Gold medals. She witnessed the Hindenburg explode. She lived through both world wars. And now, at almost 98 years old, Adelaide Cummings will become a poet laureate.
>
> Cummings, a resident of West Falmouth for more than 50 years, will be named the first resident poet laureate of Falmouth at a ceremony from 3 to 5 p. m. today at Highfield Hall.

Writer Emily Atteberry needs the second graph to set up the context and bring readers up-to-date.

A writer in a company's corporate communications department needs to tell employees about payroll changes. She must do so in a way that is informative, pertinent, and clear:

> Long Branch Entertainment employees will see in their paychecks next month some changes that represent good news and bad news.
>
> The good news is the company's across-the-board 3 percent pay raise.
>
> The bad news is each employee with a family plan will pay $52.22 more a month in health insurance premiums and employees with individual plans, $26.32 more a month.

The three-paragraph summary lead contains information essential to employees: how the company's health insurance plan will change and how much their raises will be. The writer wanted employees to know right away that they were about to be hit in the pocketbook and why. Employees who want to know more about how and why the changes occurred will continue to read the message.

Multiple-Element Leads

The Long Branch lead on health care also illustrates how a writer presents more than one aspect. Often, a lead has multiple elements or more than one point it must convey to readers. A multiple-element lead summarizes information for readers and sets up what will be covered in the rest of the copy. It presents a challenge to the writer, who must be wary of complex or convoluted sentences. The best approach is to rank the elements, put the most important in the first sentence, and then create a second or third paragraph to present the other points:

> A group of university students has presented a list of concerns to Chancellor Paula Walls, asking foremost that the university put a moratorium on tuition increases.
>
> The letter, hand-delivered to Walls on Wednesday, also asks the administration to name more students to campus-wide committees, to recruit minority faculty members, and to renovate the Student Union.

From this lead, readers have the most important information first: the list of demands and the high-priority demand. And they know the content and structure of the message. For writers, the lead sets up how to organize the story: in order of the points listed in the lead.

Delayed-Identification Leads

Another type of summary lead is the delayed-identification lead. When individuals in a news story are not prominent, their proper names are not given in the first paragraph. Rather, they are identified by a generic label: "An Orange County woman died when…" or "A Lockwood High School student has been named a National Merit Scholarship winner…." Immediately, in the next paragraph, the individual is named. If more than one person is in the lead or first paragraph, the individuals are renamed in that order in the next paragraph. The lead shown earlier in this chapter of the woman running barefoot to raise money to buy shoes is an example of a delayed identification lead:

> DES MOINES, Iowa—An Iowa woman is running barefoot across the United States to raise money to provide shoes for needy children.
>
> Rae Heim, 18, of Carroll, started her cross-country trek in Boston in April and hopes to reach Huntington Beach, Calif., in October.

Other Lead Formats

Although the summary lead is the most useful, writers sometimes find other lead formats better suited to the kind of message they need to send. Some types of leads, such as anecdotal or descriptive, are popular in media writing. They can be risky if they don't hook readers soon enough. They must be well written to entice readers to stay long enough to find out what the message is about.

In general, when using other lead formats, make sure you get to the point by the fourth paragraph. If you are writing for a newspaper, for example, the story might have jumped to another page before the reader ever gets to the point. Let's evaluate some types of alternative leads.

Anecdotal or Affective Leads

Many publications, whether traditional or online, have developed a lead style that uses an anecdote to illustrate how one person is or has been affected by a social, health, political, or economic problem. The lead makes readers understand abstract events on an interpersonal and even emotional level. The abstract then becomes real.

In a story about a heat wave that blanketed Texas, Talia Richman of the *Dallas Morning News* used an anecdote to lead into a story:

> Arthur Hale spent last summer in and out of the hospital.
>
> It wasn't because of his debilitating arthritis, which confines him to a motorized wheelchair. Hale, 48, kept getting seizures brought on by dehydration and record-breaking temperatures.
>
> Hale feared that this summer's heat would torture him like last year's—he has already gone to the hospital once, he said, pointing to his white wristband.
>
> On Friday, however, volunteers from Dallas County Health and Human Services installed an air conditioner at Hale's three-room home in Sandbranch, hoping to ensure that he doesn't become a statistic in a heat-related death count.
>
> With donations from the Dallas Foundation, the Meadows Foundation, the Harold Simmons Foundation and the Communities Foundation of Texas, the county health department is installing window air conditioners in the homes of the disabled and elderly. Work started on June 1 and will continue for four months, or until high temperatures have dropped into the 80s.

The key to using the anecdotal or affective lead is to keep it short and get to the point right away. Writers must quickly reveal the message's social or economic issue. Writers should refer to the anecdotal example throughout the story, not solely use it as a hook and then drop it after the lead.

Descriptive Leads

Like an anecdotal lead, a descriptive lead puts emotion or a human element into a message. It sets the scene for the reader. A descriptive lead can be a few sentences or a few paragraphs. The danger is in writing a descriptive lead so long that writers lose their audiences well before they get to the point.

Consider this lead from the *Silver Spring Gazette*:

> The paint on Shari Daniels' back porch was peeling, the clapboard was rotting and the single mother didn't have the time or the money to maintain the house she took such pride in when she moved in more than 20 years ago.

> So the volunteers, many from other places, who spent last week repairing Daniels' Takoma Park home were more than timely help. To Daniels, they were a blessing.

Just the few words describing the paint peeling and the clapboard rotting let readers know the deterioration of Daniels' home.

Question Leads

Question leads should be avoided. They rarely are successful. In most cases, they are the lazy writer's way out, and they turn off audiences. In almost every case, they give the audience the option to turn elsewhere.

> Who will pay to build the county's new schools?

The reader might say, "Not me, and I don't care who pays." Think of another angle such as:

> The average Cityville resident will end up paying the cost for building new schools, a local watchdog group stated today.

On rare occasions, a question lead can work, as in this one from the *Arkansas Democrat Gazette*:

> What's a prairie dog worth?
> Two to six years, Little Rock police say.

The reader at first mentally guesses a dollar figure, but then is surprised immediately that the correct answer is a prison term. The reader is hooked into the story on prairie dog-napping.

Quote Leads

Quote leads should be used sparingly because rarely does someone sum up an entire speech or premise for a decision in one simple quote. A quote can be used if it is short, is relevant to the rest of the message, and does not need any explanation. It must be clear within itself. Look at this newsletter lead:

> "Graduates should take advantage of the different opportunities to become entrepreneurs and solve the world's problems," said the graduation speaker at Cityville University on Sunday morning.

The lead here is empty and nonspecific. It fails to point out that the speaker has made millions from entrepreneurial ventures and has the experience to make him qualified for such a statement. A stronger lead would have focused on his accomplishments:

> A self-made millionaire from four successful start-up companies told graduates on Sunday that they can solve the world's problems if they are willing to be entrepreneurial and take some risks.

A partial quote is used effectively in this example from the Associated Press:

> Smoking and drug use among U.S. teenagers are increasing after a decade of decline, a study showed Monday, and its author warned that "the stage is set for a potential resurgence of cocaine and crack use."

Direct Address Leads

The direct address lead talks straight to the reader or consumer. It usually gives advice or has a "hey, you" aspect to it. Consider this summertime lead in *The Washington Post:*

> You know it's bad when relief means the temperature has dipped to 102 degrees.

Or this *Post* lead about a bakery that plans to install a 24-hour cupcake-dispensing machine:

> It's 2:00 a.m. The bars have just closed, and you're craving the sugary goodness of a cupcake. Trouble is, bakeries are closed, too. So your best bet is the prepackaged Hostess snacks selling at 7 Eleven.
>   Not for much longer.

Most of us were taught not to use "you" when writing papers for English class. But in an article with broad human interest, a direct address lead might be just the technique needed to grab readers' attention.

Writing Leads for Digital Media

Sometimes the medium can dictate the type of lead. The more time you anticipate a reader will spend with a story, the longer you can make your lead. Anecdotal leads, for example, are particularly well suited for longer stories often found in magazines or in the Sunday editions of newspapers, whether print or online. However, online readers often quickly skim stories. They might see only the headline and first paragraph before deciding whether to click and read the whole piece, view the video, or move on to another story.

For example, CNN posted on its home page a lead to attract viewer interest to a video. The sentence read: *A man dressed as Darth Vader probably should have used "The Force" to help talk his way out of a traffic ticket.* Viewers could then click on the video to see the man covered in his head-to-toe black Vader costume and the interaction with police.

Writers who work for online publications can increase the chances of their work being found on the Internet by considering a technique called search engine optimization. Search engines use the first dozen or so words of cached Web articles to deliver the pages that are most relevant to a person's search terms. Online writers, therefore, should make an effort to use in their leads keywords and phrases that potential readers might use in a search.

The need to use keywords and phrases could change the leads on the same story for the print versus the online version. An anecdotal or descriptive lead might be shelved and the graph that contains the point substituted for the online story because it would contain key elements that are searchable.

This lead was written for a story published online by WebMD Health News:

> Intense control of blood glucose levels in type 2 diabetes helps reduce the risk of kidney and eye complications, but not cardiovascular risks such as heart attacks and strokes, researchers said at a news briefing during the annual meeting of the American Diabetes Association in San Francisco.

Count the number of nouns that someone with type 2 diabetes might use as search terms to look for information about treating the disease, and the potential side effects of the treatment: "blood glucose," "type 2 diabetes," "kidney," "eye," "complications," "cardiovascular," "heart attacks," "strokes," and "American Diabetes Association." Now, look where those keywords and phrases are located in the paragraph. "Blood glucose" and "type 2 diabetes" are the most widely used keywords, and they appear high in the lead. The writer emphasizes the results of the study, saving the attribution information until the end of the paragraph.

You may also have noticed other nouns, such as "San Francisco," that are popular search terms—probably even more popular than "diabetes." But someone looking for this information probably doesn't care where the meeting was held. And someone planning a vacation in San Francisco probably isn't interested in attending a meeting of the American Diabetes Association. Remember: Only the relevant keywords are important.

Now, compare the WebMD to this lead from a *New York Times* article on the same topic:

> Two large studies involving more than 21,000 people found that people with type 2 diabetes had no reduction in their risk of heart attacks and strokes and no reduction in their death rate if they rigorously controlled their blood sugar levels.

This story also has some keywords and phrases—"type 2 diabetes," "heart attacks," "strokes," and "blood sugar"—but not nearly as many as the Web MD article, and they aren't as high in the lead. This lead puts sources for the news—"two large studies"—and even some details about the scope of the studies—"involving more than 21,000 people"—ahead of the findings. While a study's size is important, people with diabetes probably are less interested in "two large studies involving more than 21,000 people" than in information about "intense control of blood glucose levels in type 2 diabetes."

Before writing their lead, online writers should ask themselves a few questions:

- Is this story valuable to readers because of its immediacy or because of its in-depth and relatively timeless account of a subject in which people will be interested for some time to come?
- What are the key search terms most likely to be used by people interested in my story? More detail about online writing is covered in Chapter 8.

Choosing a Lead Type and Elements

In many cases, the information will dictate the type of lead. A crime story, for example, generally will use a summary lead. A story on a city council meeting will need a multiple-element lead to cover the council's different actions. Lack of prominence will dictate a delayed-identification lead. But sometimes a writer must ponder and decide which lead will set up the story best.

Remember to read through your stories carefully and ensure that your leads are honest and set up for the reader what the story covers. Review the checklist in Box 5.1. In addition, remember that deaths, injuries, or substantial loss of property are other items that should be included in leads. All relate to news elements and values that capture audience attention.

Readers will be disappointed if they believe that a story is about one topic only to discover that it is about another. Writers will lose credibility if they make false promises in their leads.

You can become a good lead writer, whatever the topic, by focusing on what is important to your audience, learning the guidelines of good writing, and reading good leads that are specific and present information accurately, clearly, and concisely. Look for such leads in everything you read.

Exercises

1. Read the following lead. Identify the elements and the news values present:

   A third elementary school in Johnston County will be delayed for a year because school officials have asked architects to revise the plans to include more space for computer labs, the school board chairman announced Monday.

   The school will be a model for schools across the state and will take about 14 months to build.

Elements
Who:
What:
When:
Where:
Why:
How:

News Values (identify only those present; not all will be)
Conflict:
Timeliness:
Proximity:
Prominence:
Magnitude:
Impact:
Oddity:
Emotion:

2. Read the following lead. Identify the elements and the news values present:

Two fishermen whose boat capsized in the Atlantic Ocean were rescued Sunday after spending 24 hours floating in life preservers.

George Blackburn and Brian Livengood, both of Wilmington, Del., went fishing off the coast early Saturday. Their boat capsized about 2 p.m. that day after a fire burned a hole in their boat. The Coast Guard rescued them about noon.

Elements
Who:
What:
When:
Where:
Why:
How:

News Values (identify only those present; not all will be)
Conflict:
Timeliness:
Proximity:
Prominence:
Magnitude:
Impact:
Oddity:
Emotion:

3. Read the following lead. Identify the elements and the news values present:

WASHINGTON—Hospital leaders told members of Congress Tuesday that reductions in Medicare and Medicaid could have great impact on the people they care for.

    The federal budget calls for $115 billion less for Medicare and $21.6 billion less for Medicaid. More than 1,000 hospitals across the country depend heavily on the two federal programs for about two-thirds of their annual revenues.

Elements
Who:
What:
When:
Where:
Why:
How:

News Values (identify only those present; not all will be)
Conflict:
Timeliness:
Proximity:
Prominence:
Magnitude:
Impact:
Oddity:
Emotion:

4. Read the following lead. Identify the elements and the news values present:

The Cityville Town Council approved a 3-cent property tax rate increase for the coming fiscal year budget and more programs to assist in low-income housing.

    The tax rate increase means a person who owns a home valued at $100,000 will pay $30 more a year.

Elements
Who:
What:
When:
Where:
Why:
How:

News Values (identify only those present; not all will be)
Conflict:
Timeliness:
Proximity:

Prominence:
Magnitude:
Impact:
Oddity:
Emotion:

5. You are a reporter for the Cityville Chronicle. Write leads for the following information. List for each exercise *who, what, when, where, how,* and *why*. You may want to list the news values to help you determine what information should go into the lead. Think about the local audience. Write just the lead, not the entire story, for each.

   ■ A Johnston Community College student died yesterday. He was working at a construction site at Town Hall. The construction company he worked for was building an addition to the Town Hall. He was dead on arrival at Cityville Hospital. He died when scaffolding he was standing on collapsed and he fell three stories to the ground. One of the cables holding the scaffolding broke and he slipped off the scaffolding. A board from the scaffolding, which came apart, fell on his head as he lay on the ground. He worked part time for the construction company while he was in school.

   ■ The Natural Resources Defense Council had a news conference today in Washington. The NRDC is a national environmental lobbying group. It said that smog is getting worse in metropolitan areas across the country and is reaching the stage of "a public health emergency." The group also said the government is seriously understating the problem. Smog is the polluted air that irritates eyes and lungs and causes long-term health problems. The Council said unsafe levels of smog occur in many large cities twice as often as the federal Environmental Protection Agency says they do.

   ■ The Cityville Planetarium has regularly scheduled programs at 7 p.m. and 8 p.m. on weekdays and 10 a.m. Saturdays. This weekend, the planetarium will expand its offerings to the afternoon. "Sam, Space Cat" will be at 1 p.m. and 3 p.m. on Saturday and Sunday. The film "Beyond the Earth" will be shown at 2 p.m. each day. The planetarium director said the additional showings will allow more people, particularly those who work during the week, to see the special offerings.

   ■ Workforce.com, a local company in the Cityville Research Park, employs 85 people. Company officials have announced a restructuring that will lay off 60 employees and that they hope will allow them to save the company. Profits have dropped 40 percent in the last six months. Workforce.com was founded five years ago. It is an online employment company that had targeted a national clientele, but company officials said the number of clients did not reach expectations.

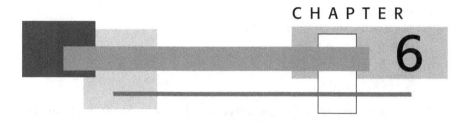

Beyond the Lead:
Writing the Message

Once writers have fashioned the lead, they face the task of organizing the rest of the message. They must decide what will come after the first sentences or paragraphs that hook the audience. The ranking decisions discussed in Chapter 5 that help them write the lead are invaluable in helping them develop the body of the message. Again, with audience needs and interests in mind, the writer outlines how the message will evolve.

As mentioned in Chapter 5, journalists traditionally have used the inverted pyramid style of writing to get to the point quickly and to set priorities for basic news stories. The principle behind the inverted pyramid—to order information according to its value to the audience—is valuable in much writing today and is becoming more valuable as news is updated every minute on digital sites. Audiences today read more news through multiple delivery modes, and they spend less time with each message they read there. The process of ordering information for the inverted pyramid involves critical thinking, an essential skill for writers.

Specific styles of writing that are alternatives to the inverted pyramid might be suitable for certain audiences or for a particular medium. Students will find a variety of organizational styles in newspapers, magazines, company newsletters, blogs, microblogs, and so on. If you find yourself reading an article from start to end, study it to identify the elements that pulled you into and through the message. Save it. Someday you may want to adopt the style for a piece of your own.

This chapter discusses

- the inverted pyramid style of writing,
- the news peg and nut graph,
- other organizational formats, and
- how to unify writing.

The Inverted Pyramid

Leads must get to the point quickly, and messages must provide important information right behind the lead. Newspaper editors have recognized that need for decades. Henry A. Stokes, as an assistant managing editor for projects at the *Commercial Appeal* in Memphis, Tennessee, once wrote in a staff memo that reporters had to ensure stories attracted reader attention.

Stokes told staff writers they were to "tell the news in an identifiable, functional format that guarantees the reader will receive the best information we can provide, written in a way that the reader can quickly and easily understand."

As a result, the newspaper adopted the four-paragraph rule: Tell the essential message in the first four paragraphs of the story. Details that could be cut would follow.

The format Stokes advocated was the inverted pyramid style of writing, long a standard in journalism. With the inverted pyramid, information in a message is organized in descending order of importance. The most important and compelling information comes first and is followed by information of lesser value. His advice from years ago still applies in today's digital world where important information must be stated immediately and in a style that audiences can relate to and understand immediately.

To be successful at using the inverted pyramid, writers must be able to evaluate and rank information, and they must know what is most important to their audiences. This simple model shows how the inverted pyramid works:

Lead summarizes information. Next few paragraphs back up the lead

Next section provides background and additional important information

Next section has information of lesser importance about the topics introduced in the lead

Final section contains least important information, which could be cut

In the inverted pyramid, the lead paragraph or paragraphs summarize the most important news values and elements and hook the audience.

The next paragraphs usually give additional crucial information that would not fit into the lead. Background information to provide context comes next. From there, subsequent paragraphs develop the topics presented in the lead, introduce other important information, expand the significance of the information, and give details.

Each section will vary in length, depending on what the writer has introduced in the lead and whether he or she is building the message with quotes. A local government reporter, for example, might devote four or five paragraphs to dialogue from a meeting before moving on to other city council actions set forth in the lead paragraph.

For breaking news or evolving events, the inverted pyramid allows writers to create the initial story, then write new leads that focus on the latest or new information as it emerges. Even with Twitter, the latest posts are building on earlier tweets. For example, a writer covering a trial can post developments as the jury is charged, deliberates, and returns with a verdict.

The inverted pyramid helps a writer organize information logically, whether the topic is a single subject or has multiple subjects or elements. If the writer plans to develop several issues in the message, the summary multiple-element lead would set up the organization in the following way:

> The Cityville City Council voted unanimously Tuesday night to renew the
> city manager's contract for three years, with a raise each year, and to annex
> 325 acres south of town and just west of the Newtar River.

Through the inverted pyramid, the writer sets up the order of importance in the lead and how the message will be organized. The most important item is the city manager's contract, which includes a pay raise. Because no one objected to the annexation of acreage, it carries less importance because it is not controversial. It can be discussed second. The important point, the action of annexation, is contained in the lead. The rest of the story follows the lead like this:

> In discussing City Manager Larry Morgan's new contract, council members agreed
> that Morgan had done an exemplary job in his six years as manager.
> "Larry is an excellent manager," said Council Member Dick Haynes, who
> made the motion to give Morgan a 10 percent pay raise in the first year of the
> contract and 5 percent in the second and third years.
> "We have maintained quality town services with only modest tax increases
> while Larry has been here," added Council Member Loretta Manson.
> The council voted to annex the Heather Hills subdivision following a public
> hearing in which no one objected to the annexation plan. Residents who spoke
> said they wanted to come under the town's water and sewer services and to gain
> improved fire and police protection.

The inverted pyramid is more than just an organizational tool. It has been identified traditionally as a writing style that uses simple words, short sentences, and one idea to a paragraph. Those principles are found in today's platforms that feature frequent posts, such as Twitter and Facebook.

The inverted pyramid also represents critical thinking: It forces writers to evaluate information and rank it in order of importance. Some critics have said the inverted pyramid puts pressure on reporters to craft an attention-getting, information-packed lead, leaving them little time to follow through with a well-organized message. To be successful, writers must do both: write a compelling lead and organize a story logically. In reality, time constraints or deadline pressure might interfere with both functions.

Why Use the Inverted Pyramid for Media Writing?

Traditional media have used the inverted pyramid style for two primary reasons: to give audiences the most critical material quickly so they can move to other stories if they wish and to allow a story to be cut easily from the bottom, leaving important information intact at the top of the story.

Print editions of newspapers, for example, have a limited news hole, or space, to fit editorial content, so story lengths can change at the last minute, depending on where a story is placed on a page. For online sites, the story length is potentially limitless, but online writers and editors know audiences have limited time and attention, so their work must capture and retain readers.

Many beginning writers question why they should follow the inverted pyramid style when they plan careers in public relations, multimedia, advertising, or marketing. They object to what they see as a rigid way of writing or formula writing—a basic format devoid of creativity.

At first glance, the objections seem valid. But as students use the inverted pyramid, they will discover plenty of opportunities to develop their own styles. They will also learn that their audiences expect upfront delivery of essential information and that critical thinking goes along with the inverted pyramid style. For the inverted pyramid, writers must gather information, list or rank information, write a draft, and rewrite, as outlined in Chapter 1.

John Sweeney, professor in the School of Journalism and Mass Communication at the University of North Carolina at Chapel Hill, teaches advertising courses. He advises all students, no matter their major, on the value of learning the inverted pyramid structure.

"Before you can develop your own style, you have to master the basics," he tells introductory writing students. "You have to be taught to be meticulous—to say it succinctly, concisely, precisely. You have to be able to distill information, whether it's a 30-second TV spot, or a piece of newswriting, or an ad distilled from a 100-page document on product data.

"Writing also has to have access: Anyone can read it and understand it," Sweeney advises. "You have to focus on what's key, get to the heart of the matter, and put the issue in perspective."

Communicators first must be able to master the traditional before they can be avant-garde. Mastering the inverted pyramid gives any student journalist or communicator the basic plan for writing any messages to focus on what is important and emotionally compelling for the audience. Whether intended for print or online publication, the inverted pyramid organizes information so that it is accessible, appealing, simply stated, and easy to understand.

The Inverted Pyramid for Other Media

Research supports the belief that the inverted pyramid retains value today when messages are short and more direct. Consider broadcast messages, which usually begin with a short, catchy lead that grabs the viewer's or listener's attention and then summarizes the main points. Because broadcast news stories are short, it is imperative for TV and radio reporters to fit in as many compelling facts as possible in the few seconds allotted. The inverted pyramid allows for the speedy, information-rich writing that broadcast demands.

Corporate communication offices and nonprofit agencies, whether staffed by professionals or volunteers, also follow the traditional inverted pyramid style. It puts their agendas where readers and editors can see them. Advertising depends on the inverted pyramid, communicating to consumers in an abbreviated way a product's qualities and the reasons for buying it. The inverted pyramid is ideal for tweets and online postings, where writers need to connect quickly to share information with their niche audiences.

Although it works best in shorter pieces, the inverted pyramid can be adapted for longer, more complex pieces, many of which use the inverted pyramid early in telling a story and then other organizational patterns later. For example, nondeadline writing, such as feature stories and documentaries, attracts readers best by getting to the point and summarizing first. Simple pyramiding in nondeadline writing can attract readers by creating a mood, setting the stage for more detailed information, or providing a memorable image.

The growth in online news consumption has made the inverted pyramid more important than ever. Many audiences are constantly checking their smartphones for tweets from organizations or individuals they follow or skimming the headlines on online news sites. Bombarded with an increasing array of media, online readers want to know quickly the point of a message and its relevance to them.

In one sense, online news sites themselves are giant inverted pyramids. News sites put the most important information on their home pages, often in the form of brief one-paragraph story summaries called "blurbs." If the blurb entices a reader, he or she may click to go deeper into the site to get the full news story. And from that news story, the reader may have the option of linking to original source documents, archival material, audio or video clips, or other news stories related to the original article. Because the online reader can decide to click links for further information, online writers don't have to cram tangential information into every story. But they do need to think about ways they can construct an inverted pyramid of links that will make it easier for the reader to gain more information if he or she desires. More about online writing can be found in Chapter 8.

Organizing a Story

The basic work of organizing a message in inverted pyramid style is done when you use the steps outlined in Chapter 5 for writing leads. The writer first identifies news values and the elements needed to structure a lead. News values and elements introduced in the lead will be developed in greater detail within the message. The writer will use the remaining news values and elements in subsequent paragraphs based on ranking information important to audiences.

In summer 2012, a Mount Rainier ranger died while assisting in the rescue of four Texas climbers who had fallen on a glacier. Initial stories reported the death, then followed up with efforts to get all the climbers plus the ranger's body off the mountain, a feat delayed because of weather.

Reporters had basic information to consider:

Who: A Mount Rainier ranger
What: Died
When: Thursday
Where: Slopes of Mount Rainier, Washington
How: Lost his footing and slid 3,000 feet down the mountain
Why: Assisting in a rescue as part of his job

Look at the news values we discussed in Chapter 5 and determine which ones apply here. The human interest angle is crucial as is the timeliness as the news is updated. Conflict and oddity could be relevant in man versus the mountain and the death of a rescuer. Other news values such as impact, prominence, or magnitude might not apply.

Consider the lead from the Associated Press when the story was first reported:

LONGMIRE, Wash. (AP)—A Mount Rainier ranger slid more than 3,000 feet to his death on Thursday as he helped in efforts to rescue four injured climbers who fell on a glacier, a National Park spokesman said.

The lead identifies the elements *who*, *what*, *when*, *where*, *how*, and *why*. The second and third paragraphs identify the ranger and give more detail attributed to a park spokesman.

Ranger Nick Hall was helping to prepare the climbers to be taken off the 14,411-foot Cascade Range peak when he fell before shortly before 5 p.m., said Mount Rainier National Park spokesman Kevin Bacher.

Bacher said Hall, 34, didn't respond to attempts to contact him and was not moving, and he was dead when other rangers reached him at the 10,000-foot level several hours later.

Later paragraphs give information leading up to the death, such as the climbers' fall, the conditions on the mountain, and other related accidents.

In media writing, information comes in paragraphs of varying lengths. In an essay or composition, a paragraph can be a whole presentation or argument on a topic. But in media writing, a paragraph is identified as a single unit of timely information and usually is one to three sentences long. It conveys a solitary fact, thought, or "sound bite" from the larger message. When a writer is concerned with transmitting information quickly, his or her ideas about paragraphing change.

As mentioned in Chapter 4, journalists rarely use the word "paragraph." In the newsroom, a paragraph is a "graph." This abbreviated word symbolizes the abbreviated form that paragraphs take in news stories. A graph generally will contain several sentences, but on occasion it might be only one sentence long, transmitting a single news element or news value.

News Peg and Nut Graph

Newspaper reporters talk about the *news peg* when developing stories. The peg, just like a peg on the wall where you hang a coat, is what a writer hangs the story on. It is the reason for writing the message. In the ranger story above, the news peg comes in the lead: A Mount Rainier ranger died while trying to rescue climbers.

Every piece of writing—whether it appears in print or is posted, aired, or shared—has a news peg. Writers, no matter their skill or medium, have a reason for composing a message. Remember the tweet from Joan Rivers in Chapter 5? The news peg that the message hung on was Madonna's current tour. For a complete story on Madonna's tour, the news peg would be spelled out in the *nut graph:* the paragraph that defines the point the writer is making. The rest of the message expands and clarifies the singular idea in the nut graph.

In some cases, the lead serves as the nut graph, particularly if it is a summary lead, and sometimes the nut graph is more than one paragraph. The nut graph should be in the first four to five paragraphs or writers risk losing audiences who want the point quickly. When writers use anecdotal or descriptive leads, as described in Chapter 5, they must summarize and focus the message for audiences soon after drawing them in.

Look for the nut graph in this MSNBC story by Scott Stump:

> May the Force be with him.
>
> Max Page, the 7-year-old who played a miniature Darth Vader in Volkswagen's popular Super Bowl commercial in 2011, will check in to the Children's Hospital Los Angeles on Wednesday to repair a congenital heart defect, according to ad agency Deutsch LA. The goal of the surgery is to repair a hole in his heart and replace his pulmonary valve.

In the second paragraph, readers learn the reference to the Force and what is happening with the pint-sized Darth Vader.

Remember the anecdotal lead from the *Dallas Morning News* in Chapter 5? The nut graph appears in paragraph 5:

> Arthur Hale spent last summer in and out of the hospital.
>
> It wasn't because of his debilitating arthritis, which confines him to a motorized wheelchair. Hale, 48, kept getting seizures brought on by dehydration and record-breaking temperatures.
>
> Hale feared that this summer's heat would torture him like last year's—he has already gone to the hospital once, he said, pointing to his white wristband.
>
> On Friday, however, volunteers from Dallas County Health and Human Services installed an air conditioner at Hale's three-room home in Sandbranch, hoping to ensure that he doesn't become a statistic in a heat-related death count.
>
> With donations from the Dallas Foundation, the Meadows Foundation, the Harold Simmons Foundation and the Communities Foundation of Texas, the county health department is installing window air conditioners in the homes of the disabled and elderly. Work started on June 1 and will continue for four months, or until high temperatures have dropped into the 80s.

By graph 5, readers learn the news peg that is included in the nut graph: With donations, health department workers are installing air conditioners to cool at-risk individuals.

Other Organizational Styles

Although the inverted pyramid works for much writing, other formats might seem better for a particular message because of the event reported. Some formats use the inverted pyramid format to introduce material, then move into another organizational pattern.

Chronological Format

In some cases, making the decision about how to organize the body of a message is easy. Chronology—telling events in the same order in which they occurred—often can meet audience needs. A breaking news story about a bank robbery, for example, would have a summary lead telling that the robbery occurred, where, and when. Then, after the nut of the news is clear, events would be revealed chronologically. The writer would organize the rest of the story by using time elements, as in the following article:

> A masked woman robbed the First Guaranty Savings and Loan on Main Street shortly after 9 a.m. today and escaped into a thickly wooded area nearby. Police have made no arrests.

The robbery occurred when the woman entered the bank and approached a teller. She handed her a note asking for money and saying she had a gun in the sleeve of her sweatshirt.

Although the teller did not actually see a gun, she gave the woman an undisclosed amount of cash. The woman put the money into a purple sack, ran from the Savings and Loan, and disappeared in the woods behind the bank's parking lot.

At 6 p.m., police were still looking for the suspect, who was described as a white woman in her mid-20s. She weighs about 150 pounds and stands about 5 feet 6 inches. She has shoulder-length blonde hair. She wore a purple sweatsuit and had pulled a stocking as a mask over her face. Bank employees could not describe her facial features.

Here, the lead, or the first paragraph, states *who* did *what*, *where*, and *when* and the latest information. Graph 2 states *how* events unfolded. In graph 4, the time element tells readers the status of the investigation at the newspaper's deadline.

In breaking news stories that are continually updated, such as those online, chronology works well as a format. New information can be added in the lead and first few paragraphs before beginning the chronology of events. All the details that have unfolded chronologically can remain. Any additional information that adds to the timeline can be inserted easily. In the case of the bank robbery, the first online version would report that the robbery occurred, as noted above. Subsequent versions would update information in the lead about police progress in finding the suspect and making an arrest.

While some messages can be developed chronologically, organization generally is not that simple. Not all messages involve action that evolves over time. For example, a high school principal writing in the school newsletter cannot use chronology to inform teachers about changes in ordering classroom supplies. Although teachers might be interested in the events that led up to the changes, they want to know the specific changes immediately. That is when another format, such as inverted pyramid, is needed.

Hourglass Format

Some writers have adapted chronological development to longer stories in what they call the *hourglass format* of writing. Using inverted pyramid style first gives readers the most important information in four to six paragraphs, allowing them to stop at the end of the inverted pyramid segment. Then the writer sets up more information with a simple statement by a source, such as "The police chief described the events this way."

Beyond the transition statement, the message unfolds chronologically. Writers can use the style for many kinds of stories, such as telling of the details surrounding a missing child and the chronology of the search, recounting the life of a popular singer after reporting her death, or bringing out the details of a baseball game after the lead tells who won the game. Electronic media writers often use the hourglass format. For example, a local television station aired a story about a crime that police had been unable to solve. After noting the latest information, the reporter said, "Here's how police have re-created the sequence of events." The details that followed were a chronological account of the crime from several years earlier. The story ended with the reporter showing the local telephone number for Crimestoppers.

Mapped Format

Professor Jacqueline Farnan and newspaper copy editor David Hedley discussed another variation on the inverted pyramid style called the *mapped format*. They noted that the inverted pyramid becomes confusing for longer pieces, but they believed it served as a way to introduce the most important elements of the message.

Mapped format is a technique to indicate points of interest within the message, just as a map includes highlights for its readers. The mapped format aids readers in finding information of particular interest to them in longer stories. Look at the complete story on Bertine Bahige found in Appendix C. Writer Nathan Payne used subheads or a mapped format to guide readers through a long story.

A mapped message is organized into sections. The first is the inverted pyramid lead. Following the lead, a series of subheads using action verbs defines categories of information. Readers can quickly find the segments of information that most benefit or appeal to them.

Subheads for an expanded story on the bank robbery would look like this:

Robber Approaches Teller
Escape into Woods
Police Still Searching

The mapped format can also help the writer organize. Assume you are writing a story on the cost of funerals and the alternatives to traditional burial. Your research finds categories of information: reasons why funerals are expensive, caskets and their costs, funeral home expenses, cost of burial plots, cost of cremation versus burial, memorial services, and how to cut costs. After drafting the lead, you can group categories of information under subheads, which help organize the story and readily identify parts of the story for readers.

Media, both old and new, use mapped formats. For example, CNN .com uses subheads in its full stories. This style helps readers quickly find information they want and need.

Numerical Format

A writer might organize a message numerically or by points. For example, a city council votes on three issues: water and sewer rates, a rezoning application, and the town manager's contract. The writer would list in a multiple-element lead the actions taken and the votes, thereby setting up the three points to be expanded, in the same order, in the body of the story.

Writers covering a speech will often use a numeral or point-by-point format that follows the organizational structure of the speech. For example, a speaker discusses three major risk factors in heart disease. The writer notes the three risk factors in the lead: smoking, lack of exercise, and lack of a well-balanced diet. The points serve as transitions from the lead to the sections of the message. The reporter's story might read:

> Cardiovascular disease is the number 1 cause of death in the United States, but it can be reduced with lifestyle changes such as no smoking, regular exercise, and a well-balanced diet, the chairman of the American Heart Association's Wayne County chapter said Tuesday.
>
> Gus Rivas said Americans should pay attention to the risk factors at an early age and get children to be aware of healthy lifestyles.
>
> More than 3,000 children smoke their first cigarette every day. This number will translate into more adults who are at risk for cardiovascular disease.
>
> "Children consume more than 947 million packs of cigarettes in this country per year," Rivas said. "More than 25 percent of high school students who smoke tried their first cigarette while in the sixth grade."
>
> Youngsters need to exercise, he noted. Studies show that today's youth do not get enough regular exercise.
>
> "Riding a bike, walking, even doing household chores can establish fitness patterns," Rivas said.
>
> A well-balanced diet low in fat is essential to reduce the risk of heart disease, Rivas said. About one out of four children is obese, and obese children are at a risk for obesity as adults.

The writer followed the order laid out in the lead, using the three points or risk factors as a way to organize and unify the story.

Unifying Writing

Any story, memo, news release, or online message needs unity to be a coherent and complete piece. Each graph must follow the preceding graph logically and build on previous information. Each section of the piece must fit the subject or theme. Even where a new lead updates a story, the transition from the new to exiting information must be smooth. Unifying writing takes careful thought and planning, and it requires rewriting or reorganizing after a first draft is done.

Transitions and repetition of certain words are ways to unify writing and to move readers from the beginning to the end. The first two or three paragraphs set up many of the unifying elements—for example, people, places, things, controversy, or chronology.

Repetition of Words

Some writers are uncomfortable repeating words in their writing. They pore over the thesaurus or dictionary, looking for synonyms that might not be as good as repeating the word itself. Repetition is okay; it offers unity in a message and gives readers familiarity. Repetition is also clearer; readers are not stopping to match synonyms and words.

The topic will determine the words repeated. A memo that covers changes in employee benefits should use the word "employee" throughout rather than switching from "worker" to "staff" to "professional." The same applies in writing about an organization; "organization" or the organization's name can be used throughout rather than "group," "agency," or "company."

Transitions

Transitions are cues for readers. They set up changes in location, time, and mood, and they keep readers from getting lost or confused.

A simple sentence or word might be needed as a logical bridge from one section of the message to the next. Any transition should wrap up the previous thought and introduce the next one. Here's an example of smooth transition:

> "We must continue our efforts to reduce teenage pregnancy, and our programs are aimed to do that," the governor said.
> While the governor defended his policies, others in state government cited lack of action on welfare issues for his dwindling popularity.

The second sentence uses "while" and "others" to indicate a shift from the governor's words to those of state government officials.

Most writers are accustomed to simple words or phrases as transitions. Look at some of the following words and phrases that give readers certain information about where a story is going:

A change in opinion:	but, on the other hand, however
Clarification:	in other words, for example, that is, to illustrate, to demonstrate, specifically, to clarify
Comparison:	also, in comparison, like, similarly, on the same note, a related point
Contrast:	but, in contrast, despite, on the contrary, unlike, yet, however, instead of

Expanded information:	in addition, an additional, moreover, in other action, another, further, furthermore, too, as well as, also
A change in place:	above, higher, beneath, nearby, beside, between, across, after, around, below
Time:	while, meanwhile, past, afterward, during, soon, next, subsequently, until then, future, before, at the same time

Look at how a few of these easy transitions work. In developing news chronologically, time serves as a transition. Refer to the First Guaranty bank robbery story earlier in this chapter. The time elements pull the reader from shortly after 9 a.m., when the robbery occurred, until 6 p.m., when the woman still had not been caught. In other stories, time-oriented words and phrases could be "at the same time," "later that day," "Tuesday," and "last week."

A story about voter reaction on election day uses polling sites around town as geographic transitions: "Voters at Precinct 35 (Town Hall) said...," "Those voting at Precinct 15 (Main Street Presbyterian Church) said...," "Precinct 2 voters (Blackwell Elementary School) said...." Other geographical phrases would be "on the other side of town," "at his father's 25-acre farm," "next door," and "at the White House."

Tone to Unify a Message

Familiarity with your audiences will help determine what tone to set in organizing and writing a message. The tone of a story can act as a unifying device. An editor of a newsletter for parents knows that her audience is busy, fast-moving, and distracted by children, work, day-to-day routine, and a deluge of information. She knows her audience is in need of quick tips about kids and school. She must write lively copy with short, pithy sentences and paragraphs. Active parents need newsletter copy that looks like this:

> Spring cleaning may leave you with trash and treasures. Please donate them to Southview School's Trash and Treasure sale! This year's sale is planned for May 9.
> Jennifer Chen will begin receiving donations April 26 at her home, 3221 Dale Drive. For more information, call 499-2342.

In contrast, a lead in *The Wall Street Journal* about a shift in the nation's diversity has a more formal, serious, thoughtful tone that will continue throughout the article:

> For the first time in U.S. history, whites of European ancestry account for less than half of newborn children, marking a demographic tipping point that is already changing the nation's politics, economy and workforce.

A writer's knowledge of audiences will determine the mood or tone that will best maintain interest and retain it throughout the message.

Quotes to Unify Stories

Quotes can be effective transitions that unify writing. They add liveliness and allow people to speak directly to readers and listeners, helping them feel more connected to personalities and events. They can supplement facts and add detail. News stories and news releases should have a good balance between direct and indirect quotes. Information on direct and indirect quotes, attribution, and punctuation of quotes is given in Chapter 10.

Nathan Payne used quotes in his piece on Bertine Bahige to show the teacher's earnest pleading to encourage a student to stay in school:

> "You only have 30 days left until graduation, that's only 15 days in each class," he said. "Make sure you get your work done. You're almost there."

And later, when Bahige explains why he had to creep silently away from the rebel camp as he escaped:

> "I knew I didn't have a choice for failure," he said. "Death was not an issue. There was no prison. You have to overcome fear."

Closing quotes can refer to the lead and wrap up a piece at the end; they can leave the reader looking to the future; or they can add a touch of humor. But sometimes writers have to be careful in using a quote at the end. If the story is cut from the bottom, readers should miss only a chuckle, not important information.

Unifying Devices in Practice

Let's go back and look at the short article on the woman running barefoot across the country. The story was first reported in the *Des Moines Register* and then rewritten in a shorter version by the Associated Press and distributed across the country. Look at the Associated Press version. What are the unifying devices? First, see what the lead sets up.

> DES MOINES, Iowa—An Iowa woman is running barefoot across the United States to raise money to provide shoes for needy children.

Throughout the story the writer refers to running, barefoot, and shoes. The second paragraph identifies Rae Heim and outlines her goal to run from Boston to California.

> Rae Heim, 18, of Carroll, started her cross-country trek in Boston in April and hopes to reach Huntington Beach, Calif., in October.

Graph 3 gives context for how the reporter did the interview.

The Des Moines Register (http://dmreg.co/NsclC1) caught up with her this week in Iowa as she crested a hill near Victor in 91-degree heat.

Graphs 4 and 5 give context for how she started the venture and how she is feeling.

Heim stopped to talk but wasn't out of breath. She said she started running barefoot after breaking a toe last year and shedding her running shoes for comfort. Shoes now feel like dead weight to her, although she wore them through New Jersey, where broken glass and nails littered the highway, and dons them on gravel roads.
    The bottoms of her feet are like slabs of leather. When they start burning in the heat, she puts on toe socks.

Graph 6 gives her philosophy in a direct quote.

"We are born to run barefoot," Heim said.

Graph 7 sets up the next quote in graph 8.

She told the newspaper that she hated to run and even dreaded rounding the bases while playing softball.
    "It was like a punishment," she said. But then Heim realized that people thought she couldn't run, and she set out to prove them wrong.

Graphs 9 and 10 flesh out the background on she came up with the idea to run across the country and as a fund-raiser.

She entered road races and last summer met a middle-aged man who ran across America, which inspired her.
    What started as a personal adventure has become a fund-raiser for Soles4Souls, a charity that supplies shoes to needy kids.

Graph 11 uses a quote to explain how raising money keeps her running.

"When I feel like quitting, I think of the $2,900 I have raised," Heim said. "That's 2,900 pairs of shoes."

Graphs 12 and 13 follow the quote with information that tells what have been the challenges.

There have been a few bumps during her trek.
    After the first week of 40-plus mile days, she had a twisted ankle, painful Achilles tendon and sore knee. She sat on the side of the road, crying, and then called her mom.

Graphs 14, 15, and 16 wrap up the story with how she overcame the difficult moments and create an ending using her own words.

> Now, she's averaging 20 miles a day. She carries her belongings in a backpack. Her mom watches her every move with a GPS and has friends set up along the route to check on her.
> Heim said most of her journey has been pleasant.
> "The kindness I've seen in people surprised me. You always hear all the wrong with the world," she said. "But I've seen nothing but good in the world."

Moving Forward

Writing is a series of choices—choice of language, pertinent facts, introductions, organizational pattern, tone, quotes, and topics—to unify copy. All need to be made in an informed way, based on what writers know about their audiences.

Books about writing and advice from other writers can give you tips on how to organize your stories better. The best way to learn is to apply the techniques through your own efforts. Do not let organization just happen. Remember the stages of writing. Make an outline. Consciously apply a certain organizational style to your writing. Let someone else read your piece to see whether it makes sense.

Good organization helps you reach your audience. Remember Nathan Payne's story about Bertine Bahige who fled his war-torn country? The reporter uses all the strengths of simple writing, repetition for unity, and quotes as transitions to pull readers through an emotionally compelling story that could have been just another routine immigrant story. He framed a student's story within Bahige's story, both leading to the same resolution. The following chapters will guide you further in writing for your audience.

Exercises

1. You are a reporter for the *Cityville Chronicle*. You have picked up the following police report—written last night—from the town police department. Write a message with a summary lead, then develop the message in chronological order.

   > Report: Tony's Restaurant Robbery
   > Investigating Officer: Sgt. Rodney Carter
   > At 10 p.m. a robbery at Tony's Restaurant was reported. Owner Tony Hardy said he was working late preparing the payroll when a man wearing a stocking mask entered the back door of the kitchen at about 8:40.
   > Hardy said the man told him to go into the office and open up the safe. Hardy took almost $3,000 out of the safe and put it into a blue, waterproof sack.

The restaurant closes at 9 p.m. Hardy said he thought the robber knew he was there alone, but he didn't think the robber was a Cityville resident.

Hardy said he got a good look at the man: a stocky white man, about 5'6", and round-faced. He estimated the man's age to be 24. Hardy said the man's shoulders were so broad that he might have been a weight lifter. Hardy suggested that if the thief wanted to lock him up somewhere, the storage closet off the kitchen was as good a place as any. The thief agreed and locked him up there. The thief wrapped a clothes hanger around the door. He told Hardy he had a partner, and that Hardy wouldn't live to see his family and relatives if he came out of the closet before 15 minutes had passed.

Hardy said he waited the 15 minutes even though he didn't believe the story about the partner, or at least a partner who would be stupid enough to hang around for 15 minutes. He had no trouble getting out and then called the Cityville police.

We have some leads on the suspect and the investigation is continuing.

2. Write a new lead for the story produced in Example 1. The new information: Police arrested Albert Campbell, 45, of Boston, Mass., in the robbery. He has been charged with armed robbery and assault. He is being held in the Johnston County jail. His first court appearance will be tomorrow at 11 a.m.

3. From the following information, write a summary lead for the *Cityville Chronicle* that focuses on *who*, *what*, *when*, and *where*, plus human interest. Then develop the message in hourglass format.

From the Cityville police chief, Alston Powers, you learn the following:

Two sisters were playing at a Laundromat about 5 p.m. yesterday. The girls are the daughters of Nancy and Phillip Childs of Cityville. The girls were with their aunt, Janice Childs. The 3-year-old, Jennifer, climbed into one of the washing machines. Her sister, Elizabeth, 7, closed the door. The machine started filling up with water. When she realized the washer was running, Elizabeth ran to get her aunt. Ms. Childs tried to open the washer door but could not, because the washers are equipped with automatic locks on the doors.

Powers said the girl was trapped in the washer for more than five minutes before she was rescued. He said a customer had put coins into the machine before the little girl crawled inside, but the customer hadn't used the machine because he thought it wasn't working.

On the telephone you talk to Chris Gibson, of 124 Basketball Lane, Cityville. He was on his way home from work and stopped at the Glen Rock Shopping Center to buy groceries. He heard screams coming from the Glen Rock Laundry and Dry Cleaner. He ran inside the Laundromat to see what was going on. Ms. Childs ran up to him and asked him to save the child. She asked if he had any tools, so he ran back to his toolbox in the back of his truck and got a hammer. Gibson said he took the hammer back inside and smashed the glass in the washing machine door. He then reached in and pulled her out.

A Cityville Hospital spokesperson said Jennifer was admitted yesterday afternoon and was listed in good condition. Her parents could not be reached for comment.

4. You are a reporter for the *Cityville Chronicle*. You are to write a story from the following information. Focus on a summary lead with a local angle. Organize the story in inverted pyramid.

A group of 55 cyclists from the United States arrived in Ho Chi Minh City in Vietnam yesterday. They ended a 1,200-mile course through Vietnam. The trip took them 20 days. The course was fairly grueling through some of the country's mountainous areas as well as flat parts. The group camped and stayed in villages along the way.

The U.S. Cycling Federation, which arranged the tour, said it planned to organize another event next year. Officials said the tours are a way to allow U.S. residents to get a close-up look at the country and their people.

When the group arrived it was greeted by firecrackers, flower necklaces, and cold towels. Bob Lester, 33, of Cressett, was one of the cyclists on the trip. He said, "This trip was the most amazing thing I have ever done in my life. I would recommend the experience to anyone who can pedal a bike." The cyclists are expected to return to the United States in two weeks.

The tour was part of an effort to open up Vietnam to outsiders and to present a different picture of the country than people had come to expect from the Vietnam War.

Among the cyclists were seven Vietnam veterans and three Vietnamese Americans, all from the United States. The 55 cyclists were from 23 states.

Several of the Americans said the journey had erased any doubts they might have held about Vietnam and its people.

References

Farnan Jacqueline, and Hedley, David. "The Mapped Format: A Variation on the Inverted-Pyramid Appeals to Readers." Paper presented at the Association for Education in Journalism and Mass Communication Conference, Atlanta, GA, August 1993.

Fedler, Fred. *Reporting for the Print Media*. New York: Harcourt Brace Jovanovich, 1989.

"Newswriting for the Commercial Appeal," produced by Lionel Linder, Editor, and Colleen Conant, Managing Editor, 1989.

Zinsser, William. *On Writing Well*. New York: Harper & Row, 1976.

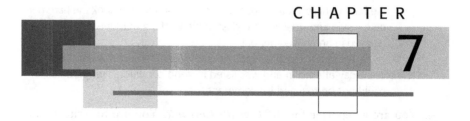

Specific Story Formats

Media messages are written for many reasons: Some messages break urgent news stories or give consumer information; some explore newsworthy personalities or places; others present opinion, analysis, or criticism. The reason or purpose of a message can determine the format. A story about a hotel fire, for example, will use a different format and tone from a profile of an award-winning teacher. A tweet or a post on Facebook will use specific style and length to tell followers where to find the best consumer deals.

Writers might follow one of the organizational formats outlined in Chapter 6 or develop a combination that works for the specific piece they are writing. For example, a breaking news story will have a summary lead, background, and chronology. What works for a bank robbery will be inadequate for longer pieces that must communicate more complex information. Consumer information pieces might use an anecdotal lead followed by specific tips.

Entire textbooks have been written on how to research and construct specific types of articles, such as features. Websites such as www.poynter.com and other sites created by media organizations also give tips on formats for messages. No basic text can cover in depth all types of articles and how to write them. Beyond news, among the more common story types that writers develop are features, obituaries, and speech stories.

In this chapter, you will learn

- the difference between features and news,
- some guidelines for features,
- the parts and style of obituaries, and
- the basics of writing speech stories.

News versus Feature

Apart from breaking news, most articles today are news-features or features. Features can be developed on any subject for any reason, and they inform or entertain audiences. A writer might be curious about the craft of making a basket he bought while on vacation in Charleston, South Carolina, or the sudden sound of cicadas around his home at night.

Features must be complete, clear, accurate, and fair. Some features will be more concise than others. Features use quotes and adequate attribution, and they mix indirect with direct quotes. Features carry the same news values discussed in Chapter 5—prominence, conflict, oddity, proximity, and especially human interest.

Traditionally, writers have used one value to distinguish news from features: timeliness. Features have a timeless quality. They can be published at any time and remain useful and entertaining. News, however, must be released immediately. The death of a nationally known fashion designer is news; a story about fashions is a feature. In sum, *news tells*, a *feature shows*.

Some features, however, are linked to news stories. When Osama bin Laden was killed, additional stories focused on al-Qaeda and its history, description of the Pakistani town in which he had been hiding for years, and individuals' reactions. Such sidebar features can stand alone; that is, they are complete stories themselves but have been written because of a news event.

Adding the Visual

To the traditional distinction of timeliness, writers must add another consideration: How much will the reader see or imagine? In other words, will the story create images to take the reader to the scene? Did the writer make the reader feel he or she were there? It has been said that journalism becomes literature when it tells the reader not just what happened but what it was like. Erik Lawson wrote in *Isaac's Storm*, his book on the hurricane that struck Galveston, Texas, in 1900:

> The wind neatly sliced off the top floor of a bank, leaving the rest of the building intact. It stripped slate shingles from houses and turned them into scimitars that disemboweled men where they stood. Atmospheric pressure fell so low, a visiting British cotton official was sucked from his apartment trailing a slipstream of screams from his wife.

Just as in good literature, feature writing must carry sensory impact. Although electronic media and improved technology increase writers' ability to add audio and video to a story, writers must still be able to describe in words the scene they witnessed. The feature's job is to flesh out the headline and to paint the picture, whether it is of the magnitude of a hurricane, the beauty of a ballet, or the courtroom tension in a high-profile murder case.

Written feature stories that appear in a publication today generally will also appear on its website. Because of the multimedia capability of the Internet, an editor could add to the text a video where readers see the person interviewed and hear the distinctive accent in her voice. The video could add context to where the person lives or works. Embedded links in the online version of the feature story would take readers to sites for more detailed information.

At the heart of today's feature writing is what Gene Roberts, retired executive editor of the *Philadelphia Inquirer* and former managing editor of *The New York Times*, expected of his writers. His expectations are aptly described in the text for the Eugene L. Roberts Prize awarded to qualifying students at the School of Journalism and Mass Communication at the University of North Carolina at Chapel Hill:

> The Eugene L. Roberts Prize is meant to encourage and is dedicated to the story of the untold event that oozes instead of breaks; to the story that reveals, not repeats; to the reporter who zigs instead of zags; to the truth as opposed to the facts; to the forest, not just the trees; to the story they'll be talking about in the coffee shop on Main Street; to the story that answers not just who, what, where, when and why, but also "So what?"; to efforts at portraying real life itself; to journalism that "wakes me up and makes me see"; to the revival of the disappearing storyteller.

The "so what" aspect that Roberts notes is critical for any feature writing. Just as in news stories, many features have a nut graph or news peg. Readers need to know why the story has been written. As noted in Chapter 6, the nut graph might be found within five or six graphs. In a feature story, readers might have to look a little longer, but the nut graph should be clear. Consider this lead from *The Kansas City Star:*

> Here at the corner of 22nd and Brooklyn, an ailing Lou Gehrig took his last at bat. A quarter of a century later, the Beatles played a concert here in front of 20,000 screaming teenyboppers.
>
> And it was here, for nearly half a century, that Kansas City sports fans cheered their hometown heroes—their Monarchs, their Blues, A's, Royals, Spurs and Chiefs—before old Municipal Stadium was abandoned in favor of two new ones further east.
>
> Today, unless you know the history or happen upon a historical marker on the corner, you'd never know the stadium ever existed, much less that the first of baseball's two 1960 All-Star Games was played there.
>
> But that's about to change as city officials try to capitalize on that storied past in an effort to attract home buyers to the half-finished subdivision that sits on the site of the former stadium.

Reporter Mike Hendricks uses a descriptive lead to set up the story. The fourth graph is the nut graph where readers begin to learn the point of the story: The subdivision has not met expectations for the development, and city officials are hoping that marketing the historical aspect of the neighborhood will make a difference.

Writing the Feature Lead

Lead types, which were covered in Chapter 5, apply to writing features. Writers have the freedom to use direct address, descriptive, question, or other leads to attract readers to stories. For example, reporters writing stories in advance of the state fair might lead with:

> Come one, come all, to this year's state fair.

Or:

> Food. Rides. Ribbons. Pigs.
> That's what brings Martha Bryson to the state fair each year.

Or:

> For Matt Rutger, vacation is 10 days at the state fair where he has operated his family's foot-long hot dog stand for 20 years.

Whether topics are light or serious, most features do not use summary leads in the same way news stories do. A summary lead might be used in a sidebar or supplementary story in a package of feature stories. Rather than the straightforward *who-what-when-where* news summary format, the summary feature lead might tally reaction in an informal poll or synthesize data. For example, a story that uses an anecdotal lead to introduce an economic story about downsizing of the furniture-building industry in the state might have a sidebar story giving the latest unemployment figures and trend data. The lead might read:

> The state's unemployment rate reached 9.2 percent in June, its highest since August 2010, according to statistics released today by the state office that tracks such data.

The article goes on to reveal other economic woes in the state.

Probably the most common leads for feature stories are descriptive and anecdotal. Many news-features use those lead types to set up stories grounded in a news event. When reporters use an anecdotal lead, they must remember to carry that example throughout the story. For example, if a campus reporter writes a news-feature about the increased cost of textbooks, she might use one student's experience as a lead into the story. The body of the feature would cover the increased costs, why textbook prices are going up, what percentage the campus bookstore gets, and comments from the student in the lead, as well as from other students. The end of the story would use a quote from the student introduced in the lead.

The Wall Street Journal has utilized this approach to the point that it is often called *Wall Street Journal* style. It takes the reader through the hard facts of the story—the background, analysis, and details that form its hard core—but focuses on an individual, a project, or a family. Look for the features on the *Journal's* front page to study this writing style.

Feature Formats

No single format defines a feature story. A feature might be as simple as the local reaction to a well-known high school athlete's death: a summary lead followed by a unified telling of family members' and school friends' recollections. Some investigative writers might spend months examining records, conducting interviews, writing articles, and producing video clips for a package of pieces on one topic.

Most writers agree that a feature, whether in print or in video, has a beginning, a middle, and an end. Within that framework, a writer uses description, quotes, unifying elements, and tone to pull readers through the story. Narrative devices, such as suspense and action, can also capture readers.

The purpose and content of a feature story might dictate a format. For example, a how-to feature on improving study habits will describe why study habits are important, then outline where to study, when to study, how to organize notes, how to review, and how to gauge success. A feature on reducing the risk of heart attack might begin with an anecdotal lead, focusing on a heart attack survivor, then outline in a mapped format three criteria—lack of exercise, poor diet, and smoking. A story on a retiring faculty member might use chronology as a primary format for chronicling the teacher's career. Each online piece could be supplemented with video and photographs.

Feature Organization

Writers often look for fresh ways to portray a subject who has been covered time and time again. At the retirement of a living-legend baseball star, a writer assigned to the story with a horde of other reporters noticed the star's wife standing several feet behind him, and to the side. The writer told the story through her reaction to the tributes offered to her husband and his farewell words. While working on a routine story of children going off to camp, a writer noticed that one child's parents had a hard time saying goodbye; they'd kiss the child, send him off toward the bus, then call him back… again… and again… and again. The writer told the story from that family's perspective.

Writing formats change. Many writers today have adopted more narrative styles of writing, using anecdotal and descriptive approaches. These stories are generally longer and pose challenges in presenting and organizing a lot of information from research and interviews. With more content moving online, writers are learning to record interviews so that through video and audio clips subjects can tell their stories in their own words. Time will be the test of whether new formats attract and retain audiences.

Types of Features

As noted earlier in the chapter, feature stories are written simply to entertain or inform, standing on their own or complementing news stories. While feature stories contain similar elements, such as description and quotes, they sometimes can be classified by type.

- *How-to* features are included among consumer features that instruct readers or viewers. Experts give tips on topics ranging from how to build a coffee table, make strawberry jelly, find day care, or evaluate dating sites. Stories should include additional resources and step-by-step guidelines. The story might use bullets to list information, such as specific ingredients and where to buy them for a specialty recipe. Many such stories posted online allow consumer commentary at the end. Some writers have developed blogs that focus on do-it-yourself projects.

- *Personality* features can be two- to three-page pieces that focus on one aspect of an individual's life or a 60-inch profile that gives an in-depth look at a person. For example, when the president identifies a Cabinet or U.S. Supreme Court nominee, the media will write extensive profiles on the individual's professional—and sometimes personal—career.

- *Historical* features recount events in an earlier time. Often, the anniversaries of events, such as the Battle of Gettysburg, generate such features. With the 100-year anniversary of the sinking of the Titanic, stories reflected the ship's construction, the voyage, and the fateful night. Researching such stories might mean looking at archives and other historical records as well as oral histories from people who remember.

- *Place or travel* features tell readers or viewers what they will find at a particular destination. These stories can also be how-to articles containing information about where to stay or eat and what to see. Detailed description sets the scene so audiences can see the place in their minds— beyond the accompanying photos or other visuals—and be enticed to visit. As a note, most publications will not publish a travel feature if the writer has had his or her expenses paid by a business or group.

- *Color* features are just that: They describe in great detail a colorful event. For example, a reporter assigned to cover a street festival would use language and description that relate to all the senses: sound, taste, smell, touch, and sight. Writers must be careful to use original and fresh description and avoid clichés or superficial language.

▪ *Brights* are news stories that can be a short news-feature, generally no longer than six to seven paragraphs and with a twist at the end. Such stories must be well crafted and succinct. Consider this bright, including the end quote, from the *Los Angeles Times*:

A pig squealed on itself yesterday and wound up in the arms of the law. And if the policemen involved have their way, he'll wind up at a barbecue.

Radio Officers Fred F. Thomas and Lee Manning had just warned a "road hog" at 103rd and Juniper Sts. in Watts when they heard the furious barking of a dog interspersed with a few terrified "oink oinks" emanating from an alley.

With Officer Thomas calling upon his latent talents as a hog-caller, the Berkshire was rescued from the dog and transferred to Ann St. Animal Shelter.

And if the pig, already named Daisy Mae, isn't claimed in the legal time allowed, Thomas Manning and other policemen of the 77th St. Station have collected a fund to pay the pound fee as a prebarbecue requirement.

Reprinted with permission of the *Los Angeles Times*.

Putting It Together

After all the research, interviews, and critical thinking about story approach, a writer has to attack the task of creating the piece. As noted earlier in the chapter, the move online has given writers the ability to enhance their stories with more visuals. But, the need still exists for writers who can fashion compelling description, whether of scenery or individuals; who can select quotes that reflect individual's personalities or opinions; and who can set the scene with suspense or humor.

With longer stories, such as 2,500 words, the challenge is even greater for writers to hook and keep their audiences. Look at the feature by Associated Press writer Kathleen Hennessey. Her story has all the attributes of good feature writing: quotes, description, prominent characters, suspense, and humor. She uses simple language and varies sentence types.

LAS VEGAS—Tempest Storm is fuming. Her fingers tremble with frustration. They are aged, knotted by arthritis and speckled with purple spots under paper-thin skin.

But the manicure of orange polish is flawless and matches her signature tousled mane.

She brushes orange curls out of her face as she explains how she's been slighted.

She is the headliner, you know. She is a star. She is classy.

"I don't just get up there and rip my clothes off," she says.

Indeed, the 80-year-old burlesque queen takes her clothes off very slowly.

More than 50 years ago, she was dubbed the "Girl with the Fabulous Front" and told by famous men she had the "Best Two Props in Hollywood." Since then, Storm saw the art that made her famous on the brink of extinction. Her contemporaries—Blaze Starr, Bettie Page, Lili St. Cyr—have died or hung up the pasties.

But not Storm. She kept performing. Las Vegas, Reno, Palm Springs, Miami, Carnegie Hall.

Her act is a time capsule. She knows nothing of poles. She would never put her derriere in some man's face. Her prop of choice is a boa, perhaps the occasional divan.

It takes four numbers, she says adamantly, four numbers to get it all off. To do it classy.

But the producers of tonight's show, just kids, they want her to go faster. She gets just seven minutes.

They gave her trouble last year, too. They even cut her music before she finished.

There may not be a next time for this show, she says. The threat lasts just minutes.

"No, no. I'm not ready to hang up my G-string, yet. I've got too many fans that would be disappointed."

FAMOUS FRIENDS

Stardom and fandom feature prominently in Tempest Storm's life—and in her neat, two-bedroom Las Vegas apartment.

Visitors are greeted by photos of a young Elvis, her favorite rock 'n' roller and, she says, a former lover.

The relationship ended after about a year because Elvis' manager didn't approve of him dating a stripper, she says.

But she could not change who she was. Stripping already had made her famous.

It put her in the room with Hollywood's heavyweights. Frank Sinatra, Dean Martin, Mickey Rooney, Nat King Cole.

She dated some, just danced for others. The evidence is framed and displayed on tables and the living room wall.

That's Storm and Vic Damone. Storm teaching Walter Cronkite to dance. Storm and her fourth and last husband, Herb Jefferies, a star of black cowboy films who swept her off her feet in 1957 when such unions were instant scandals. They divorced in 1970.

"When I look at this picture I say, 'What... happened between this gorgeous couple?'" she says.

Storm is rarely wistful. She has no doubt she still is what she once was. Although she performs just a handful of times a year, she would do more, if asked. She chides those who think age takes a toll on sex appeal.

"Ridiculous," she says.

There are just as many recent photos in the room: Storm and her daughter, a nurse in Indiana. Storm and her fiance, who died a few years ago. Storm and a beaming older gentlemen, just a fan who approached her for a photograph.

"That stage saved me," she says as she leaves a sound check hours before the night's performance.

She had been expecting a much smaller space, and she is relieved. She's a "walker," she explains. She needs room to move.

It is a direct and once-racy style, the signature work of Lillian Hunt, the choreographer at the Follies Theater in Los Angeles where Storm became a star.

She was Annie Blanche Banks then. The 22-year-old sharecropper's daughter had fled sexual abuse, two loveless marriages and poverty in small-town Georgia, she says.

She was working as a cocktail waitress but wanted to be a showgirl. First, she needed her teeth fixed.

"Do you think my bust is too big for this business?" she asked Hunt at her audition.

Hunt put her in the chorus line, told her not to gain a pound and called a dentist.

In Storm's telling, she didn't stay long in the background. She got a new name. ("I really don't feel like a Sunny Day.") She took to the spotlight quickly.

NO REASON TO STOP

On Sundays, Storm tunes in to a televangelist who tells her anyone can overcome odds. It's the only religion she's ever taken to.

She believes this is the lesson of her life. Be a survivor. Never stop doing what you love; it makes you who you are.

"If you want to get old, you'll get old," she says.

There have been men who disappointed her, financial strain, brain surgery.

After it all, she sits on her couch and exercises in front of the television on a small stationary bike. She doesn't smoke or drink or eat much.

"I'm just blessed, I think. And I know when to push myself away from the table."

If some might see all this as chasing after lost youth, she says she cares little. Younger dancers tell her she is an inspiration to them, and she has no reason not to believe them.

"I feel good about myself. And I enjoy it," she says. "I have fun when I'm onstage, and the audience loves it. Nobody ever said it's time to give it up. Why stop?"*

Stories such as Hennessey's are examples to keep as models for descriptive writing, including the use of quotes, particularly to end the article.

Obituaries

When people die, reports of their deaths, called obituaries, usually appear in local media and often are among the most-read articles in the paper. They chronicle an individual's life and follow a specific format set by the particular medium. Obituaries generally are two types: news obituaries or paid death notices. The news obituary is written by a member of the news staff and published in a news section. The paid death notice is handled by the advertising department, might appear in a smaller type size than news columns, and can be written by a family member. Media publish obituaries, whether news or paid, in specific locations familiar to audiences.

Major media, such as *The New York Times*, have obituary files on prominent individuals as do the major news wire services, such as the Associated Press. Background information, photos, and even articles are stored, ready if the person dies unexpectedly—or not. Biographical material is ready even for younger celebrities. With the depth and multimedia capability of online sites, when singer-celebrities Etta James and Michael Jackson died, readers could click on links to their music to get deeper emotional impact and greater understanding of the individuals' contributions.

Basic Information

Obituaries contain the news elements and the life history of an individual. Each obituary should note the complete name of who died, when he or she died, where, how, and why. (The "what" is that the individual died.) "How" someone died, such as unusual or tragic circumstances, might make that death a news story, such as a teen mauled by a tiger. Often why a person died will not be revealed based on the family's request. Many media do not include the cause of violent death unless it can be attributed to a medical examiner, particularly in the case of a suicide.

Obituaries also outline a person's life, particularly career details, accomplishments, contributions, volunteer work, organizational membership, or other personal information. For a prominent individual, a reporter might interview coworkers, family members, or others to have quotes in the obituary. Clips from speeches or other appearances might be included. The notice will also list funeral arrangements, visitations, survivors, and where to send memorials or contributions.

For survivors, immediate family members are included. Ex-husbands and ex-wives are not, unless you are writing an obituary of someone who has had a number of spouses. Their names would be part of that person's life story.

Funeral homes provide most information for obituaries. Some media will not accept obituary information from family members. People have played practical jokes on friends by placing a death notice when the person turned 40 or 50 years old. Reporters who are writing news obituaries will get information from place of employment, interviews, biographical sources, the Internet, and government documents. For obituaries written in advance of a person's death, an interview with the individual might make up part of the file.

Accuracy is critical in obituaries. Often families cut out obituaries and keep them with family records or in a family Bible. In a time of mourning, a family's sadness and stress increase if an obituary reports the wrong age or misspells a name. In compiling information, reporters must ensure the information is correct. They should get the birth date and calculate the person's age. Pitfalls of research are discussed in Chapter 9.

Format and Structure

Each media outlet has a format it uses for writing obituaries. For example, the obit might simply state:

> Kevin D. Smith, 33, New Orleans, Saturday. Funeral: 10 a.m., Tuesday, Jones Funeral Home. Surviving: wife, Katherine; children, Thomas, Renee, Gretchen of the home.

In paid death notices, the family pays according to the length, generally measured in column inches. The family can write the notice as long as it wants, including such detail as the person's parents and grandparents, career path, organizational membership, even personal information, and where to send memorials. Sometimes individuals will write their own obituaries before they die.

In a news obituary lead, a writer would focus on *who*, *what*, *when*, and *where*, along with *what* the individual is known for, such as a professional career or volunteer efforts. A dateline could tell where the person died or the location would be included in the story.

Writing styles will differ from publication to publication. Major newspapers, such as *The New York Times*, will generally be straightforward in writing and use the word "died" to tell what happened. The writing might be more casual in local reports, such as this one from the *Virginia City News*:

> A Nevada icon, Chandler Laughlin, aka Travis T. Hipp, has passed on peacefully to the great radio station in the sky.
> A bagpipe rang out as he was buried Silver City style in a plain pine box crafted by his friend, Tom Byron, in the Silver City Cemetery.

From the leads, readers learn *who* died, *when*, *where*, and *why* they will be remembered. The body of the obituary will put the events of the person's life in order, usually chronologically. The general format for obituaries is the lead, contributions, career and life, survivors, funeral services, and memorials or donations. Norma Sosa, a former obituary writer for the *New York Times*, notes that the *Times* follows a specific format that has a kicker, when appropriate, as the last paragraph. She says:

> *Use a quote or anecdote that you feel reflects a stand-out aspect of a person's life, views, work, or contribution. It's the thought that remains in the reader's mind—what you, the researcher and writer, felt was the single most important or interesting thing you learned about the person. It could be something counterintuitive, funny, sad, surprising, or poignant.*

Sometimes quotes from the individual as well as from others can tell the story, as in the obituary on writer and filmmaker Nora Ephron in *The New York Times*. Quotes from colleagues, such as fellow writer Sally Quinn, offered insights into Ephron's personality, such as Ephron keeping the diagnosis of a pre-leukemic condition from many people. The obituary also included detail, such as Ephron's attention to her hair.

Links throughout the article took readers to reviews of and information about her writings and movies. Readers could post comments at the end.

Speech Stories

Writers today rarely produce stories solely from speech content, such as the president's State of the Union address or a commencement address. In covering such events, writers will note others' reactions to the speaker's comments, background information to give the speech topic some context, and sometimes references to previous speeches by that individual.

In some instances, links are inserted to transcripts often available through a government or organization website if the speaker is a leading figure. Readers who follow politicians, for example, like transcripts because they can track what people are saying. Speech articles today often include video or audio that allows reporters to add clips of certain comments or quotes that illustrate the topic or the mannerisms of the speaker.

Getting the Quotes

Writing articles about speeches presents challenges to note taking and organization. Taking notes during a speech is much more difficult than during an interview. In an interview, you can ask an interviewee to wait a few seconds while you fill in your notes. During a speech, you cannot stop the speaker; you have to keep up with what he or she is saying.

Many writers use tape recorders so that they can ensure accuracy with quotes or upload audio files to supplement the written piece. Writers using a recorder should make sure that the equipment is working and they are comfortable using it. Most writers, even when using a recorder, will take notes as a guide to locating the key quotes in the audio file. Notes also help if you need to ask a clarifying question after the lecture is over or post a tweet before you write the full story.

In some cases, you might not be able to record. You may find that developing a shorthand is the easiest and fastest way to get complete notes in these situations. Put quotation marks around remarks you know can be used as direct quotes to help when you finally sit down to write.

Good note taking means listening carefully to what speakers say. Ears can deceive. Consider the following errors made when writers did not listen carefully and then did not think when writing the story.

> "Bureaucrats are never seizing in their efforts to keep information from the public," he said.

The speaker actually said "ceasing" not "seizing."

> The council member said she would vote to resend the cell phone ban ordinance.

She actually said "rescind" not "resend."

> "The creation of new toxic dumb sites has all but been eliminated," Browner said.

She really said "dump" not "dumb" sites.

> She saluted American industry, small business, schools, and American citizens for banning together to solve the country's environmental problems.

The speaker said "banding" not "banning."

> People in countries have "the need to create extinct, stable governments," he said.

The speaker said "distinct" not "extinct."

> "Canada stepped outside its democratic laws to get the treaty written," she said.

The speaker actually said "diplomatic" not "democratic."

Sometimes writers hear the right word but misspell it. This error damages their credibility and can be embarrassing. For example, one writer called a school's lecture series the "Wheel" lecture when it is named the "Weil" lecture. Another referred to a river as the "Noose" River when it is spelled "Neuse." Consider these:

> "Investigators found millions of land mines sewn into the earth," Williams said.

The writer should have written "sown."

"Our commitment cannot waiver," she said.

She said "waver."

"Congress is trying to role back the progress of 25 years of environmental legislation."

It's "roll" not "role."

"America should be neither a claste nor a classified society."

The speaker said "classed" not "claste."

"Ronald Reagan was applicable with the press during his presidency."

The speaker said "affable."

"The accident does not pose any immediate treat to nearby residents."

The writer made a typographical error. The speaker said "threat" not "treat."

Tips for Writing about Speeches

- When you start to write, always look for the theme. Ask yourself: What does the speaker want us to know? In one speech, the theme may be the importance of democracy, in another the value of higher education, and in yet another public service. It may be in the speech title, or the speaker may deviate and pick out a pet subject on which to elaborate. The theme will be a clue to the lead. Generally, in the lead, a summary of what the speaker said will go first, and then attribution will end the first sentence. An exception is made for a prominent speaker, such as the president or a local government official. Then the name goes first.
- Rarely will the first paragraph be a direct quote. Few speakers summarize their comments in 20 words or fewer. The lead may use a partial quote.
- Write a lead that states what the speaker said. Use attribution verbs such as "said" or "told."
- Do not write a label lead that simply identifies the topic or theme of the speech. That means do not use attribution words such as "discussed,"

"talked about," "spoke about," or "expressed concern about." See the difference:

> Label Lead: Three members of the Broadcasting Board of Governors held a panel discussion on the future of international broadcasting on the university campus last Wednesday.

> Summary Lead: U.S. government broadcasts to regions all over the world can explain democratic values to people living in countries that have repressive governments, according to a panel of experienced broadcasters and journalists who spoke at the university last Wednesday.

- Have a second graph that follows and supports the lead, usually a direct quote rather than background that could bog down the story.
- Have a balance of direct and indirect quotes.
- Look for a direct quote as a good way to end a story. Or end the story with more background about the speaker.
- Make sure your story has adequate attribution, even if you cover only one speaker.

When President Obama made stops at three college campuses in April 2012 to galvanize support for legislation to keep college loan rates low, Dane Huffman of NBC 17 in Durham, North Carolina, wrote:

President Barack Obama arrived in Chapel Hill Tuesday, speaking to a packed house at Carmichael Arena and stressing the value of a college education to a young, energetic crowd at the University of North Carolina.

"We can't price the middle class out of a college education," he told the audience of about 8,000.

Obama opened with some light-hearted banter, chuckling when someone in the audience yelled out their affection for him.

"I love you back. I do. I love North Carolina," he said. "Every time I come to this state, I love it that much more. The thing about North Carolina is the folks who don't vote for me are nice to me."

He even mentioned the UNC basketball team that was knocked out of the NCAA Tournament after star point guard Kendall Marshall was injured.

"I want to tell you, I picked UNC," he said. "If Kendall hadn't gotten hurt, who knows where we might have been."

But Obama soon turned serious, addressing the crowd in a white shirt with sleeves rolled up. He spoke about how he and his wife, Michelle, did not come from wealthy families and had to pay off heavy student loans.

"When we married, we got poor together," he said.

In fact, he said, they didn't pay off their student loans until about eight years ago.

He urged the crowd to contact their Congressional representatives to urge Congress to not let the student loan interest rates double on July 1.

*Reprinted with permission: Dane Huffman for WNCN-NBC 17, Raleigh, NC, a Media General television station.

Huffman's story included statistics on unemployment and a comment from the N.C. State Republican Party chairman. The story package had photos, video, and a link to a transcript of the president's remarks.

Exercises

1. Find a news article that also carries a sidebar or companion piece that is a news-feature or feature. Compare the language between the two stories. Identify how the sidebar might carry more description by highlighting the words. Look at the organization of both articles. How do they differ?

2. Based on Exercise 1, look at how the stories are presented visually, such as with photos or video. Can readers find additional information? What do these elements add to the information or entertainment value?

3. Go to today's *New York Times* website, and click on obituaries. Look at a lead and how the writer has focused on a well-known individual's life. Look at the last graph. How did the end (usually a quote) wrap up the individual's life? If possible, compare *The New York Times'* obituary to an obituary on the same individual in your local or regional newspaper. How did the obituaries differ?

4. Prepare an advance obituary for a national figure, either in politics or the media. Find at least five online sources, for example, the state website for a governor, a campaign website for another politician, or a news station's website that includes employee biographies. Try to find an article by or about the individual so that you can use quotes. Write the obituary with all the information; leave the lead blank where date, time, place, and cause of death would be included.

5. Go to a political site, such as the home page for the Republican National Committee or Democratic National Committee. Check for transcripts from major speeches. Then do a search for news stories to compare how media covered the speeches. How were the leads different? The quotes used? Background? Additional information?

6. Check CSPAN's latest offerings of videotaped speeches. Select one and play the speech. Write a news article of 500 words and then do an online search to compare your version to coverage in media.

References

Sosa, Norma. Lecture on how to write obituaries. Midweek Special. School of Journalism and Mass Communication, University of North Carolina at Chapel Hill. Spring 2001.

Writing for Digital Delivery

Most writers who work for any media today produce content with an eye and ear toward digital delivery. Traditional print and broadcast news sources are pushing more breaking news coverage and other features with video and audio to their online home pages. A city government reporter covering an event might gather audio and video along with notes and tweet updates periodically about what's happening at a city council meeting before the full story is up on the local news page. A social media marketer posts teasers on the company's microblog to attract followers to new products.

Increasingly, all types of companies expect entry-level writers as well as experienced staff to choose the right medium to share messages and to know how to collect and edit information whether it is text, still images, video, audio, or animated and interactive graphics.

More and more, online content is connected. What gets posted in an online article can be shared, emailed, tweeted, liked, or pinned to people with similar interests. Information is delivered to people's fingertips via smartphones and other mobile devices. Apps, short for applications, can be downloaded so people can reach their go-to locations in a few seconds. Audiences can tailor their media diets to what they want to get instantaneously and regularly.

In a multimedia world, writing remains a critical and essential skill. The boom in unedited and unverified content that appears alongside accurate information online has made it even more challenging for people to organize, sift through, and validate vast amounts of information.

Understanding and knowing audiences and how they access information are crucial, particularly when media are competing for audience attention. Information that is relevant, concise, accurate, and complete is just as important for online content as for any other medium. Media consumption habits will continue to change as people rely more and more on mobile phones and other portable devices connected wirelessly for information. At the same time, writers must be aware that a huge part of the population still relies on

155

community newspapers and nondigital sources because some people cannot afford the devices that link them to the digital world or because high-speed Internet or wireless is not available to them.

In this chapter you will learn

- what to consider when writing for online formats,
- why news values and the inverted pyramid are important to online content,
- how online formats, such as microblogging, reach and serve today's audiences, and
- what's coming next for digital delivery.

The World Goes Online

The growth of the Internet as a communication tool ranks as one of the most important revolutions in publishing. Like the revolution set off by Johannes Gutenberg's invention of the printing press in the early 15th century, the growth of the Internet in the final decade of the 20th century made the publication and distribution of the written word much cheaper and more widely available.

The Internet opened the door for digital delivery of many kinds. Digital communication perhaps has had the greatest influence on modern lives, from the way people conduct business, participate in the political process, shop, and learn about distant people and places.

Using the Internet, people all over the globe can communicate via email, instant messaging, blogs, microblogs, and even in real time, transcending the boundaries of time and geography. Its multimedia capabilities allow for video, audio, photos, graphics, and animation to be distributed without the expense of broadcast towers or government licenses and even without the delay of emailing a video file.

Before the Internet, consuming a news medium such as a newspaper, magazine, or television newscast generally was the same for every member of the audience. A subscriber to the local paper received basically the same content at basically the same time of day as every other subscriber. Viewers of a television newscast saw the same program at the same time of day as every other viewer of that newscast.

But with the advent of the Internet and other digital technologies, audiences now have much more control over what messages they read, how they view those messages, and the time and place they read them. Those choices extend to how they communicate with friends through social networking to how they search for products and services. Digital video recorders have made "time-shifting" more prevalent among television audiences who literally move a program from the time a broadcaster sends it to another time that is more convenient for them to watch it.

Media have moved to digital delivery to extend audience reach. For example, National Public Radio's news reports, once available to an audience only at the top of the hour, are available anytime via NPR's podcasts and links through Twitter posts. Followers can access their favorites on the programs' Facebook pages or topics from music to politics on NPR's YouTube site.

The Internet Is Born

The Internet developed within the federal government, primarily the Department of Defense. The explosion of the Internet as a news source in the United States dates only to about 1996 when computer scientist Tim Berners-Lee created a new system for physicists around the world to share data. Berners-Lee called his set of computer programs "the WorldWideWeb project," and he made the code generally available for others to use for free.

In 1993, a group of professors and students at the National Center for Supercomputing Applications at the University of Illinois at Urbana-Champaign developed Mosaic, the first Web browser. The Mosaic computer program made it easy for a person who didn't know computer programming to read text and view images stored on a remote computer that connected to the Internet. Unlike many computer programs, Mosaic was also available for free to most users.

Newspapers made their first foray into online publishing by posting stories to gated online services that hosted websites. Visits to newspaper websites quickly increased as people stormed the Web looking for election returns in November 1996.

In 1996, 12 percent of Americans went online to get information on current events, public issues, and politics. News events such as the Clinton-Lewinsky scandal, the Super Bowl, and the terrorist attacks of September 2001 each led to a higher plateau in the numbers among the online news audience. By 2000, one in three Americans went online for news at least once a week. In 2010, more than two out of five Americans said they went online for news through Internet or mobile digital sources, while close to the same number said they got news from traditional sources. More recent numbers from Forbes.com indicated that more than 70 percent of Americans access the Internet each day.

Today, going online is a routine activity for those in search of information, shopping, entertainment, and social networking. Entrepreneurs such as the late Steve Jobs of Apple, Bill Gates of Microsoft, and Mark Zuckerberg of Facebook have led developments in applications, hardware, and software that have brought down the price and increased ease and access to online products and services.

Considerations for Online Content

Technology allows anyone to become a citizen journalist, blogger, or creator of online content, using text, video, photos, audio, graphics, and interactive software. Any media or other organization can post or update information instantly.

For communicators, the access and depth of online delivery allow almost anyone to watch or read content you generate. Information can be repurposed, retweeted, or forwarded to groups well beyond those you intended to reach. Writers must exercise judgment and editorial skills so that audiences can be confident in the reliability and accuracy of information they find in digital venues. More and more, professional writers need to practice not just news judgment, but also media judgment—the ability to know which storytelling and digital techniques to use for a particular story.

Media entrepreneurs such as Arianna Huffington, who created The Huffington Post, have shown that online sites can expand beyond a single article or video uploaded online. Stories posted online can add in experts via Skype and audience interactivity. And the information is available 24/7, whenever people want to go searching.

Some online writers must grapple with tighter limitations on space as well as the pressure to post quickly. They also produce for an online audience that tends to skim content at a faster pace than do print news audiences. A compelling lead or microblog is essential for audiences to click further or continue with reading. Writers must produce content that keeps audiences and also brings them back.

Writers have three primary advantages when they publish online. They can go beyond text, incorporating still images, audio, video, animation, and links. Online writing can be made more relevant. Online space is virtually unlimited, so writers can explain many more details than in print publications. Online writers must remember, however, that the audience still has limited time, so long-format writing must be compelling from the first paragraph to the last.

Although online writers can employ these benefits, professionals know that not every storytelling technique or digital format is suitable for all writing. For example, a piece about new enrollment figures at the local college might include many numbers, making it appropriate for a long, explanatory text story with graphics but not necessarily video. A human interest story about a local personality, however, might warrant video that reveals his facial features, mannerisms, and diction. For a story on the local housing market, a writer might work with a motion graphics designer to create a database so that readers could look up home sales in their neighborhoods by typing in their zip codes.

Another way online writers make their work more relevant is engaging the audience in online conversation. This dialogue can take the form of a live chat, a blog post, microblogs, social media threads, reader comments, or discussion boards.

Such exchanges with the audience take a more conversational tone that inherits some style from broadcast media, such as call-in radio talk shows. Writers in such interactive roles must be able to think quickly and clearly so that they create accurate and well-edited messages, especially when posting frequently.

Online News and Information

Audiences go online to find out the latest news, do research, get directions, find recipes, and locate other specific information. Some material is created in specific formats, such as entries in Wikipedia. Much writing, however, is produced by professionals who are reporting breaking news or developing longer stories on a particular topic, such as an overview of the impact of bills passed in a legislative session.

For the purposes of this textbook, the focus in this section is on writing that has immediacy and considers news values to attract audiences. Many of the same principles can apply to blogging and other types of online writing.

Applying News Values to Online Writing

Because of the "always-on" nature of online information, particular news updates must be made quickly when new facts are available. When filing breaking news online, writers must write a story with as much information as they can verify, even if it is clear that more is coming. This pattern follows the long tradition of broadcast news, when networks interrupt their regularly scheduled programming with short news briefs in the event of major happenings, such as canceling the New York City Marathon after the destruction to parts of the city by Hurricane Sandy.

News values generally are much the same for online as for any other medium, but the continuous nature of online news can create a new struggle between the value of immediacy and other news values, such as prominence and conflict. Even online writers must stop collecting and organizing information at some point so that breaking news, features, or blog posts can be published.

The advent of on-demand news specifically puts a larger burden on the online news writer to balance currency with proximity, prominence, and impact. Most online news sites (with the notable exceptions of sites with a blog format) do not emphasize immediacy to the detriment of all other news values. And online readers still choose which pieces to read, at what time of day, and in what order.

Online sites are in competition for audiences who use email, RSS feeds, blogs, references from friends, and social networking sites to find information. An uncertainty for online is that writers don't know when a reader is going to come back. Surveys by the Pew Internet and American Life Project indicate that members of the online news audience are slightly more likely to say they read news online for its immediacy than to say they read online news for its depth or breadth.

Audience behavior can affect news judgment in another way. News outlets from Yahoo! to *The Washington Post* display lists of the most read, most emailed, most discussed, or highest-rated news stories. Prominently featured, these stories become self-fulfilling prophecies, driving still more readers to them.

As audiences consume content in real-time, writers and editors are paying attention to which events they should cover further, display prominently, and explain more deeply. Popularity of a story topic is becoming a predictable element of news judgment among professional journalists.

While writers use news values in structuring content, online editors use news values to determine where to place content. Editors of a news site might place one set of stories on the home page in the morning because they think those stories are the most important for readers to see.

By the end of the day, tracking will show which stories received the most audience attention and how deeply into the site readers went. That data, possibly in conflict with what editors thought would be popular, informs where the stories go as newer pieces change the order of home page content.

In a world where more people are reading more online, writers must work much harder to differentiate their articles from all the other similar reports online. With so many choices for audiences, writers increasingly need to seek unique angles, target specific audiences, and dig deeper for uncovered facts.

Getting Readers into Online Content

As with any article, headlines give audiences the first clue about message content, whether on a news release, breaking news, or feature in a company newsletter. The same is true for online writing. With online writing, however, below the headline usually comes a blurb, a few sentences of summary information. The blurb can give details that are not laid out in the lead but that entice readers to go further and look at the lead. Typically, clicking on the headline or the blurb will take the reader to the full article.

The characteristics of a good lead—short, to the point, and attention-getting—are essential when writing for an online audience. Online leads should be brief and full of information because online audiences quickly skim information and want to know the relevance as soon as possible.

As noted in Chapter 5 on leads, writers of online leads have to think about key words that will aid search engines in locating their stories. But overall, online leads should be written primarily for people and not for computerized search engines. Good techniques for search engine optimization, however, can also be good techniques for writing a more clear and concise story.

This example from the *Los Angeles Times* shows how the three parts—headline, blurb, and lead—work:

Queen Elizabeth II is Britain's 'most familiar enigma'

For Britain's Queen Elizabeth II, royalty and celebrity don't overlap, a distinction observers credited with helping to preserve the monarchy's appeal.

The story by Henry Chu had this lead:

> LONDON—Her face is everywhere: on stamps, coins, mugs and book covers. Her likeness has just been reproduced for the 23rd time at Madame Tussauds, London's famous wax museum. More visitors come to gawp at her house than probably any other residence in the world.
>
> Yet after reigning over Britain for longer than most of her subjects have been alive, Queen Elizabeth II is the country's "most familiar enigma," in the words of one TV presenter.

Because blurbs usually appear directly below a headline, both must work well together, avoiding redundant information where possible. In the example, the headline and the blurb complement each other to interest the reader in the full story, the "familiar enigma" phrasing in the headline setting up a twist. The lead continues in that vein, the first graph showing the queen's public face and the second graph setting up the fact that people really know little about her.

Although online stories have practically unlimited space, audiences do not have unlimited attention. The inverted pyramid remains one of the best-suited story formats for online writing. The inverted pyramid has even become a metaphor for the structure of websites themselves. The home page of a site contains the essential information about a broad range of stories, and as visitors delve deeper, they can gain more and more details by clicking to the full story. From there they can choose related stories from the archives, links to primary source documents, video, audio, or other uploaded material.

Consider how the inverted pyramid works for reporting information online about a shooting at a local high school. Reporters know that concerned parents who can't get through the jammed phone lines on campus will likely turn to the local newspaper's or TV station's website for updates. It's possible that no one was injured, but it's also possible that several students were killed. Public safety demands that a writer post even cursory information online as fast as possible.

An early version of the story might be a single paragraph that includes only the *what*—that a shooting has occurred. And it might directly acknowledge which important news elements remain unknown. It might read something like this:

> Shots were fired at Central High School shortly after 11:30 a.m., according to police reports. It's unknown whether anyone was injured in the shooting or exactly where on campus it took place.

While the reporter is still waiting for more information, the story could be fleshed out with background about Central High School or school shootings across the country. A second paragraph may look like this:

> Central High School is no stranger to violence. Last year, two students were sent to the hospital after they were stabbed in a gang-related brawl.

When the reporter learns the police have someone in custody, that important information could be reworked in to a new lead.

> Police are holding a former student in custody in connection with a shooting at Central High School this morning. It's unclear whether the student is a suspect, and it is also unclear whether anyone was hurt. Police reported that shots had been fired on the campus shortly after 11:30 a.m.

The story now has some information about *what, where, when,* and *who* was involved. When the reporter receives news of injuries, the lead will need to be rewritten again, perhaps like this:

> Three students were wounded this morning in a shooting at Central High School. The names of the victims have not been released, but police identified them as two girls and one boy. Police are holding a former student in custody in connection with the shooting that took place shortly after 11:30 a.m.

The key news element shifted from the *where* and the *when* used in the original lead to the *who*—albeit an incomplete version—in the latest variation of the lead.

Each of the new leads replaces the previous one, and older information moves farther down into the story. Most news organizations also print at the top of the page the time the story was updated so readers can gauge the currency of the information. Audiences today expect updates and know that information might eventually change.

News organizations are also requiring reporters to create microblogging sites, such as Twitter. In such situations, writers post breaking news items, and editors can repost with a link to the website for more details. Writers have to learn how to write a "headline" or short lead within the limited character link. Subsequent posts, like the updates on a news story, can provide new information to followers.

Imbedding Links

Links are an important tool of any online writing, but they must be used with care. Done well, they can improve the transparency of research and build audience trust because audiences can examine the original reporting. Done poorly, they can erode confidence in the reporting as much as any misplaced comma or misspelled word.

Incorporating links into a story allows a writer to omit nonessential details that might interest only some readers. Links can be especially helpful to readers who might be skeptical about the information in the article or to readers with immediate or deep interest in the topic.

A writer might add different types of links to an online story on weight loss, such as:

1. Primary source documents, such as actual studies cited in the story.
2. Audio or video of full interviews with a source quoted in the story.

3. Older stories on the same topic.

4. Other sites that contain material related to the story, such as organizations that assist with weight loss.

5. Other sites where a source might make a longer or more nuanced argument in support of a weight-loss plan noted briefly in the story.

Writers who include links in their stories must be aware of two pitfalls. While links to other websites are not explicit endorsements of the information found on those sites, they imply a level of validity from the writer to the reader. Linking to another website that contains false or defamatory information can tarnish the writer's reputation.

Also, broken links that lead nowhere or to the wrong page can also erode trust. If possible, writers should check their links before they are published. If that's not possible, they must verify their links as soon as possible. Such checks are part of the online editing process and are as important as checking for spelling and grammar.

Editors can use two ways to link from a story. "Inline" links are made from words inside the body of the story. "Sidebar" links stand alone, often in a bulleted list, in a separate space adjacent to the story. Inside the story, editors must choose which words to link so the audience understands where they will go when they click on the link.

Here are some guidelines:

1. Link no more than three words in a row. Longer links often are difficult to read on a computer screen.

2. Choose nouns or verbs that describe the destination of the link. For example, if linking to a police report, choose the words "police report" for the linked text.

3. If multiple places in the story reference the destination page, place a link only on the first reference.

4. When placing links adjacent to the story, write three to five descriptive words as the text of the link. Emphasize nouns and verbs, such as "action unfolds at Olympic venues."

5. Use single-word descriptions to tell the reader important information about the medium or style of the destination link. For example, if the link goes to a video of the high school football game, good link text might be "Video: Friday's Game Highlights."

6. Readers have a difficult time choosing from more than three to five links. If your organization has thousands of archival stories on a topic, don't link to all of them from the space adjacent to the story. It is better to place a long collection of links on a separate page or at the end of the story under "related links."

Correcting Online Copy

As noted briefly earlier in this chapter, because messages live online long past the time when the information first appears, it is important to correct quickly, permanently, and transparently any error of fact that might make its way into publication. What happens if a writer has to change a story because a fact is wrong? That is when it is essential to print a correction clearly described elsewhere on the page. Without a description of the correction, a reader who returns to the story might see the changed information and become confused about whether the old information or the new information is accurate.

The *Washington Post* has created a way for readers to post errors at www.washingtonpost.com/corrections. ESPN posts its corrections at http://espn.go.com/espn/corrections, a resource for examples of wording for online corrections.

Corrections need not always be formal. Some opinion columnists and bloggers use a more informal tone to alert readers to their errors. Regardless of the tone, placement, or content of corrections, professional writers aim to make them rare. Errors of style, grammar, or fact compromise the trust a writer has established with the audience.

Blogging

An explosion of websites laid out in the blog format started in 1999 with the widespread adoption of the first Web-based, free publishing system called Blogger. Blogs—short for "Web logs"—grew in popularity first as a tool for amateur diarists to publish text to the Web without the need for any technical knowledge. Other self-publishing tools also made it easier to publish photos, videos, audio, or just about any combination of media online—often for free. Technorati, a company that tracks blogs, keeps an eye on more than 112 million bloggers.

Since then, bloggers have become professionals as diarists, commentators, or even reporters in every niche category imaginable. Blogs appear as stand-alone columns or related to news or features. The format has become widely adopted at traditional news organizations, such as *The Washington Post* and the *New York Times*.

Marketers know that a blog can enhance their company's or organization's reputation and visibility and start a conversation with consumers who can comment on products, services, or special offers. Many bloggers, however, are amateurs who do not consider themselves journalists and do not adhere to a tradition of professional ethics. They develop some expertise and write for niche audiences, so anyone accessing those sites as part of research must be aware of the limitations. Blogs generally have these characteristics:

1. A blog consists of "posts," which can be of varying length. Posts, like news stories or articles, are about a single topic or event. But unlike

articles or news stories, they do not necessarily follow the same inverted pyramid structure.

2. Posts are laid out vertically on a blog's home page in reverse chronological order. The most recent post is at the top of the page and the oldest at the bottom.

3. Professional news blogs are almost always on a single topic. In newsrooms, those topics often are called "beats." Music, schools, parenting, technology, food, politics, a certain sports team, or a specific television show are all common topics for a blog.

From these basic similarities, blogs can take on all sorts of optional forms. They can be filled with straight news or pure commentary and often are a mixture of both. They might contain dozens of participants' views on an event, such as those of hometown supporters who attended the 2012 Summer Olympics. Many allow their followers to comment on each post. Most are written by a single author, but many news blogs have several reporters who post to them. Most bloggers make prolific use of links within their posts to footnote their commentary or to demonstrate transparency by allowing readers to view original source material.

An online search can uncover dozens of tips about creating and maintaining a blog as well as building followers. One major piece of advice: Don't start a blog unless you can add posts on a regular and continuing basis. Followers will not stick to blogs that are updated on a random schedule. Most note that establishing a blog and a following can take up to a year.

Other tips are:

■ Select a topic and stick with it.

■ Keep the tone conversational.

■ Create a tag line or short summary so people know what your blog is about.

■ Don't just post the news or rehash. People go to your blog because they want to hear from you and they are looking for something different. Some bloggers say that just rehashing news releases is a no-no; followers want context or commentary.

■ Monitor your traffic, do surveys, track which blog posts people read most. Ask people to repost a blog to gain attention.

■ Think about posting a photo or an "about you" section so followers can establish a bond with you. If you want followers, you might have to forego some privacy.

■ Keep posts short.

While creating a blog appears to be a fairly cost-free process, remember that it requires a computer or tablet; high-speed Internet or mobile data access; and time to research, write, and post. Some bloggers today create their blogs on specific sites that cater to bloggers, such as Tumblr. Having a blog in one location that is part of a network of other blogs could increase the likelihood of gaining followers. Different services offer software that accommodate specific users' needs.

Going Shorter: Microblogs

A microblog is different from what is considered a traditional blog because its content is smaller. People write short messages and include links to share information in what some people call microposts. The best known of these probably is Twitter, where 140 characters is the maximum length.

Anyone can create a microblog for free and access others for free once they are members of a particular microblogging service. People are followers, meaning that they are friends and can see what people they follow are writing. Some might be followed by people that they themselves don't follow; for example, many people follow Twitter accounts of celebrities, who in turn don't follow each of their thousands of followers.

Through their microblogging accounts, people can share what's going on around them, from picnics to sporting events. They can get breaking news, fashion updates, or celebrity talk. Public relations and marketing firms have microblogs that post information students or other job seekers would find relevant. Some students, for example, might have a Twitter account for personal use and a separate one tagged for professional sites that they follow. Microblogs join the mix of accounts that people use to organize how they get and share information.

Content in a microblog should consider the same ground rules as for any writing: accuracy, relevance, correctness in spelling and grammar, and ethics. When false information is posted on a microblog, it can be corrected, but the people who saw the first post might not see the correction. And the information can go viral, as it did in 2012 when a rumor circulated that S.C. Gov. Nikki Haley was stepping down. In this case, the reporter posted the information on his Twitter account, apparently without confirming the details with the governor's office. Within minutes, the news appeared on national media—only to have to be retracted later.

In addition to keeping an eye on accuracy, microbloggers often have to follow a style for abbreviations and focus on the main points or news elements. Symbols such as # can be used to search for subjects and @ before a username will connect to the owner's feed.

To keep the post as short as possible when including a link, writers can go to http://tinyurl.com/ to convert long Web addresses to a more condensed link that won't use too much space.

People who do any microblogging also have to be aware of privacy settings that can limit what is seen. Some individuals have learned through embarrassing lessons that a post they meant for specific people was accessible to a much wider audience.

Companies, whether media, public relations, marketing, or retail, can use micrologging sites, such as Twitter, in several ways. Jeffrey Mann of Gartner Research notes the most obvious is through a Twitter account that establishes direct contact with consumers. More indirect means would be to establish their reputation as a source of information, such as reposting tweets or citing relevant research.

Mann also suggests using such accounts to monitor what users are saying about your company, a move that could forewarn of pending issues or problems. He cautions about using microblogging for internal communications because of inadvertent security risks. A casual mention could tip a competitor.

Social Media

By the time you read this book, some of the social media names included here might have faded from popularity, and assuredly many new ones will have surfaced. Almost daily, people have more social media sites to try out beyond the more established ones, like LinkedIn for job networking, Facebook and Google+ for building communities, Instagram and Snapchat for photo sharing, and Twitter for microblogging. Others, such as Pinterest, have gained popularity among people who have hobbies or specific interests.

Social media allow people, companies, organizations, and others to share information, whether it's niche material such as recipes or politics; headlines to drive audiences to media content; or personal details, such as family photos or favorite books. Because of the ease in setting up social media accounts, individuals often are complacent in what they post or upload. Some college coaches have banned their athletes from using social media accounts; in interviews recruiters have asked applicants for access to their Facebook accounts. People who use social media must be circumspect about how they are sharing personal information about themselves or others.

Those on social media sites can build followers by creating content that followers will see on their feeds or posts. The can "like" or tag other people's content to draw attention to their own sites, or they can cross-list among multiple sites. For example, a company could post on its YouTube site a video on a community event that it sponsored and also link to YouTube with a post on its Facebook page.

More and more companies are hiring recent college graduates who grew up in a digital world to manage their online presence. They are looking for people who can maintain websites or implement and grow social media strategies within a comprehensive marketing program. The titles might vary from social media marketer or manager to online community manager. Responsibilities could include managing website content, posting to social media sites, staying current with social media trends, overseeing innovation, and measuring the impact of social media as part of marketing efforts.

Such companies are also looking at *social media governance*, a term suggested by three German researchers to outline how much time, resources, and planning a company should devote to social media. While companies have strategies for using social media to reach audiences, most have no basic internal structures to govern the efforts.

The Media's Adoption of Social Media

Social media tools are becoming mainstream through the ways reporters gather information and writers share bits and pieces that wouldn't make a complete story. Managing editors are buying smartphones for reporters so they can tweet about events they are covering in real time. Some reporters have Facebook pages where they post stories that might interest their followers. Quirky stories, for example, might be one reporter's specialty and attract a following, while another might focus on political quips.

Social media tools present a new model for journalists. Traditional journalism has been one-way—that is, a story published on a newspaper page and then distributed. Most social media are interactive. Followers can post comments, redistribute material, and share links. With that interactivity, reporters have to avoid getting too involved in a "conversation" that goes beyond the expectations of good journalism.

Some media companies are beginning to see writers almost as a brand, bringing with them their followers on their social media. Some companies have launched advertising campaigns to promote the writer and his or her specialty areas via Twitter, Facebook, and other sites. Such focus elevates writers to celebrities or even independent contractors who can sell their social media ties along with their writing skills.

Recognizing the benefits but also the potential pitfalls of new media, organizations, such as the Radio Television Digital News Association (RTDNA) and the American Society of News Editors (ASNE), have drafted guidelines. The pressure to post breaking news on Twitter sets up a situation for incomplete information or the rush to publish, as in the Gov. Haley example. Reporters must remember to verify anything they see on a social media site before they repost or use the information in any way.

RTDNA includes its social media and blogging guidelines in its ethics section. It notes:

> Social media and blogs are important parts of journalism. They narrow the distance between journalists and the public.... They can be vital news-gathering and news-delivery tools. As a journalist you should uphold the same professional and ethical standards of fairness, accuracy, truthfulness, transparency and independence when using social media as you do on air and on all digital news platforms.

The ASNE guidelines note that writers should accept that everything they write eventually could find its way online. Writers who work for media and have personal social media accounts have to remember that they still

BOX 8.1	ASNE 10 Best Practices For Social Media

1. Traditional ethics rules still apply online.
2. Assume everything you write online will become public.
3. Use social media to engage with readers, but professionally.
4. Break news on your website, not on Twitter.
5. Beware of perceptions.
6. Independently authenticate anything found on a social networking site.
7. Always identify yourself as a journalist.
8. Social networks are tools not toys.
9. Be transparent, and admit when you're wrong online.
10. Keep internal deliberations confidential.

represent their employers and at some point their posts might become public and embarrass themselves and their companies. Care should be taken with privacy settings, which should be continually checked as the sites themselves change the parameters, possibly making what was once private more accessible.

The ASNE list is particularly useful because the organization's ethics committee surveyed newspaper companies for best practices in regard to social media, then developed 10 themes. Each theme is expanded with specific advice based on experience and excerpts from newspapers' social media policies and can be accessed under "Resources" on the ASNE website at www.asne.org. The advice is applicable to any online writer.

The bottom line: Writers should approach social media services as tools, as ways to share information, embracing the ability to reach audiences in new ways but also recognizing the pitfalls and even legal dangers.

What's Next with Online Content

Emerging digital and networked communication tools are changing the ways people share stories about their lives and the world in which they live. When we wrote the first edition of this textbook in the early 1990s, we used fax machines and FedEx to share edited versions of chapters. Now we work online and via email. In the first edition, we didn't have laptops but a bulky desktop computer. For the fourth edition, we didn't mention blogging, but almost before that book hit the shelves, blogging had infiltrated online writing. You will find no tweets or microblogging in edition five, but you will in edition six.

What's coming next? Who knows. But the point is that technology is changing almost daily how audiences are getting information and how writers have to accommodate their content and style to fit the parameters of portable devices.

We contend that despite the evolving delivery modes, content remains a priority. The relevance of messages will get audience attention, whether they are 2,500-word articles in *The New Yorker* magazine or a 140-character tweet on Twitter.

Good writers will need to find ways to bring information before audience members who increasingly filter out information they consider irrelevant or uninteresting. New information, new ideas, and new voices aboard new technology are needed to provide democracy with constant rejuvenation.

Along with increasing technology, writers must also be aware of an emerging "digital divide" between people who use new communication technologies and people who continue to rely on traditional media. While use of home computers, smartphones, and portable devices has exploded over the last decade, many Americans cannot afford the latest gadgets. When considering audiences, writers need to decide whether they want to reach a broad audience or a smaller, more specialized audience and how to do that.

Also, as technology develops and use expands, writers must proceed with caution so that they don't unwittingly violate audience trust. They must not post information quickly at the expense of accuracy. Standards and expectations of privacy, transparency, and professionalism—and sometimes the laws—continue to change not only in the United States but also in cultures around the world.

Media companies have had to consider their liability when readers post story comments directly to a site. Some postings contain language considered by some to be offensive, vulgar, or profane. While federal law protects online sites from libel in such postings and readers are encouraged to respond, media managers on occasion have opted to shut down and prevent postings, more for ethical than for legal considerations.

This change in the distribution system of news and information is also changing the business models of many media companies that behaved according to a long-established standard of ethics and values. Will writers pay to have their articles displayed on popular locations? Will more and more media companies charge to allow unique news and information available exclusively to their subscribers? Will readers who want high-quality information start paying premium prices for immediate or customized news alerts?

In this evolving media landscape, many of the best opportunities for writers are probably yet to be imagined. Professional communicators of the future will need to remain alert for new ways to reach audiences with the same high standards of accuracy, completeness, transparency, and relevancy that have won audience trust in traditional media. The rapid changes in digital technology seem likely to increase the pace and broaden the scope of these challenges. However, if history is any guide, writers who remain committed to providing precise and concise information to their audiences will surf the waves of change most successfully.

Exercises

1. Compare the news articles on the home page of a national newspaper's site with the news articles on the home page of Digg.com and the home page of a national television news site. Which news values are most commonly reflected in each site's story choices? Why might that be the case?

2. How do you as a media consumer use social networking or microblogs to get news and other information? Where do you get breaking news? Where do you go for additional information?

3. Do a poll of your classmates to find out if they follow blogs, identify the top two, and find out why those are most popular. Examine how each person evaluates the reliability of the blogs he or she follows.

4. You are an online editor for your campus newspaper. You have the following lead from the print edition. Write a headline and a blurb for the home page. Then rewrite the lead so the important keywords would appear in the first 20–25 words in the online story.

   > When Carmen Alvarez planned her Christmas decorating, she knew she wanted to string lights across the front of her two-story house. She bought icicle-type lights on sale, then last Saturday morning she hauled the family's ladder out of the garage, set it against the wall by the front porch and began to climb. As she reached the fifth step, the ladder collapsed. Alvarez fell on the concrete front porch steps, broke her collar-bone and suffered an upper-back injury. Her 12-year-old son heard her scream and called 911.
   >
   > Alvarez's accident is quite common. More than 500,000 ladder-related injuries are reported each year, and about 500 people die. Organizations, such as the American Academy of Orthopaedic Surgeons, publish information about how to inspect ladders and do home chores without injury. They sponsor a program called "Climb It Safe."

5. Based on the information in Exercise 4, write a 140-character tweet for a microblog on home safety. Write a second message for followers of a microblog on Christmas decorating ideas.

References

ASNE 10 Best Practices for Social Media. http://asne.org/content.asp?pl=19&sl=77&contentid=77. Accessed July 2, 2012.

Brabham, Daren. "Crowd Control: A Research Agenda for the Management of Online Communities." Conference paper presented at the International Open and User Innovation Workshop, July 30 to Aug. 1, 2012, Boston, Mass.

Catone, Josh. "Top 5 Business Blogging Mistakes and How to Avoid Them." http://mashable.com/2009/09/21/business-blogging-mistakes/. Accessed September 21, 2009.

"Ethics: Social Media and Blogging Guidelines." RTDNA, Radio Television Digital News Association. http://www.rtdna.org/pages/media_items/social-media-and-blogging-guidelines1915.php?id=1915. Accessed July 2, 2012.

Fink, Stephan, Zerfass, Ansgar, and Linke, Anne. "Social Media Governance: Regulatory Frameworks As Drivers of Success in Online Communications." Paper presented at 14th International Public Relations Research Conference, Coral Gables, Fla., March 2011, accessible at http://www.researchgate.net/publication/215689412_Social_Media_Governance_Regulatory_frameworks_as_drivers_of_success_in_online_communications

Gates, Bill. Interview with Charlie Rose, aired July 5, 2012, *CBS Morning News*.

Johnson, Kelly. Author interview on Social Media Practices of Newspapers Today, May 17, 2012, Chapel Hill, N.C.

Mann, Jeffrey. "Four Ways in Which Enterprises are Using Twitter," Gartner Research. http://www.gartner.com/newsroom/id/920813. Accessed March 12, 2009.

Miller, Lindsey. "A Twitter primer—in way more than 140 characters." http://www.ragan.com. Accessed April 9, 2009.

Research and Observation

Writing begins with an idea. While watching the musical "Wicked," a writer is fascinated with the work required to set the scenes and propel the witch skyward. He wants to write about theatrical staging. But he needs more than just his observations to write a factual, accurate, complete, and entertaining article. He must learn more.

Gathering information is like detective work. As a sleuth, you start with a clue. Step by step you add pieces until you have enough information to reconstruct events and solve the case. As a writer, you add to your knowledge until you can create an accurate and complete summary of the topic.

Writers, like detectives, gather information from research, interviews, and observations. Also, like detectives, writers gather a broad array of information to ensure their searches are objective. Such work is called reporting. Research—or reporting—allows writers to study what others have already found out. That information might be in books, magazines, letters, statistical abstracts, encyclopedias, databases, blogs, or any number of other print or electronic sources. Writers can access thousands of documents using online search engines or commercial databases. More and more information is added online every day. But it's important to remember that much of the best information in databases can't be found on the Web. To acquire background, writers often team with librarians who have information-tracking skills and access to resources.

Armed with facts retrieved in research, writers can continue reporting by interviewing expert and relevant sources who add personal comment on the topic. The personal reflections of sources give context and interest to facts. Interviews can confirm or verify online or library research. Interviewing, quotes, and attribution are discussed in Chapter 10.

Writers also take time to note their observations as part of their reporting. Student writers are sometimes reluctant to include their impressions for fear they will appear too subjective. They must overcome that fear. In the theatrical story about "Wicked," the writer would be remiss not to describe his surprise as the witch, armed with her broom, defied gravity and soared upward. Audiences want to know.

In this chapter, you will learn

- how to develop search strategies that will mine traditional and online resources,
- what specific sources to consider,
- the plusses and minuses in online and other research, and
- how observation is a part of gathering information.

Getting Started

Writers start out as generalists; they know a little about a lot of subjects. Some develop specialties or subject areas they prefer. Whether they are newspaper or electronic media reporters, public relations practitioners, advertising copywriters, or social media marketers, writers need to do research as the first step in preparing copy. A medical writer might know medical terminology, but if she wants to write about autism she must become knowledgeable about the topic. A government reporter must learn about the newly elected members of Congress before he goes to the opening session. A social media marketer might know the latest methods to reach technology-savvy audiences, but she also needs to know keywords that will entice them to click onto a site.

Writers need to find information that is accurate, relevant, and up to date. Time is their greatest enemy. Most writers have deadlines and limited time to devote to research. They need to find information quickly and efficiently.

Librarians can save you time by developing search strategies and expanding source lists. Librarians are experienced at translating between the writer's research needs and the myriad sources that can answer a question. Stephanie Willen Brown, librarian at the School of Journalism and Mass Communication at the University of North Carolina at Chapel Hill, recommends that anyone who spends more than 30 minutes unsuccessfully looking for a piece of information should contact a librarian. Her motto is that "librarians help researchers save time and find more stuff."

Most colleges and universities have librarians trained to help journalism and mass communication students in their academic research, and media companies also have librarians to help with research. In addition, public librarians are available to help all members of a community, including reporters and advertising professionals. Take advantage of library resources to save time and improve the accuracy of your research.

Brown also recommends that writers develop a set of reporting bookmarks filled with resources appropriate for their area of expertise or topic. As a start, USA.gov provides a search engine for U.S. government websites and offers information and statistics from the U.S. and state governments.

The Statistical Abstract of the United States compiles data summaries of social, political, and economic statistics about residents of the United States and is updated annually.

Newspaper search engines such as America's News, Newspaper Source Plus, or LexisNexis, available at libraries, will help locate free-to-you articles published in national, state, and local newspapers. The library will also have access to popular, trade, and scholarly journal articles through search engines such as Academic Search Complete, Infotrac OneFile, or ProQuest Research Library.

A good print dictionary, such as *Merriam-Webster's Collegiate Dictionary* or *The American Heritage Dictionary of the English Language*, is still an essential resource for all writers to keep close at hand.

Developing a Strategy

To be successful in research, you need a strategy to find information. Once you have defined your topic, you must make a list of questions, identify obvious sources, conduct searches for additional sources, review those sources for additional leads, refine your questions, and then interview.

Let's say you are a medical reporter and want to write a story on childhood immunizations. You first must make a list of the information you need to know, such as the following questions:

Initial Question List for Story on Childhood Immunizations

Who has to be immunized?
What are the state laws?
What shots do children have to have?
At what ages do children get which shots?
Are there any reactions to the shots?
How much do the shots cost at a doctor's office?
Can children get shots at public health clinics? How much do they cost?
Where are the clinics here? What are the hours for immunizations?
How many local children register for school and aren't immunized?
Is this a problem locally?
Have any other diseases surfaced locally?
Why are children not immunized?

Additional Questions after Research

What are the risks to children who aren't immunized?
Do children ever die from immunizations?
What are the reactions parents can expect after a child gets a shot?
How many children in the state aren't immunized properly when they start school?
How many immunizations are given each year in the state? In our county?

What childhood diseases are appearing again?
How are immunizations covered under current health care law?
Do we consider some diseases eradicated?
Fifty years ago, children suffered from mumps, measles, and even polio.
Now children can be protected against even chicken pox. Are we too
complacent about a resurgence of diseases?
Are there any diseases left that children need to be protected from?
If a certain number of children are immunized, does that protect other
children, as in the herd effect?
What factors prevent parents from having children immunized
at the proper time?
What immunizations do college students need?

The obvious sources for answers to these questions would be newspaper and journal articles, search engines, information at online health sites, pediatricians, and local health department and school officials. You would also interview experts and agency officials.

Eventually, your source list grows to include state health officials, state statutes that stipulate which immunizations children must have to enter school, officials at the Centers for Disease Control, legislators who allocate funds for immunizations, parents, and even children. You refine your list of questions for each source and prepare to interview your sources.

Your search strategy is similar if you are writing a story for your alumni magazine on a graduate whose first novel has been published. She is an assistant professor at a college in another state. Before the interview, you need to find information on the author. Most students and writers today go to the Internet first and use a search engine to find information. Such a search might reveal biographical information on her publisher's website, reviews of her work, or articles on her own website.

If you can find no accessible biographical history, you will have to rely on a strategy that includes interviewing former professors, roommates, colleagues, friends, and family members. You might have to call the English department where she teaches and have someone fax or email her *curriculum vitae*. You might have to consult newspaper indexes in public libraries in her home state to find specific articles about her. If one source indicates an organization to which she belongs, you might need to look for references within that organization. Articles about the organization could include material about your up-and-coming author. Newspaper search engines such as America's News might offer articles about her from her local newspaper.

Basic References

As writers search for information, they should always remember basic sources such as telephone books, city directories, and lists of people by occupation, political affiliation, or other activities. Research could include a trip to a special collections library to pore through historical documents. Many traditional sources have become available online.

Today's researchers and writers use hundreds of sources and always must be sure sources are credible and updated. Listed here are some types of publications that writers traditionally have relied on for information. Remember: Most publications have websites. Many might have a paywall or a point where you must have a subscription to access content; your library can identify free-to-you access to archived publications.

Wikipedia can serve as a basic reference, if it is used carefully. Wikipedia is an online encyclopedia that can be edited and updated by anyone, and some sections are frequently changed. Brown, the UNC librarian, suggests using Wikipedia as a first stop in a research quest because of the breadth of topics from biographies to data. The references at the end of Wikipedia articles can lead to sources and confirmation of information posted on a Wikipedia site. Any facts gleaned through Wikipedia should be checked through at least one additional source.

As another way to start a search, Brown recommends the following Google search that links to credible sites. If you are looking for information about hybrid cars, for example, type **"hybrid cars" site:edu library** into Google's search box. This tactic will yield websites created by academic librarians on the topic of hybrid cars; these websites will have links to authoritative sources of further information.

Biographical Sources.   Biographical references contain information about well-known people. Some are specific, such as *Who's Who in American Politics*. The information will include date of birth, parents' names, education, career, awards and achievements, and family data. Among other biographical sources are *Marquis Who's Who®*, *Webster's Biographical Dictionary*, *Current Biography*, *Who's Who among African Americans*, and *Who's Who among Hispanic Americans*. Many of these sources are also online. The online resources Biography Index and the Biography Reference Center have credible biographical information on a variety of famous and well-known people. Because URLs can change, writers should search for updated links to the particular resource needed.

Statistical Information.   *Statistical Abstract of the United States* is one of the most widely used reference books and is online. It provides information from the number of police officers in Albuquerque, New Mexico, to the number of houses with indoor plumbing in Lincoln, Nebraska. Data are based on information collected by the federal government and other sources. *The Decennial Census of Population of the United States* is published every 10 years and updated annually through the American Community Survey. The easiest way to search this treasure trove of data about U.S. citizens is through American Factfinder, at http://factfinder2.census.gov/. Most states compile statistical data, particularly those dealing with vital statistics—births, deaths, marriages, and divorces—and make the data available online. Writers can find information on states, counties, cities, and even sections within cities. This feature is especially helpful if they are looking for the local angle on a story. The *CIA World Factbook* provides data about all countries in the world (free; https://www.cia.gov/library/publications/the-world-factbook/). Standard Rate and Data Service (SRDS) offers for free basic demographic information for 210 Designated Market Areas (DMAs), such as household income, topic industries, and sales data (next.srds.com/resources/maps-profiles). College and university libraries may provide access to the OECD iLibrary or the WorldBank for additional international data.

Political and Government Information. The *U.S. Government Manual* contains information on departments and agencies in the executive branch. *Congressional Quarterly* publishes a weekly report that catalogues the voting records of Congress and major political speeches. States annually publish manuals that contain information about branches of government and legislatures, summaries of the state history, the state constitution, and biographies of major state officials. The Library of Congress provides a free, online directory of state government information at http://www.loc.gov/rr/news/stategov/stategov.html. Information on foreign governments and leaders and world events can be found in reference books, such as *The Statesman's Yearbook*, the *CIA World Factbook*, and other similar publications.

Geographic Data.   Writers might need to check on the locations of cities, towns, and countries. They can refer to local maps or the *Times Atlas of the World* and *Rand McNally Commercial Atlas and Marketing Guide*. Online sites, such as Google Maps, will guide writers to locations and even provide maps and directions to get there. Writers can download map apps to have information at their fingertips. Or they can find up-to-date maps of continents and regions for free at university sites such as the University of Texas' Perry-Castañeda Library Map Collection (http://www.lib.utexas.edu/maps/).

Business Information.   Writers might need data on a company or an industry, and students might need information on a potential employer. Today's competitive companies usually have extensive and interactive websites. Research on companies can also be found in annual reports on file in many libraries.

Information on thousands of companies can be found at the Securities Exchange Commission EDGAR database of public company filings and forms at http://www.sec.gov/edgar.shtml. Incorporation records must list officers, addresses, and company descriptions, and these documents are filed with states' secretary of state offices. Many businesses fall under the purview of state regulatory agencies, such as the state insurance commissioner. Information on companies can also be found in reference sources, such as *Standard & Poor's NetAdvantage* or *Hoover's*, which are available at many libraries. Also, for company information that can lead reporters to sources, check out the Reynolds Center for Business Journalism at Arizona State

University at www.businessjournalism.org. Both Yahoo! and Google offer additional financial information; see finance.yahoo.com and finance.google.com. ReferenceUSA, available at many libraries, offers basic information on 14 million U.S. businesses, including contact information, location, and sales figures.

Professional Sources. In any search for information sources, writers should consider professional organizations such as societies, guilds, and associations. These sources often have links or references to other depositories of information, can provide updates on media issues, contact names, and historical background and serve as a means to verify facts. Before writing about trends in real estate, reporters will want to look at the National Association of Realtors site at www.realtor.org and at related sites for local and regional Realtors. Similar sites are available on thousands of organizations that serve particular interests such as medicine, law, construction, government workers, architects, and others. Your library might have print or online access to the *Gale Encyclopedia of Associations*, which lists more than 23,000 organizations in business, public administration, the military, education, athletics, and more.

For background on professional issues in media, some sites worth checking are the Poynter Institute at www.poynter.org and its webinars and self-directed training; the American Society of News Editors at www.asne.org; Nieman Reports at http://www.nieman.harvard.edu/NiemanFoundation.aspx; Public Relations Society of America at www.prsa.org; American Advertising Federation at www.aaf.org; Radio Television Digital News Association at www.rtnda.org; Society for News design at www.snd.org; National Press Photographers Association at www.nppa.org; Investigative Reporters and Editors at www.ire.org; and Society of Professional Journalists at www.spj.org. Journalism organizations and issues also are a focus of Unity: Journalists of Color at www.unityjournalists.org.

Health Information. The U.S. government has created two free, credible sites for finding health information. MedlinePlus offers consumer health information, including extensive information about drugs, an illustrated medical encyclopedia, interactive patient tutorials, and latest health news (medlineplus.gov). PubMed is a search engine for scholarly journal articles about all aspects of health and medicine. Articles might not be free, but local libraries usually can assist in obtaining articles. Many states offer portals to health information for consumers, which are also useful for journalists and other writers. For instance, NC Health Info is a guide to websites of quality health and medical information and local health services throughout North Carolina (http://www.nchealthinfo.org/).

Pitfalls in Research

The hunt for information can be complex. Not all information comes in a compact, convenient form. At the start of a search, students may discover people who share the same names as celebrities, such as basketball star Michael

Jordan, television personality David Letterman, or even McDonald's mascot Ronald McDonald. Researchers must check to be sure that the person named on records or documents is in fact the same person they seek.

Information might be dated or incomplete. For example, early biographies of actor Brad Pitt would fail to include the correct number and names of his children. Students and other researchers must remember that not every reference includes every individual, and those that do might not have all the facts. Researchers must look at many sources, both print and online, to find complete information. Searching for information is rarely one-stop shopping. Using many sources helps uncover discrepancies and inconsistencies about information and ensures that information is as accurate as possible.

Writers should look continually for additional and alternative sources. The research game is a detective hunt. Names or sources mentioned in an article or in references can lead to nuggets of information elsewhere. The only constraints will be time and deadline pressure.

Government Sources

Local, state, and federal governments produce millions of pages of documents every year, ranging from official findings, such as federal Food and Drug Administration studies, to county tax records and the disposition of local traffic cases. Most government documents are open and accessible to the public. Many are free online, while some are available only by mail or at the city hall, the county courthouse, a regional federal repository, or the Library of Congress. They provide a wealth of information for writers and curious citizens. USA.gov, the U.S. government's official web portal, searches websites of various federal agencies, such as the Centers for Disease Control, military.gov, the Transportation Security Administration, and more.

Government officials and others have taken advantage of the information age to put reams of material online. Agencies maintain their own websites that provide history, facts about elected officials, agendas and minutes of meetings, and other relevant data. For information on legislation, try THOMAS, a congressional online system from the Library of Congress; *Congressional Record*; congressional legislation digests; and directories of congressional members' email addresses. Even the White House has its own website featuring news releases of the day, speech transcripts, and access to federal agencies at www.whitehouse.gov. A government documents librarian at a college or university can help navigate this data.

Public Records

Routine government documents are considered public. The documents have been created by the government, which is supported by taxpayers' money. Researchers, writers, and anyone who wants the documents can request to see them or to have copies made. All states have laws that pertain to what is and what is not a public record. The general rule most journalists follow is that any document is considered a public record unless the agency or individual who has the document can cite the section of state or federal law that prevents its disclosure. If the agency cannot, it must relinquish the information.

Media writers should know the open records laws for their particular state. State press associations can provide the law and its exceptions. Publications such as *The News Media and the Law*, published by the Reporters Committee for Freedom of the Press, can be consulted at your library. The Electronic Frontier Foundation is a valuable, free resource at www.eff.org.

Agencies can charge a reasonable fee for photocopying documents. Most states have regulations pertaining to computer storage of public documents and reasonable charges for making copies or providing access to electronic information. To find which agencies offer public records online, search for "public records" or "open records" at USA.gov.

Freedom of Information Act

In 1966, the U.S. Congress passed the federal Freedom of Information Act (FOIA). The act became law in 1967 and has been amended five times. The law is much like state laws regarding public records. Anyone is allowed to make a written request for information from any federal agency, but not all information is available. The act provides broad exemptions, such as information relating to national defense or foreign policy, internal personnel rules and practices of an agency, personnel and medical files that would constitute an invasion of privacy, information compiled for law-enforcement purposes, and geophysical information such as that related to oil well locations. Find more information about the Freedom of Information Act at foia.gov.

In 1996, the Electronic Freedom of Information Act Amendments required federal agencies to release electronic files of certain types of records created after November 1, 1996. Because of the time needed to respond to requests for electronic data, the amendments extended the agencies' required response time from 10 to 20 days. In 2002, amendments to the FOIA affected requests from foreign governments or any requester acting on behalf of a foreign government to any agency considered part of the government's intelligence community. Changes under the Open Government Act of 2007 further clarified government agencies' duties in regard to FOIA requests.

The media have worked continually to reduce the number of exemptions to FOIA. Michael Gartner, former president of the American Society of News Editors, once lamented in a speech on national Freedom of Information Day that the name "Freedom of Information" implies that the government is holding information hostage. He objected to many of the restrictions, particularly those that prevent publication of what the United States broadcasts to developing countries over the Voice of America. Homeland security concerns have added to difficulties in accessing information in some settings. To help with access, George Washington University houses the National Security

Archive, a repository of government documents and declassified material at www.nsarchive.org. Its website notes that it "is also a leading advocate and user of the Freedom of Information Act."

FOIA sets out the procedure for requesting information, the time required for an agency to respond, appeals procedures, and fees. Individuals must pay the cost of photocopying the information but can request a waiver of that cost if the release of the information is in the public interest. Writers or individuals seeking information under the act might be frustrated—delays can occur even when procedures are followed. The request must be specific and must be sent to the proper agency. When the information is uncovered, a reporter may receive a desired document, but with sections or entire pages inked out or redacted to protect exempted information. The reporter pays the cost of photocopying all pages—even the blackened ones.

FOIA searches can be time consuming and costly, but many journalists and researchers have used them to find information for fact-filled articles. The numbers of requests continue to rise. According to the national FOIA site, almost 650,000 requests were made to federal government agencies in 2011. Not all requests can be filled. In 2011, about 7 percent were denied, and only 53 percent received complete information. In other cases, information that fell under at least one exception was redacted.

The organization Investigative Reporters and Editors presents awards each year to media that produce stories using public record searches and requests. Background on the award and award-winning stories are available under the "Awards" section of IRE at www.ire.org.

Online Research

Technology has changed the way writers collect, transmit, and share information. Distance from sources has become irrelevant. A public relations practitioner in Detroit can search online for background information on the success of drugs to treat acid reflux disease and email it to a company official in Switzerland. Photographs and other color visuals can be emailed anywhere. Using a smartphone, a reporter can tweet about the unfolding events in a court case and drive followers to the online site to find more information.

A major change in the last two decades is how information is stored. People who began writing careers in the mid-1980s and earlier have seen phenomenal changes in the ways they seek information. In the old days before 1985, most searches for information centered on treks to libraries, such as those at newspapers, universities, or wherever resource books were housed. People had to handle paper to get information.

Computers have allowed anyone who produces information to store it online, usually in searchable form, so that others can access it. When people go online, they search for information; download data, photos, or text to computers; send email, blog, or IM; post a tweet; or chat. Writers can find information about an event they are covering in a matter of seconds while sitting at that event. The amount of information available online grows daily in diversity and ease of access.

The ease of using the Internet and the breadth of information found there can lull all writers into a false sense of security in regard to accuracy. As much as students and professional writers have come to depend on online sources, they must still have some skepticism about what they find. All websites are not of equal quality. With the proliferation of information has come discussion of issues on privacy, legal uses, copyright, and ethics (discussed in Chapter 12). Writers who use popular and emerging technology must become knowledgeable about securing information online and using it for publication.

Pitfalls of Online Research

Convenience is a major advantage of online research, but some important concerns persist. Online, identities might be cloaked, expertise exaggerated, and content tweaked in such a way that critical errors go undetected. Because Internet sites and social media tools have made it easy for anyone to publish, writers must realize that not everything they read online is true, just as not everything they hear on the street is true. Writers must take specific measures to establish the accuracy and credibility of sources and sites. In *Web Search Savvy: Strategies and Shortcuts for Online Research*, author Barbara Friedman suggests Web-based content be evaluated using the following five criteria:

1. **Accuracy.** Impossible facts are a giveaway that a website is bogus, although some errors may simply be clerical. Yet if a site is riddled with spelling or grammar errors, it's a safe bet the author has been careless with overall content, and the researcher should be wary of using the material. The quickest way to spot inaccurate information is to check Web-based content against traditional or nondigital sources.

2. **Authority.** What individual or organization claims responsibility for the site's content, and does it have the proper credentials to speak authoritatively on this particular subject? Use a site's contact information or a domain lookup, such as WHOIS or InterNic, to verify who's behind a site.

3. **Currency.** Websites may linger online long after their authors have stopped maintaining the content. Check the site for dates that indicate when the content was posted and last revised.

4. **Audience.** Determining the intended audience for a website will help you evaluate the usefulness of the information. A site about political campaigns designed for an audience of elected officials may be too complicated if you are writing for elementary school students.

5. **Agenda.** In the online world, many writers express strong opinions or are more subtle in their point of view. Bloggers, for example,

publish views on a range of topics using personalized language that would be discouraged in traditional journalism. That bias is not intended to make you doubt a site, but rather understand its purpose. Knowing whether a website's author is motivated by a personal or professional agenda helps you find a context for the information.

Online research might be the first and most convenient choice for writers, but it is just one step in the research process. Taking the time to evaluate the integrity of Web-based content will go a long way in establishing your credibility as a researcher and writer. Writers who follow individuals or companies on microblogging sites such as Twitter should also check the credibility of the information, which is sometimes posted quickly and before facts are completely checked. Some individuals have had to retract "news" that appeared on their sites.

Additional Online Search Strategies

When searching online, writers should remember that most search engines have advanced search functions. Google, for example, offers a step-by-step guide on how to look more precisely for information on a topic by typing in appropriate search requirements.

Writers should also be aware of the growing number of state libraries that offer a state's residents free or low-cost access to library catalogues, reference materials, and commercial search engines such as LexisNexis, Hoover's, and Academic Search Complete. For example, NC LIVE, North Carolina's statewide online library service, offers North Carolina residents free access to articles from more than 60 search engines; 7,000 newspapers, journals, and magazines in areas as diverse as business management, education, history, literature, nursing, and science; and free assistance with research via chat. Similarly, iCONN provides access to Connecticut newspapers, as well as scholarly articles, online encyclopedias, and eBook, free for all Connecticut residents (iconn.org). Most public university libraries permit members of the public to search their online resources for free while on campus; large public libraries have many of the resources mentioned in this chapter and are also open to anyone.

Any savvy searcher should be familiar with advanced search engine options. Randolph Hock's *The Extreme Searcher's Internet Handbook* helpfully explains search features of Google and Yahoo! These include tips such as using site:gov to limit results to a U.S. government website or filetype:pdf to require results be available in PDF format.

What You Can't Find Online

Writers today must remember that online information is a recent phenomenon. Most history is buried in letters, memos, newspapers, magazines, and other written material not catalogued in online databases. When writer Nadine

Cohodas began researching her book, *Spinning Blues into Gold: The Chess Brothers and the Legendary Chess Records*, she went hunting. Her research included visits to the Chicago neighborhoods where brothers Phil and Leonard Chess had offices and where the great blues singers performed.

Cohodas produced a book that brought information to readers they would not have gotten on their own. Finding the details required hours and hours of reading trade journals, such as *Billboard* and *Cash Box*, to understand the evolution of the record company; poring over Chicago newspapers; and scouring public records, such as old liquor licenses, to trace the brothers' business beginnings, city phone books and directories to confirm relevant addresses, and the Federal Communications Commission archive for details about their radio stations. "You have to love the hunt," she said.

Every now and then, Cohodas had "eureka" moments when she found something that provided the telling detail for a piece of the story. For example, she needed information about the history of the Macomba Lounge, owned by the Chess brothers. She explains how she found it:

> *To find out what the Macomba Lounge had been, I photocopied about 30 pages of the Chicago Yellow Pages in the tavern listings, then read them one by one to find the same address. Lo and behold, the Congress Buffet showed up at 3905 S. Cottage. I used that name to request the liquor license for that venue so I could trace the history further.*
>
> *Meanwhile, I found the only ad anyone knows of for the Macomba Lounge by going through the now defunct* Chicago Bee *week by week in the first or second year Leonard and Phil were in the club and that's when I saw the ad—a sweet moment.*

The result of nearly three years' work was a fascinating account of two Polish immigrants who built a company promoting black singers, such as Muddy Waters, Chuck Berry, Bo Diddley, and Etta James. Writers today must follow the research trail to get the nuggets of information essential for their stories.

Observation

Observation—an old method of research—still is a key tool in gathering information. At the same time a writer is interviewing someone, notes should describe the source's mannerisms, age, and attire. At a speech, the writer should record how the crowd reacts to comments. Such details are part of the observation process.

Many students and inexperienced writers, however, are reluctant to include too many details. New writers might not have trained themselves to be good observers. In an online, technology-driven world, they become too easily distracted and lose focus. Or they fear that audiences will doubt their descriptions. They believe using description borders on being subjective when, in fact, leaving out description might distort an event. For example, a story might reveal a speaker's eloquence and pointed remarks on U.S. trade with China, but the reporter might not mention that only 22 people were seated in an auditorium that holds 550 people. Although the speaker might have been eloquent, the speech's title failed to attract a sizable audience.

Seeing Isn't Enough

Many people notice their surroundings or the events happening around them in one dimension. They see. Rarely do people consciously smell, taste, hear, or touch their environment. Even using only sight, most people miss much of what goes on. So do writers. They have not trained themselves to observe events that happen simultaneously. At the state fair, a reporter might notice the lines in front of concessions but not see the child wailing for more cotton candy, the youth loaded with three bright green teddy bears, the overflowing garbage at a nearby trash can, and the cigarette hanging from the hawker's lips. The unobservant writer does not smell the odor of fried dough, taste the grease in the air near the Ferris wheel, hear the ping-ping from the shooting gallery, or feel the slap of heat from the barbecue cookers.

Reporters who go out with a video recorder also might be one-dimensional, turning the camera toward the most visible action, but failing to capture more subtle, but telling reaction along the sidelines.

To be skillful observers, writers must hone all their senses. To be complete and successful writers without supporting audio or video, they must describe scenes to absent audiences. Even when viewers see events on television, they still need the reporter's or news anchor's observations. When television covers the annual Thanksgiving Day parade in New York City, for example, reporters must identify floats and provide background on performers. Viewers need the information to understand what they are seeing.

General Observation

Many people exist on autopilot. They drive the same route to work, live in the same house or apartment for years, and work in the same office. They become less and less observant. What about you?

Any person or writer can sharpen observation skills. Try this experiment: Take a piece of paper. Describe what your roommate or friend wore to school or work today. Note colors and types of fabric, if possible. What did you eat for breakfast? Can you remember the smell as well as the taste? What about the color or feel? What sounds do you hear in this room? Can you name more than three?

Keep a notebook in your car, backpack, or pocket. Start recording what you see and hear in multidimensional ways. Use your cell phone to capture the visual and even audio. Although most people can note different sounds, it is harder to catch and record events happening simultaneously. The oft-told adage is that two people on a street corner would give two different accounts of an accident both witnessed. Think of ways to compare what you see with events or items that are common knowledge.

Remember the story on the burlesque queen? Writer Kathleen Hennessey uses simple language to describe Tempest Storm's physical attributes from the color of her hair to her fingernail polish. She notes the dancer's fingers "tremble with frustration. They are aged, knotted by arthritis and speckled with purple spots under paper-thin skin." Hennessey describes Storm's apartment, including her exercise bike and the photos that catalogue her relationships. Readers get a sense of Storm's physical surroundings as well as her philosophy of life.

How Observation Changes the Action. The act of reporting, of being an observer, might have the unintended effect of changing the behavior of an individual you are observing. Think about a friend who would rush to pick up living room clutter when you pull out your cell phone and take a picture. Your presence can change the way events unfold.

The same tendency holds true when reporters attend a meeting or a rally or when they participate in an online discussion. Their presence affects how people behave. The town council members sit up straighter and look busy when the public access television channel is airing the meeting. Rally organizers look efficient and engaged when photographers approach. Store managers beam smiles of success on the first day of business.

The trick to accurate observing is to observe over time. Most people can maintain a facade for some time, but they cannot keep it up forever—even when they know a reporter is in the room. You might have to observe for more than a few minutes, taking notes or photographs unobtrusively. Two hours into a meeting, the mayor might forget the unobtrusive camera and rail against the accusations of an unhappy citizen.

With advanced technology, people can be observed and recorded when they don't know it. Those images can appear on video or photo-sharing websites, social networking sites, or other Internet venues—much to a person's surprise. As a reporter, you must be careful not to invade an individual's privacy, discussed in Chapter 12, as you record your observations. When people are involved in events considered public, such as a rally or a plane crash, they do lose their right to privacy. But if they are partying in the privacy of their apartment, they have an expectation of privacy, an expectation that they will not become visuals for a story taken surreptitiously with a cell phone.

Participant Observation

Social scientists have long used observation as a means of getting information about groups. They join a group as participants to observe individual behavior within a group and the individuals' interactions. In the popular TV show "Undercover Boss," a company CEO or president assumes an identity to work alongside his employees. A camera records the action, but audiences might wonder just how much the apparently unsuspecting employees really know and how that could influence their interaction with the disguised boss.

Journalists also have adopted the practice, gaining admission and recording the interactions of the group. Such intrusion by journalists affects the way people interact. Over time, however, reporters become accepted, and other members might forget their role.

Because their presence does affect how members relate, some journalists have opted to become members of groups and not to identify themselves as reporters. In the 1890s, reporter Nellie Bly pretended to be a mental patient to get a true picture of how the insane were treated at New York's Blackwell's Island asylum for the mentally ill. Some writers have joined cults, ridden with motorcycle gangs, or gotten jobs in nursing homes to observe from the inside. One reporter in her mid-20s enrolled in a Philadelphia high school to observe it firsthand—and was invited to the senior prom. Before resorting to undercover work, reporters and their editors must determine that a change of identity is the only way to get the story.

In either case, problems can arise when it is time to produce the video or story. Writers might feel a kinship to the group and have difficulty setting themselves apart. Journalists who become group members put their impartiality at risk in writing a story. Writers might become too emotional or too attached to sources and not be able to distance themselves. They also run the risk of not knowing completely whether their presence altered the group in any way, as in "Undercover Boss." Writers might also get complaints from group members who feel betrayed when the article appears. Writers should double-check their reactions and observations by interviewing a balanced mix of sources who are familiar with the subject.

Nonverbal Communication

Although writers get the bulk of their information from sources and from interviewing, they can add details from nonverbal communication. Such cues come from the way people move or act when they say something. A politician might raise her eyebrows at a constituent's question. A child might shift his hands behind his back when leaving the kitchen. A teacher might frown while correcting student essays. Each action implies a thought or behavior to the observer. The politician might be surprised. The child might be guilty of swiping a cookie. The teacher might be unhappy about a good student's low grade.

When recording nonverbal cues either in note taking or with a camera, writers must be careful. They must think beyond the obvious because the same cue could carry different meanings for different observers. Furrowed eyebrows might indicate puzzlement or anger. Waving hands can mean agitation or enthusiasm. A smile might be sincere or forced. Generally, one action alone is not sufficient to indicate how an individual is feeling. The gestures must be catalogued in addition to words and other body movements. A reporter might have to go so far as to ask an individual what a particular posture meant. For example, pacing during an interview may not be a result of nervousness; the interviewee may suffer from restless legs syndrome, but no reporter could tell that simply by observing.

In addition, nonverbal actions have different meanings across cultures. In some cultures or ethnic groups, individuals do not make eye contact while speaking. An ignorant or inexperienced reporter might show cultural bias by being suspicious of such behavior. When U.S. business leaders engage in negotiations with Japanese officials, they have to learn etiquette and protocol. For example, the Japanese consider it offensive to write on a business card, while in the United States, executives and others make notations or add home telephone numbers to business cards. The good reporter learns about cultural differences or asks questions to clarify behavior. Such sensitivity and awareness are essential to accurate reporting.

Dangers in Observation

John Salvi was charged with murdering two people and injuring five others in shootings at two abortion clinics in Boston. When Salvi was arraigned on weapons charges in conjunction with the shootings, Gary Tuchman of CNN gave a live report and description for audiences who were not in the courtroom.

Tuchman described Salvi as wearing a blue blazer, white shirt, white socks, loafers, and nice pants. The description implied that Salvi had dressed conservatively and neatly. A print news account reported that Salvi was wearing "an ill-fitting blazer." The implication here contradicted the neat appearance of Tuchman's report. Which account was right? Audiences who heard and read the two accounts might have noticed the discrepancy and been puzzled. Or maybe it just added to their belief that you cannot trust the media to be right.

Tuchman also took his reported observation one step further. He noted to viewers that if they had a stereotype of someone who would be charged with committing murder, Salvi did not look like that stereotype—that is, Salvi did not look like someone who would commit murder. Viewers may have wondered: "What does the stereotypical murderer look like? Why didn't Tuchman give us a description of that stereotype?"

Observation plays a major role in writing, but we must be circumspect about the descriptions we use. As will be discussed in Chapter 11, we as writers carry our prejudices and biases with us as we collect information and write. We must be careful. Think about Tuchman's reference to a stereotypical murderer. Can you describe one? Of course not. If murderers were readily identifiable, people who have been killed would have had some warning. But murderers vary in shape, size, age, gender, skin tone, hair color, and clothing preference. They do not have greasy hair and shifty, beady eyes and act furtively or in a suspicious manner.

The Importance of Accuracy

As noted, Tuchman's observations might have been distorted by his experiences. He might have a stereotypical idea of what a murderer looks like. Writers can bring biases to observation, just as they can to any aspect of reporting.

Just as you double-check facts, you should be circumspect about your observations. Take emotions into account. If you covered an anti-abortion rally, you might have found your emotions surging if you are pro-choice. Despite your role as a journalist, your feelings might not be neutral. Your feelings could influence your description. Be aware.

To ensure accuracy, you should record impressions in your notebook or on your electronic equipment at the scene and then review to add context as soon as possible afterward. Smartphones make recording simple and allow a spur-of-the-moment decision to record. The longer you wait, the fewer details you will remember accurately. Memory fades over time.

Like other kinds of research, observation leads to a more complete message. Description that is simple, clear, fair, and complete also will aid accuracy. Writers should lay out description alongside other facts and allow audiences to judge for themselves. Audiences invariably will apply their own biases to the description and form their own opinions, but a writer's choices of words should not be the deciding factor.

Exercises

1. Hillary Clinton, former presidential candidate and secretary of state, is coming to campus to give a lecture. Before the lecture, she will have a news conference, which you will attend for the campus newspaper. First, you need to find out more information. Using three biographical sources, answer the following questions. Cite the reference used. One reference should be online.

   a. When and where was Clinton born?
   b. Where did she go to college?
   c. What jobs did she hold before joining the Obama administration?
   d. What has she done other than be secretary of the State Department?
   e. Has she won any awards? If so, list them.

2. Identify a reporter in your college community or in your hometown by reading articles, blogs, or other writings in the respective paper. Call the reporter and ask what sources he or she uses in researching stories. Note whether the reporter uses online sources to retrieve information. Find out how the reporter ensures accuracy in using sources. Share the information with your class.

3. You are the public relations coordinator for a child-advocacy organization. You have been contacted by a wire service reporter who is developing a

story on parents charged with killing their children. Your organization president wants more information before making a statement. Your task is to prepare a memo that lists six references to substantial articles on parents charged with killing their children. The references need to be annotated; that is, they should be accompanied by explanatory notes as well as enough information to enable the president to find the articles and gain oversight on the issue before she responds.

4. You discover that many adult day-care facilities exist in your area, and you want to make a case to your editor that a multimedia feature story about these facilities would be a good one. Search online for information on these facilities and identify at least three in your area. Prepare a strategy for developing the story with audio and video as well as any limitations, such as access, that could arise in completing the assignment.

5. Pick a place on campus or attend a town government meeting as an observer along with another student. Use your senses to take notes on what transpires outside the actions of passersby or officials. Write a description of what you observed. For the meeting, for example, describe aspects such as the room, the mood, the speakers' attitudes, the officials' attitudes, the tone of the meeting, and how many people attended. Then compare your account with the other student's accounts. See what each of you chose to include and chose to ignore. Compare the language you used in your description, then discuss what made your observations different.

References

Cohodas, Nadine. "Using documents." Interview via email, October 2001.

FOIA Data at a Glance. www.foia.gov.

"FOIA Legislative History." http://www.gwu.edu/~nsarchiv/nsa/foialeghistory/legistfoia.htm.

Freedom of Information Act, 5 U.S.C. 552, 1966. Amended in 1974, 1976, 1986, 1996, 2002.

Friedman, Barbara. *Web Search Savvy: Strategies and Shortcuts for Online Research.* Mahwah, NJ: Erlbaum, 2004.

Gartner, Michael. Speech in honor of national Freedom of Information Day. Washington, DC, National Press Club, March 1989.

Hock, Randolph. *The Extreme Searcher's Internet Handbook: A Guide for the Serious Searcher.* Medford, NJ: CyberAge Books, 2010.

McGuire, Mary, Stilborne, Linda, McAdams, Melinda, and Hyatt, Laurel. *The Internet Handbook for Writers, Researchers, and Journalists.* New York: Guilford Press, 1997.

Paul, Nora. *Computer Assisted Research: A Guide to Tapping Online Information,* Fourth Edition. St. Petersburg, FL: The Poynter Institute for Media Studies, 2001.

10

Interviewing, Quotes, and Attribution

Asking questions and collecting answers—interviewing—is an essential skill for all media writers. Becoming a skilled interviewer takes practice; it is not something someone does naturally.

Most of us interview in a casual way when introduced to someone new. We ask questions: Where are you from? Are you a student? What year are you in school? What is your major? We hope to get responses that help us learn more about the person.

But if you are going to write about that individual, your questions must be much more specific. You hardly have enough for a story if you know that Steve Monroe is a junior from Lake Geneva, New York, majoring in information and library science. You need more detailed information, perhaps his career objective and his views on information storage and retrieval.

Good interviewing is more than just carrying on a casual conversation. It takes skill, and it takes practice. This chapter will start you on the road to becoming a good interviewer.

In this chapter, you will learn

- how to prepare for an interview,
- how to conduct an interview in person, by phone, or online via email or in real time,
- how to handle off-the-record information,
- how to use quotes, and
- the importance of accuracy, attribution, and punctuation in quotes.

Interviewing as a Challenge

Writers do interviews in different ways. The medium they work for, deadline pressures, the accessibility of sources, and people's willingness to talk affect how well a writer can plan and do interviews. More and more, writers are on the move as they tweet, blog, and become mobile journalists, or mojos, capturing quotes and filing stories from cars or coffee shops. In addition to a paper notepad or electronic notebook, today's writer will need a smartphone and perhaps audio and video equipment to record the best sound and visuals for online postings. In today's media world, stories can be multidimensional, as noted in Chapter 7 on online content.

Writers face challenges as they work diligently to reach as many sources as possible before a deadline. They become detectives as they figure out just whom they should interview and how. Like anyone else, writers feel nervous and even excited when they have the chance to interview a well known newsmaker or celebrity. And they feel great satisfaction and accomplishment when a source answers their questions and gives them something extra.

Reporters usually interview multiple sources to get the information they need for a story. Often those sources are quoted directly, such as in a piece on fires in Colorado that would require talking to homeowners, firefighters, police, military personnel who are assisting, insurance adjusters, and so on.

In other cases, writers would interview people to re-create a scene, as Jim Trotter did in a *Sports Illustrated* story on Junior Seau, the NFL player who committed suicide in May 2012. Through detailed interviews with those who knew him well, Trotter re-created how Seau might have spent his last day or days. The lead sets the scene for readers so they see his daily routine, then Trotter reminds them in paragraph four that Seau died.

While only seven people are directly quoted, other information is indirectly attributed, and Trotter refers to family and close friends as sources. When writers conduct in-depth interviews with many sources, they can re-create accurately a timeline of events, often in a narrative that resembles a novel. The technique is often used in crime stories. (*Sports Illustrated* does not grant permission for excerpts of stories to be used, only the full story, thus the lead is not reprinted here. The authors recommend that readers find it online.)

Research before Interviewing

Whether you are a journalist or a blogger, the first step for any writer in interviewing is to know the topic, and that requires research. Before any interview, you should have knowledge of your topic and the people you will interview, whether by phone, via email, or in person. The general rule is not to go into an interview cold. You will have more success if your source quickly sees you are prepared. Preparation shows that you are serious about the interview, and it flatters the source.

Because of deadline pressure imposed by online news cycles or the need to keep Twitter feeds or blog posts current, some writers might find that they do not have time to do research before they have to be on site to cover an event or update a story. On some occasions, you might go into an interview unprepared. Experienced writers will tell you that such an experience is uncomfortable and often embarrassing. No one wants to walk up to the newest Nobel Prize winner for medicine and ask, "Now just what was your work that caused you to win?"

With the advantages of technology today, a reporter can be on his or her way to an interview while a researcher combs files for background information. The reporter can get data from the researcher and arrive somewhat prepared. Or the reporter can stop and do some quick online research via his or her cell phone.

Writers—whether print or broadcast reporters, online journalists, freelancers, public relations practitioners, graphic designers, bloggers, social media marketers, or advertising copywriters—look in their own files first for information, then move to the company's or community's library. They might find other articles, videos, or commentary about their topic, or they might consult research materials such as government sites. Specific sources are noted in Chapter 9.

Sometimes as part of research, media outlets will conduct an informal survey of people's opinions or search recent polls done by other media or polling organizations. Often media, such as CNN or NPR, will post questions and ask viewers to call in with their responses. Those are tallied and aired later in programming.

Polling firms spend millions of dollars each year interviewing voters about their favorite candidates and consumers about their favorite products and services. Marketers use the results to promote everything from a specific politician to toothpaste. Their questions have to be worded carefully to avoid bias and to obtain relevant, pertinent, and accurate information. Such firms have professionals who draft questions, oversee interviews, and compile results. Examining polling research allows writers to uncover public sentiment and determine whether conflict exists over an issue.

Getting the Interview

Once you have sufficient knowledge, you must determine who is the best person to interview. For a story on credit card fraud, a local bank president might be a primary interview. But you must also talk to experts in the financial services industry, consumers, and whoever is knowledgeable about the subject. Some names might appear during research, and some could come as referrals in other interviews.

Setting Up the Interview

When you know the specific person you want to interview, you need to determine the best method of interviewing and make an appointment, whether the interview is by telephone or in person. Some interviews can be conducted by email. Online questions and answers are fast and convenient, but remember: They have serious limitations. The source might not be known to the writer. The writer who interviews only via email loses the candid spontaneity that comes with live interviews, as well as any sense of the source's surroundings and personal characteristics. A low chuckle or a timely grin are impossible to detect in an email.

In setting up any interview, you might have to go through a secretary or a public relations person who maintains the source's schedule, and that process can be time consuming. Or you might be able to call the person directly.

Make sure that a source has firsthand information. If you are working on a story that requires expert opinion, for example, be sure your source is an appropriate one. The primary surgeon for a lung transplant is a much better source than a hospital public information officer or a physician who assisted during the operation. People who have never been involved in a child abuse case and are just giving you secondhand or hearsay information are not good sources for a story on that subject. A few filter questions up front can eliminate unnecessary interviews: "I am looking for people who tried to break into the country-western music market. Did you ever sing professionally? Or perhaps prepare a demonstration tape for an agent?"

In setting up an interview, be sure to specify the amount of time you will need. Don't underestimate, or you will lack time to ask all your questions. Some people might be willing to be interviewed on the spot when you call, so be ready with your questions. Others will want to set a specific time at a later date. Ask for more time than you will need.

Select a comfortable place for any face-to-face interview. The source's terrain is best because he or she is usually more relaxed in a familiar environment. The reporter also has the opportunity to observe personal items, such as family photographs or collected memorabilia, that can add to the story.

Avoid doing interviews during meals. People have difficulty talking while eating, and a discussion over who should pay for food—source or writer—can be uncomfortable. If the individual is from out of town and staying at the local hotel, you might choose to do an interview over coffee—a fairly inexpensive way of meeting and talking.

Dress appropriately for the interview. If you are interviewing the chief executive officer of a Fortune 500 company, wear a suit. If you are meeting a peanut grower in his fields, shuck the cashmere coat. And, if you are meeting with teenagers at the local hangout, jeans are okay.

What to Work Out in Advance

Do not agree to pay for an interview. Only in very rare situations should you consider paying for information. A news organization might agree to pay because the source's information is newsworthy, but any payment should be worked out ahead of time and be consistent with company policy. If you are a freelancer, you should not agree to pay for information; publications might not buy your work if sources were lured by profit.

Work out arrangements if you plan to use an audio or video recorder or a smartphone to record information digitally. Do not just show up with the equipment. Sources might want to be prepared, particularly in regard to their physical appearance if they are to be filmed. A tape recorder is advisable if you are planning a long interview or one that might contain controversial or important information. You might want a tape as a backup if you suspect a source might question your quotes in the printed article. One good way to have a source agree to be taped is to stress your need for accuracy in getting quotes right. Few people will argue.

Of course, you will need audio equipment if you know you will be writing an online version of the story and sound will be part of the package an editor will prepare. The same applies if the online editor wants video clips. Be sure to reserve equipment in advance, make sure it is working and has batteries before you leave the office, and review any operating instructions so you can use it comfortably.

If you are doing an interview by email or telephone, establish a time period for questions and answers so you will get responses by your deadline. You also might want to agree on a code word that the source will include at the end of responses so that you know the source answered the questions and not someone who had access—whether legally or illegally—to the email account. Some writers use email only as a follow-up to a telephone or face-to-face interview. Be sure to note in the story which quotes came from email interviews, just as you would note "in a telephone interview."

Some people will want to see a list of questions before they agree to an interview. Such a request can be honored if sources need to collect specific information, such as statistics. People who are not used to being interviewed might want some time to formulate responses. Or, if you are getting a quote to use in a broadcast, a source might want a few minutes to prepare a response so he or she will have a script to follow. In many cases, your deadline will determine whether you have the luxury of submitting questions and waiting for responses. In any case, don't give up the right to ask a question that is not on the list.

Some sources will ask if they can see the article before it is printed or listen to the tape before it is aired. Of course, if you are a public relations practitioner or an ad copywriter, your source—who might be your client—will have final approval. But in the news business, the answer is *no*. Deadline pressure generally precludes allowing time for a source to review the message. Sources can become editors, wanting to change more than what applies to them.

If a source insists on previewing the piece, check it out with an editor or producer. You might want to find someone else to interview. Be clear if the answer is no. One inexperienced reporter caused herself and her newspaper some unpleasantness because a source thought he would have the right to edit a story citing him before it was printed. The reporter did not flatly say no, and the source misunderstood, believing he could review the story in advance. When the story appeared, the source felt deceived.

Writing the Questions

Interviewers, no matter how skilled or practiced, should write a list of questions before an interview. The list can be typed and printed, put in the "notes" app on a smartphone, or scribbled on an envelope. The questions ensure that all important aspects are covered during an interview. A reporter can review the list before ending an interview to make sure all points were asked. Questions also serve to keep an interview on track. For example, a minister might sidetrack an interview to a discussion of the writer's religious beliefs. The writer can refer to the list and remind the minister that she is there to interview him. The list can also fill in lags in the conversation.

Covering the Basics

Obviously, when you are planning questions, you want to ask the basics: *who, what, when, where, how,* and *why.* But you need to ask other questions to get more information and to make the message complete. One formula for interviewing is called *GOSS,* an acronym for *Goals–Obstacles–Solutions–Start,* devised by Professor LaRue Gilleland of the University of Nevada. It can be applied to many interviews and is based on the assumption that people have goals, that obstacles loom before goals, and solutions can be found. Talking about goals, obstacles, and solutions gives the source plenty to discuss. During the interview, you may discover that you need to "start"—to go back to the beginning of an event or topic to get a more complete understanding.

For example, you might interview a chemist who does research on polymers. Using GOSS, you would ask about the goals of the research, the obstacles to discovering new uses, and the solutions to overcome the obstacles. "Start" would lead you to ask more broadly about the field of polymer research and what is happening in this particular laboratory compared with others.

Ken Metzler, author of *Creative Interviewing,* has suggested two more letters to Gilleland's GOSS: *E* for *evaluation* and *Y* for *why. Evaluation* suggests a need for an overall assessment of the situation—seeking meaning beyond the facts. To get such information, the writer asks for the source's interpretation:

What does all this (polymers and research) mean to you? The *Y* is a reminder not to forget to ask why a situation has occurred and why particular research is important.

Think about quantitative questions. How many times has the baseball star struck out? How many ounces of marijuana were confiscated, and what is its street value? How many tons of concrete are needed for the runway, and is that equal to filling the high school football stadium to the top row 15 times?

When formulating questions, think of the unusual aspects. Don't hesitate to include questions you and your audience would like answered. You might even ask friends or colleagues what questions they would include if given the chance to interview a particular source.

Conducting an Interview

Always be punctual for any interview, whether face-to-face or by telephone. Making a source wait is rude and could cost you the interview. Call to let the individual know if you will be late and offer to reschedule.

If you are interviewing a celebrity or high-ranking official, avoid appearing to be a fan or worshiper, nervous or excited. Few people would be calm the first time they interviewed an Oscar winner or a country's head of state. Butterflies are to be expected, but you should show respect rather than adulation.

Getting Started

When you introduce yourself, always give your name and identify yourself professionally—as a reporter, blogger, social media marketer, or whatever your title. Also state your employer or where you expect to have the story appear, and give a summary of what you need from the interviewee. That introduction puts the interviewee on notice that anything he or she says is on the record or for publication in some format.

After you introduce yourself, start an interview with some questions that will set a relaxed mood. For example, if you are in the person's home, comment about trophies, collections, or decor. Show you are interested. Don't ask weighty questions right away.

Avoid starting an interview by asking people what they do or other routine information. They will know you haven't done your homework, and they could be insulted. You might need to verify such information with them, however. A student who interviewed author Barbara Victor discovered in a biographical source that she was born in 1944. A question revealed that Victor actually was born a year later, in 1945.

Before beginning an interview, ask yourself the questions in the checklist shown in Box 10.1.

Box 10.1   Checklist for Interviews

- Have I researched my subject and source thoroughly?
- Have I selected the right people to interview?
- Have I set up the interview in a place conducive to the interviewee?
- Have I allotted adequate time?
- Have I worked out with the source the use of a tape recorder? A video camera? Other recording device? Is the equipment in good working order?
- Have I written a thorough list of questions, including extra questions to fill surplus time?
- Have I dressed appropriately for the interview situation?
- Do I feel prepared and confident?

Using Recording Equipment

Even if they don't edit the stories, reporters might have to collect raw video that online editors can scan to find relevant images to the story being told. Most reporters can learn to use recording equipment in a few lessons and also through trial and error.

If you are using a voice recorder, hold the microphone about six inches below your interviewee's chin to get good audio free of distortions from your interviewee's breath.

For audio alone, be sure you let sources know when the tape recorder is on. Most states require that you notify people if they are being recorded. If you are conducting a telephone interview and plan to record it, you must ask the individual's permission before you turn the recorder on. Rarely, if ever, will you need to hide a tape recorder in your briefcase or under your clothing. In some states, concealing recording equipment is illegal.

If you are using video equipment and doing the recording yourself, get cover or overall shots first so that you can then focus on the interview. If a videographer is doing the shooting, use the time he or she is setting up the equipment to ask questions to put the person at ease and draw his or her attention away from the equipment. Many recorded interviews are done in offices where the lighting can be enhanced and where little outside noise detracts or interferes with the sound.

Remember, when recording outside, noises can interfere with the quality of the recorded interview. Stay away from streets, try to avoid wind, and watch the person's head position so he or she doesn't turn away from the recorder. Visually, what's going on in the background might distract viewers from looking at the interview subject as they watch the action behind.

Remember to think of your microphone as if it were a camera lens. If you want the sounds of an event, move back to capture the jumble of noises as well as the panorama. Then move in close for the more specific sound of the interview.

Asking the Questions

Ask the easy questions first. This technique allows the person to relax and feel comfortable when responding. How to ask the tough questions is covered in the next section.

Be straightforward and specific in questioning. You can preface a question with a statement, but don't talk around a question—ask it. "Mr. Rich, you have investments and inheritance that have many people asking the question: Just how much are you worth?"

As you take notes, be sure to read back any confusing quotes to ensure you have complete and accurate statements. Sometimes a person will talk quickly or start a sentence, stop midway, and begin again. You might need to repeat part of a quote and ask the speaker to confirm or clarify what he or she said.

Maintain control. Don't let the person lead you off track and away from your intended questions. Keeping an interview on track might be difficult for a student writer or inexperienced reporter. Someone accustomed to being interviewed could have an agenda or might have what seem like canned responses. A politician, for example, might ignore a question about changes in tax laws and answer instead about his or her plan for economic development. If the person digresses, wait for a suitable pause, then steer the person back to the subject. Use your list of questions as a reference. If you interrupt, you could be cutting off some valuable comments.

Try to keep yourself out of an interview. Often a person being interviewed will throw questions at the interviewer. Be polite and firm, and remember—and perhaps even say—that you are there to do an interview, not to be interviewed.

Watch your body language. Avoid any behavior, such as nodding your head, that could subtly indicate you agree with comments. If the source believes you are sympathetic and empathetic, he or she might expect a positive story.

Maintain a friendly but professional distance. Do not become the source's friend. Writers who get too chummy with their sources can create tension when the article is published. The source might believe the writer betrayed confidences.

Leave all preconceptions and misconceptions at home. You might be a single working journalist with no children, and your interview is with a stay-at-home mother with five children. Mask any feelings of envy of her domestic life or notions that her job is not as fulfilling as yours. Do not be antagonistic if you disagree with a person's philosophy. Some people will open up, however, if they sense that you do not agree with them.

Listen to the source. Be aware of inconsistencies. Be willing to divert the conversation from the prescribed list of questions if you hear a tidbit that should be developed through another line of questioning. If you do not understand a response, ask for clarification. Remember: If you aren't clear about information, you'll never convey it clearly to audiences.

The Tough Questions

Save all embarrassing and controversial questions for the end of the interview, such as those dealing with a person's gambling debts or reports that a political candidate has had an extramarital affair. Of course, if a suitable occasion to ask such a question occurs during an interview, ask it. Be aware that you run the risk of having an interview terminated if you ask a particularly sensitive question. When asking these questions, be straightforward. If you act embarrassed, you will transmit that feeling and possibly fail to get a response.

The fact that a person does not answer a tough question is often noteworthy in a story. A former foreign service diplomat who settled in a small town was arrested on charges of shoplifting. When he refused to answer reporters' questions after his trial, one reporter noted his refusal in the story. His silence supported statements that he was close-mouthed about his current life. But don't shy away from asking a question in the expectation a person might not answer it. You might get a response.

Many times writers must interview people who have suffered trauma or witnessed a traumatic event. An individual might have endured years of repeated physical abuse, survived a plane crash, been a hostage in a domestic dispute, or been wounded. A person might have witnessed a friend's drowning, seen a fiery truck crash, or found a house full of diseased and starving animals.

Writers must understand that people who have suffered trauma or an atrocity recover from those events in different ways and at different times, depending on the particular trauma and their personalities. Judith Lewis Herman notes in her book, *Trauma and Recovery*, that part of the healing process is remembering and telling the event. People seeking quotes and information might find individuals who are have survived trauma and are quite willing to talk and others who refuse to be interviewed. Herman writes:

> *People who have survived atrocities often tell their stories in a highly emotional, contradictory, and fragmented manner, which undermines their credibility.... It is difficult for an observer to remain clearheaded and calm, to see more than a few fragments of the picture at one time, to retain all the pieces, and to fit them together. It is even more difficult to find a language that conveys fully and persuasively what one has seen. Those who attempt to describe the atrocities that they have witnessed also risk their own credibility.*

Reporters must be aware of the psychological state of people who have just experienced a tragedy or atrocity, such as a subway bombing. Interviewers should ask the questions but understand when they do not get complete or even accurate responses. Interviewing more than one source might be required to get a full picture of what actually happened. Reporters might have to come back for follow-up interviews well after a traumatic event occurs.

Just as it is difficult to approach victims and witnesses, it is hard to interview victims' families. The media, particularly the electronic media, have drawn criticism for asking family members of victims "How do you feel?" only minutes or hours after a relative's death. Although some people view such questioning as aggressive, others regard it as heartless. In some instances, reporters might find that a family member is willing to talk and is helped by remembering the individual. Writers must use judgment and good taste in how far they should go in trying to get information. Reporters must try to ask the questions, but they must respect a person's right not to answer.

Interviewing during traumatic situations takes special care. The Dart Center for Journalism & Trauma at the University of Washington has an informative website—www.dartcenter.org—that defines trauma, gives specific advice on interviewing trauma victims or witnesses, and outlines how interviewing might add to their stress.

Off-the-Record Information

In the middle of an interview, a public official says, "The following information needs to be off the record." Stop the official. Don't let him or her talk any longer. Off the record means you cannot use the information. As a writer you don't want information you cannot use. Politely refuse the information. Then you can proceed to clarify what the official means. People have different definitions of what off the record means:

> Don't use the information at all;
> use it but don't attribute it to me; or
> use it to ask questions of others, but I never said it.

Sources might want to go off the record because they fear retribution if certain comments can be attributed to them. Sources also might have an ulterior motive in sharing what they imply is a secret, so reporters must be sure the information is valid and can't be learned any other way.

If you refuse to accept off-the-record information, the source might open up. People who have juicy information usually feel important and want to show they know something you don't. Think about it. Has a friend told you some gossip about someone else and sworn you to secrecy? Within 24 hours, had you shared it with someone else, despite your promise? Few secrets exist that are known only by one person.

As an interviewer, you must remember that many people who have information want to share it but might not want to take responsibility for making it public. They will let you as the writer reveal it anonymously, or let you find someone else to confirm it and become the public source. Be careful. Audiences do not necessarily believe information attributed to "a source close to the president" or "a high-level State Department official."

Some people will want to do interviews for background or just to educate you about a situation or to give you context. That means they are giving you information not to be attributed to them. For example, a bank executive might give you background on lenders and home mortgages and foreclosures. The information helps you in explaining the mortgage process to your readers or in asking questions of executives at other banks.

A final warning: Make sure you and the source are clear on how the information can be used before you accept it. If you agree to use the information but not the individual's name, you can use the information but not for attribution. If you agree the tidbit is confidential, you must not publish it. You might want that person as a source again. If you act unethically and violate the agreement, you can write that person off your source list, and you might attract unflattering attention to yourself and your employer.

Note-Taking Tips for Interviews

Most people talk faster than an interviewer can write. If you are not using a tape recorder and if you have trouble keeping up, politely stop the source and ask for a moment to catch up on notes. You could preface it by saying, "I want to make sure I record this correctly, so I need a moment to complete your last comment." Few sources would respond: "I don't care if you get it right. I want to keep talking."

Be sure when you are writing comments that you get them completely rather than in bits and pieces that might not fit together when you write the article. Complete notes help you avoid taking quotes out of context or misinterpreting quotes later.

If you have a quote that is complete, put it within quotation marks in your notebook. Then you will know you have the speaker's exact words when you review your notes and are ready to write. If you are using a tape recorder and hear a quote that you know you want to use, you can quickly check the counter on the recorder and write the time next to the quote in your notebook.

You might find it handy to flag your notes as you take them. Put a word or two in the margin to indicate where certain information occurs. For example, you may have a wide-ranging interview with the incoming Democratic speaker of the state legislature. "Welfare," "tax cuts," "power," and "education" would remind you where each topic was discussed. If you're using a tape recorder, it might also be useful to write down the timestamp—the number of minutes and seconds after the start of the recording—of each interesting statement by the source. That can help you write not only the correct words in a text report, but it will also reduce the amount of time you spend on editing audio if you are doing a multimedia report.

At the end of an interview, take a few moments to ensure you have asked all your questions. Most sources won't mind waiting while you double-check. If a quote is not clear, ask the source to repeat it. "You said earlier, Mr. Speaker, that changing the rules will help the House pass legislation faster. Could you clarify the parliamentary procedure a little more?" You also might want to ask if you can telephone or email if any further clarification is needed when you are producing the story.

After an Interview

Take time soon after you leave an interview to review your notes. Fill in any blanks that might appear confusing later. Note your feelings, the qualities of the source, any additional description, and other details while they are fresh in your mind. If you did not use a recorder, you should transcribe your notes as soon as possible to retain important details or impressions. If you store your notes on your computer, you can call them up easily to refresh them when it is time to create the piece.

After an interview, you might want to write the person a thank-you note.

Selecting and Using Quotes

You have pages of notes from your interview. How do you determine which quotes to use? The same rules for using quotes from interviews apply to selecting quotes from speeches, presentations, or even published works. Selected quotes should be vivid, show opinion, reflect the speaker's personality, support the speaker's thesis, and unify a piece of writing.

When to Use Quotes

In organizing material, writers have to decide whether to quote an individual, then whether to use that information in an indirect or direct quote.

Direct quotes give the exact words of the speaker. The quotation marks signify to readers "here's exactly what was said." Direct quotes are used for colorful statements, opinions, and emotions. Direct quotes can convey an individual's personality and manner of speaking. Here's one rule to follow: Use a direct quote if it is better than any paraphrase.

Direct quotes can be either complete quotes or partial quotes. Here is a complete direct quote:

> "Congress needs to take action to ensure that all individuals' health care needs are met," the senator said.

Or:

> Triathloner Jim Birch, 70: "The runs are okay. And for the swim, I'm fine as long as I'm in a wetsuit. Out of one, I'm a hair faster than a rock."

A partial direct quote would be written as:

> The bear "is on the move, heading toward a campground" about a mile away, the ranger said.

Or:

> Triathloner Jim Birch, 70, said he wears a wetsuit during the swim because without one, he is "a hair faster than a rock."

In the partial quote above, care was taken not to switch person when using a partial quote. In the example below, the writer switches ("the senator") to the first person ("my influence"):

> The senator vowed to "use every last little bit of my influence" to block the bill cutting military spending.

A grammatical sentence would use the words "his influence' to agree with "senator" but then the quote would be inaccurate. To be correct requires a rewrite to:

> The senator vowed "to use every last little bit" of his influence to block the bill cutting military spending.

As a note, most writers avoid using what are called orphan quotes—that is, quotation marks used for emphasis on a single word.

> The special envoy said the cease-fire represented a "monumental" effort.

Why use quotations? "Monumental" is hardly an inflammatory phrase or an unusual adjective. A writer might use the rare orphan quote if a speaker labeled an individual in a colorful way, such as calling a political opponent a "knucklehead."

To Paraphrase or Not

Indirect quotes are used to summarize or paraphrase what individuals say, particularly if they have rambled about an issue or topic. Indirect quotes do not use a speaker's exact words and are not set off with quotation marks. Writers use indirect quotes to keep quotes relevant and precise.

Many writers find indirect quotes particularly valuable when speakers have digressed from the main topic, when the statement is longer than can be used, or when a speaker inject jokes or anecdotal material that cannot be used.

When U.S. Sen. Olympia Snowe of Maine decided not to seek a fourth term, she issued a statement. Her comments proved longer than what most media would have used in an article, though many included the entire statement with online stories. Here is an excerpt from her comments:

> .... what I have had to consider is how productive an additional term would be. Unfortunately, I do not realistically expect the partisanship of recent years in the Senate to change over the short term.

A *CBS News* report summed up the part of her statement referring to partisanship this way:

> Snowe, a three-term senator and former eight-term House member, said she was "well prepared" for another electoral bid, attributing her decision instead to frustrations with the partisan nature of Congress.

Correcting Speakers' Grammar and Other Slips

Reporters who covered a high-level state official quickly learned that the man was not a good speaker. He had a vernacular accent for that region of the state, used incorrect grammar, and stated goals that seemed out of reach. How was the reporter to quote him?

Early in the official's tenure, some print journalists chose to paraphrase his remarks so they could clean up the grammar errors. Others chose to clean up the grammar in direct quotes, making the official sound well schooled. But they soon discovered that cleaning up the official's language was not good practice. Audiences who also watched local television broadcasts saw and heard the official as he really was. The image they derived from reading the newspaper did not match.

Writers are faced continually with deciding how to use quotes. If a speaker uses improper subject–verb agreement, should the writer correct it in a direct quote? How far should writers go in cleaning up quotes? In the case of the state official, print journalists figured out they had to be true to the quotes or else paraphrase. They could not dramatically clean up the quotes, put them in direct quotations, and thereby tell audiences, "Here's exactly what the man said." He didn't.

The Associated Press Stylebook advises writers:

> *Never alter quotations even to correct minor grammatical errors or word usage. Casual minor tongue slips may be removed by using ellipses but even that should be done with extreme caution. If there is a question about a quote, either don't use it or ask the speaker to clarify.*

Are Profanities and Obscenities Acceptable?

The Associated Press Stylebook also advises writers not to use profanity, obscenities, or vulgarities unless they are part of direct quotations and there is a compelling reason for them. Writers are cautioned to warn editors of writing that contains such language. The language should be confined to a single paragraph so that it can be easily deleted. Writers should not modify profanity, such as changing "damn" to "darn." Editors may change the word to "d—" to indicate that profanity was used by the speaker if no compelling reason exists to spell it out in the story.

Writers need to check with their publications and media organizations to determine their particular rules on profanity, obscenities, and vulgarities. Some specialized publications, websites, blogs, or television shows allow such language. Audiences who subscribe to such media are familiar with the language and either do not find it offensive or overlook it.

Sometimes reporters will not include profanity in the news story on which the interview is based, but they will when it is part of an associated full transcript of the interview. Writers who link to the transcript from the online news story may want to consider ways to warn the reader that the transcript contains language that some readers may consider vulgar or offensive.

General Rules about Quotes

- Never make up a quote. Quotes must be accurate.
- Don't take a question answered "yes" or "no" and turn it into a direct quote. For example, if an interviewer asks a high school basketball coach if he believed many students bet on the outcome of games and the coach answered, "No," the quotation in the newspaper should not read:

  > Coach Lyman Jones said, "I don't think many students bet on the outcome of our basketball games."

  All you can really say is this: When asked whether he thought many students bet on the outcomes of games, Coach Lyman Jones replied, "No."
- Watch out for redundancies when setting up quotes. Direct quotes should expand or add to the information in the preceding graph, not repeat it.

Avoid:

She said she was surprised at being chosen the school's outstanding senior. "I was so surprised when they called my name," Gonzalez said.

Prefer:

Gonzalez said she was surprised when the principal called her name. "I couldn't move or react," she added. "I felt glued to my chair in shock."

- Set up situations before using the quote so readers will have a context for quotes. In the story about the woman running barefoot across the United States, the Associated Press writer used this format:

  Heim said most of her journey has been pleasant.

  "The kindness I've seen in people surprised me. You always hear all the wrong with the world," she said. "But I've seen nothing but good in the world."

- Use "according to" only with printed or factual information. Do not use it as an attribution to a person.

  Avoid:

  The state's prison system is 3,456 inmates above the legally allowed level, according to the secretary of corrections.

  Prefer:

  The state's prison system is 3,456 inmates above the legally allowed level, said the secretary of corrections. According to prison documents, the level has exceeded capacity for the past seven years.

- Use attribution in the middle of a sentence only if it occurs at a natural break. Otherwise, put it at the beginning or the end so that you don't interrupt the flow of the person's statement.

  Avoid:

  "We can always," he said, "commission a new statue for the college commons."

  Prefer:

  "We can always commission a new statue for the college commons," he said.

  Acceptable:

  "The marine sciences lab is vital to the state's economy," he said, "and we must persuade the legislature to allocate more funds this year."

- Always use attribution for statements that use "hope," "feel," or "believes."

  The district attorney said she believes the verdict fell short of what she expected the jury to do. She said she feels that the community will be angered that Ammons was not found guilty of first-degree murder.

You as a writer are not inside another person's head; you know how he or she feels, thinks, or believes because you were told.

More on Attribution

Quotes, whether direct or indirect, must be attributed completely and adequately. Readers or listeners must know who is talking and who is making each statement. They need to know the proper sources of information. The general rule is that attribution should go at the beginning of each new quote or at the end of the first sentence, whether the quote is one sentence or more than one sentence.

If the quote goes on for several paragraphs, attribution usually is placed at least once in every paragraph, and most writers follow the rule of attribution somewhere in the first sentence. Some writers will omit attribution in a middle paragraph if they have several short paragraphs of quotes by the same speaker. The key is to ensure that readers know who is talking.

If paragraphs contain strong statements of opinion, however, the writer must use attribution for every sentence.

For many writers, particularly news writers, "said" is the attribution word of choice. "Said" carries no underlying connotation as to a speaker's emphasis or meaning; it is neutral. "Added," "continued," and "told" are also fairly neutral. Attribution words that contain subtle meanings include "emphasized," "stressed," "declared," "demanded," "ordered," "stated," "criticized," and "contended." Writers avoid most of these words.

Do not use words such as "smiled," "laughed," "grimaced," "chuckled," and so on as attribution words. They are descriptive words that tell how a person was behaving when she or he said something. Rather than writing "'Hello,' he smiled," use "'Hello,' he said with a smile." Phrases such as "she said, and frowned," "he said, and grimaced," and "she said, then laughed" are preferred.

When using attribution that includes a person's title, do not place the title between the person's name and the attribution verb.

Avoid:

The University will accept 3,475 freshmen for the incoming class, Polly Wilson, director of undergraduate admissions, said.

Prefer:

The University will accept 3,475 freshmen for the incoming class, said Polly Wilson, director of undergraduate admissions.

Punctuating Quotes

General punctuation rules are discussed in Chapter 2. Here are the basic rules for punctuating quotes:

- Attribution at the end of a quote—whether direct or indirect—must be set off with punctuation. In most cases, the punctuation will be a comma.

Fifteen barrels of sardines will be delivered Wednesday, he said.

"Fifteen stinking, dripping barrels of sardines will be delivered Wednesday," he said.

"Will you deliver the barrels of sardines before noon?" he asked.

■ Attribution at the beginning of an indirect quote is not set off with punctuation.

He said 15 barrels of sardines will be delivered Wednesday.

■ Attribution at the beginning of a direct quote requires punctuation. If the quote is only one sentence long, use a comma. If the quote is two or more sentences long, use a colon.

Johnson said, "We have spent three days examining the department's accounts and have found no evidence of impropriety."

Johnson said: "We have spent three days examining the department's accounts and have found no evidence of impropriety. We will recommend that no further action be taken."

■ Quotes within a direct quote are set off with single quotation marks.

"He said, 'Go ahead and throw it away, just like you have done every game,' and he walked out and slammed the door," Smithers said.

"I think 'War of the Worlds' was a frightening movie," she said.

■ Commas and periods go inside quotation marks in direct quotes.

"Fifteen stinking, dripping barrels of sardines will be delivered Wednesday," he said.

Matthews said, "This race should be the test of every man's and every woman's physical and mental stamina."

■ When placing the attribution at the end of the first sentence in a direct quote, the attribution is closed with a period. It marks the end of a sentence.

Wrong:

"The new gymnasium is fantastic and humungous," said basketball player Brad Jones, "We're proud to play there. We really feel important playing our games now."

Right:

"The new gymnasium is fantastic and humungous," said basketball player Brad Jones. "We're proud to play there. We really feel important playing our games now."

■ Question marks go inside or outside quotation marks depending on whether they are part of the quote.

Mark said, "Are you asking me whether I cheated on the exam?"

One of Dionne Warwick's popular renditions included "Do You Know the Way to San Jose?"

■ Consider what may be slightly confusing but correct punctuation here:

Sara asked Kate, "Have you ever seen the movie 'Gone With the Wind'?"

Here, the writer has a movie title that must be set off with quotation marks within a direct quote plus a question mark that is not part of the title.

■ If the attribution breaks up a direct quote, it must be set off with commas and the quotation marks continued.

"Go ahead and throw it away," said Smithers, "just like you have done every game."

■ If a speaker is quoted for several continuing paragraphs, the quotation marks are closed only at the final paragraph. Each paragraph must open with quotation marks to indicate the person is still speaking.

Resident John Loftis of Hollowell Road said, "We have been waiting two years for the southeast area to be annexed, and we are getting annoyed that the town council has further delayed a decision.

"I have written and my neighbors have written all the council members to say we want town services and are willing to pay for them.

"We just don't understand what the holdup is," Loftis said. "If a decision doesn't come after the next public hearing, I plan to picket city hall."

Not closing the quotation marks at the end of the first and second paragraphs tells the reader that Loftis has not finished talking. The quotation marks at the beginning of graphs 2 and 3 reopen the continuous quote from Loftis.

Writers must ensure that readers know who is speaking and when a person stops speaking. Attributing a quote to the wrong person because punctuation is incorrect could cause problems, ranging from jeopardizing a writer's relationships with sources to more serious issues of damaging credibility or even leading to defamation lawsuits. Careful writers pay attention to detail and accuracy, down to every quotation mark.

Many books have been written about interviewing and using quotes in media writing. Most writers become more and more skilled in the art of interviewing as their careers progress. But both experienced and beginning writers will benefit from a few key guidelines listed below.

Always remember:

- Be circumspect in your use of quotes. Just because you have a quote doesn't mean you have to use it.
- Look for variety in quotes when writing, and use a mix of indirect and direct quotes.
- Check *The Associated Press Stylebook* rule about correcting quotes.
- If you are not sure about a quote, follow this rule: When in doubt, leave it out. Don't try to reconstruct it as a direct quote. And be sure you have the gist of the remarks if you convert the comments to an indirect quote.
- Develop recording skills so you can use electronic equipment to add visuals and sound or to assist in long or complicated interviews.

Exercises

1. Identify a campus leader who has been in the news recently. Select a specific topic related to the leader's expertise. Set up an interview and prepare questions as outlined in the chapter. If possible, take a video camera to record the interview. While interviewing, take notes on the surroundings to add description. When the interview is over, compare your notes to the tape. Write a story that focuses on the campus leader's views. Use a mix of direct and indirect quotes. Select 30 seconds of video to use as well.

2. Assume that you are a reporter for the campus newspaper. Your editor has asked you to come up with a story based on money, specific to the campus. Ideas might be the cost of tuition or books, lack of enough financial aid, lack of funds to maintain classrooms, cost of getting settled in a job after graduation, increased student fees. Begin work on a story that would interest your audience: students. Stick to the campus for interviews. You must use more than one source. If the story relates to campus funding, you will need to talk to an administrator. You would also want to talk with a student who is affected. Be sure to have enough sources. After the interviews, write a story showing all sides of the issue.

3. Many publications reveal how average citizens feel about or react to an event. Editors will select a current topic and assign a reporter to get

public reactions. Scan today's daily newspaper and select a current topic, such as an ongoing international conflict, national legislation, a campus issue, or another major event that students and staff would have read or heard about. Interview 10 people. Ask each one the same question. If you have to ask a question that is answered yes or no, you will need the follow-up question—"Why?"—or your responses will be skimpy. Get each individual's name (check the spelling) and two other identifying labels: year in school, academic major, hometown, age, and residence. Your attribution would look like this: Jane Smith, a senior chemistry major; or Alex Jones, 19, of Whiteville. Write the story. The first paragraph should have a summary lead, giving the results of your informal poll, such as "Five of 10 university students interviewed Thursday at the student union said they believed the presidency is a tough job that receives little credit, and not one student would want the job." The second paragraph poses the question: "The students were asked, 'What is your assessment of the job of president, and would you want the job?'" Then you can proceed with each person's response.

4. Find a story in your local newspaper and the same story on the newspaper's website but with audio and video components added. Listen and view the recorded pieces. How do audio and visual elements add to the story? What can they tell that print alone cannot? Email or call the reporter and find out whether he or she was trained to use broadcast equipment and how such skills were learned. What advice does the reporter offer about how technology extends interviewing?

References

Brady, John. *The Craft of Interviewing*. Cincinnati: Writer's Digest, 1976.

Cappon, Rene J. *The Word: An Associated Press Guide to Good News Writing*. New York: Associated Press, 1991.

Christian, Darrell, Jacobsen, Sally, and Minthorn, David. *The Associated Press Stylebook and Briefing on Media Law*. New York: Associated Press, 2012.

Herman, Judith Lewis, *Trauma and Recovery*. New York: Basic Books, 1992.

Metzler, Ken. *Creative Interviewing, 2nd ed.* Englewood Cliffs, NJ: Prentice-Hall, 1989.

11

Recognizing Bias and Stereotypes

Understanding bias means considering your own background as well as the backgrounds of others. Many people believe they can write about other people without allowing any personal bias to creep into their writing. But few people can step outside personal bias because most people are unaware of how ingrained their beliefs and attitudes can be. That means we have prejudices against people, groups, or things that cause us to treat them in a manner that is considered unfair. All of us have biases or preconceived notions. At their most conspicuous, biases in writing appear as racial slurs or hate speech. But most bias is not overt. It is subtle—and it comes from who you are.

Consider your background. Did you come from a suburban middle-class home where you attended a school with little ethnic diversity? Did you speak a language other than English at home? What is your family's ethnic or racial background? Did you grow up in an urban ethnic neighborhood—Italian, African-American, or Laotian?

Did you live in a subsidized housing project, in an inner city, or in a small town of 5,000 people or fewer? Maybe you grew up on a farm or ranch, and your nearest neighbor was a half mile away. Did your grandparents or another relative live near you? Did you attend private or public schools?

What is your gender? Do you or does someone in your family have a physical or mental disability? What is your religion? What political party do you claim? Are you close to someone who is in a same-sex marriage or household?

All these aspects of your background and many others helped to build your attitudes and beliefs. For example, if you grew up in a rural community, you might have bias against individuals who come from cities. If you went to public school, you might be disdainful of acquaintances who were educated in private schools. If you have had little exposure to members of a specific ethnic group, you might misunderstand some of their cultural practices.

214

As a communicator, you must become aware of your attitudes and beliefs to curb the bias still evident in the media today. Overcoming such bias is particularly important in digital messages that can be easily and quickly distributed and spread erroneous views of certain groups and individuals.

Bias often surfaces in stereotypes that show up in adjectives or nouns used to describe certain groups. People form stereotypes from their perceptions of individuals' or groups' behavior and from their experiences and those of friends and relatives. Stereotypes are usually broad and simplified ideas about an individual, group, or thing. Often, these ideas become widely held and applied without personal knowledge that could dispel such thinking.

What about the label in the sentence "Hillary is a typical college student who wants to have a good time and study as little as possible"? As a student, you would not want people to ignore your full array of attributes and view you only as a party-goer. The generalization is not fair to you or most other students. As a writer, you must learn to confront such stereotypes and avoid perpetuating negative overgeneralizations that reflect insensitivity and ignorance of other groups.

In this chapter, you will learn

- how writers can begin to recognize bias,
- how bias in writing affects specific individuals and groups, and
- specific tips on how to avoid bias in writing about individuals and groups.

The Bias Habit

Writers' cultural values can affect the ability to be truly fair. Because of the way the brain processes information, people must categorize and label people and events. Walter Lippmann referred to this phenomenon in 1922:

> *The real environment is altogether too big, too complex and too fleeting for direct acquaintance. We are not equipped to deal with so much subtlety, so much variety, so many permutations and combinations. And although we have to act in that environment, we have to reconstruct it on a simpler model before we can manage it.*

Journalism researchers Holly Stocking and Paget Gross note that people often will select the information that confirms their existing attitudes and beliefs. This *adaptive process* means people do not consider as many perspectives as possible, or they develop a view that does not accurately reflect reality. Most important, Stocking and Gross say, people might not even be aware they process information with a cognitive bias. They do not have to make a conscious effort to be biased; in fact, they may be trying to be unbiased, as journalists do in attempting objectivity.

It is important to remember that bias surfaces in many arenas. Adjectives and nouns are ascribed to people because of where they live, their political beliefs, their sexual orientation, and their religion. Bias attributes certain characteristics to women, men, people with disabilities, children, older people, and members of ethnic and racial groups. Labels are dangerous. They often are offensive and usually imply inferiority. They can exclude or oppress. Labels do not accurately describe individuals, nor do they accurately apply to groups. Writers who do not think beyond labels perpetuate negative stereotypes and myths.

Not all stereotypes necessarily appear negative, however. For example, a majority-culture stereotype has been exhibited in several kinds of traditional U.S. stories such as cowboy stories, soap operas, or musicals where the heroes usually are depicted as tall, broad-shouldered, white, and handsome men, while women most frequently play minor roles.

Another example of a positive stereotype is the "model minority" in the Asian-American community, where people are depicted as geniuses in music, math, and science. That generalization, although it seems complimentary, is not true and affects the majority of Asian-Americans who might not have aptitudes in these particular fields.

Usage also changes as perception, the environment around inclusion, and bias change. Writers who rely on *The Associated Press Stylebook* for guidance on word choice notice the changes in each annual edition. For example, the 2012 edition notes "mentally disabled" as the preferred term, replacing "mentally retarded."

Bias in Writing

Groups can construct a shared view of "reality" because of the similarities in the way they view the world. In the early 1990s, Timothy Crouse in his book, *The Boys on the Bus*, explained the close working relationship among political reporters on the campaign trail:

> *It was just these womblike conditions that gave rise to the notorious phenomenon called "pack journalism" (also known as "herd journalism" and "fuselage journalism"). A group of reporters were assigned to follow a single candidate for weeks or months at a time, like a pack of hounds sicked on a fox. Trapped on the same bus or plane, they ate, drank, gambled, and compared notes with the same bunch of colleagues week after week.*

As early as 1950, one famous study showed how wire editors relied on their own values to select the news. David Manning White reported that "as 'gatekeeper' the newspaper editor sees to it (even though he may never be consciously aware of it) that the community shall hear as a fact only those events which the newsman, as representative of his culture, believes to be true."

While there are many more ways for people to seek information and alternative views, the gatekeeper role still exists. People write blogs about topics of their interest, deciding the viewpoint and agenda. Magazines, whether print or online, choose content for their particular audiences. Multimedia producers select the video that best tells the story. In each decision, writers and editors are influenced by their colleagues, the function of their organization, and the perceived needs of their audiences.

More than a half century after the Civil Rights Movement became a force in the United States, inequities based on race and ethnic background persist. Media have both helped and hindered the effort for equal rights in this country. On the one hand, media give voice to various social movements and allow the message of equality to reach a mass audience. On the other hand, they perpetuate misinformation and ignore a myriad of other ethnic groups.

Although the complexion of management is changing, most people who run the media are of Western European descent, and, despite cutbacks in all areas because of budget constraints, a large majority remain male. The percentage of underrepresented groups in newsrooms across the country has declined since 2007, but the annual decreases are starting to level off. According to the American Society of News Editors, most newspapers have minority populations numbering well below their representations in the communities they serve. Also, journalists as a group are well educated, and few of them grew up in poverty. They have little context, therefore, to help them know what it is like to be an African-American, Native American, Asian-American, Hispanic-American, or other person of color in the United States. Too often, stories about those communities are reported with an outsider's perspective, resulting in misinformation or stereotypes. In other cases, the stories might not be reported at all so the group and the neighborhood remain invisible.

The issue of race and the media—both how the media cover race and the racial makeup of newsrooms—surfaced in the 1968 Kerner Commission Report. The report was commissioned by President Lyndon Johnson's administration after the race riots in Los Angeles in August 1965. As part of the report, the committee looked at media and race. Ten years later, another study, Window Dressing on the Set: Women and Minorities in Television: A Report of the United States Commission on Civil Rights, noted the token roles played by women and minorities in TV news and sitcoms. The two reports are considered classic cases that started media managers looking at racial issues and prompted news organizations, such as the American Society of News Editors, to launch diversity committees.

Consider some of these other overt problems of bias in coverage:

- When NBA player Jeremy Lin became an on-court sensation, media comments about his height and his Asian heritage
- The continued belief that Muslims who are U.S. citizens might be affiliated with a terrorist cell

- The belief that teens with dyed, spiky hair and black leather jackets are drug users
- The use of black or Hispanic women as the subject of photos about welfare when the majority of welfare recipients are white, not black or Hispanic
- The concern that children in same-sex households might not fare as well as other children

Breaking the Bias Habit

Today, writers are trying, through better awareness, to overcome their own biases in addition to cultural bias implanted in the media. But old habits die hard. A first step is for writers to be aware of their own biases and stereotypes and how easily each can slip into communication. Take religion as an example. Our religious beliefs might contain opinions about others that we should not include in our writing, even though we firmly believe them. Some writers may have Biblical or "sacred text" attitudes and opinions about Jews, gentiles, African-Americans, women, and gay, lesbian, bisexual, and transgender individuals. In other words, some religions might teach us things about those who don't believe as we do.

Another important way to break the bias habit is to know your own biases. You can check yourself by taking the Implicit Association Test. Developed by a consortium of university researchers, it measures hidden attitudes, stereotypes, and biases. You can find it online at https://implicit.harvard.edu/implicit/. What's important in the real world is that communicators know themselves and check for bias in their communication.

Writers also must not fall into the habit of ascribing overused adjectives to certain groups, as noted earlier in the chapter. Writers unconsciously tend to write on stereotyped templates, such as "rural–urban or inner city," "black–white," "rich–poor," "old–young," or "rags to riches." Writers need more original and accurate categories to describe individuals.

Changes in society itself help writers deal with bias. Today a multicultural approach is being integrated into numerous aspects of society, from school textbooks to television advertisements. All types of cultures in the United States are gaining a voice. As someone disseminating information, you can learn to tap into these cultures for diverse insights.

Many organizations have developed guidelines to assist writers with language usage. Professional journalism organizations have websites that often include examples of stereotyping or negative portrayals and can guide writers on problem language.

For example, when NBA player Jeremy Lin hit the boards for the New York Knicks, the Asian-American Journalists Association advised the media on "danger zones." Among its advice was caution about applying the label "Yellow Mamba." The AAJA site noted: "This nickname that some have used for Lin plays off the 'Black Mamba' nickname used by NBA star Kobe Bryant. It should be avoided. Asian immigrants in the United States in the 19th and

---

Box 11.1   Helpful Web Sites with Cross-Links to Other Informative Sites

www.ciij.org—Center for Integration and Improvement of Journalism's comprehensive site with links to major journalism diversity organizations. It includes diversity news, resources, and media sites.

www.unityjournalists.org—The Unity website, self-described as "a strategic alliance advocating news coverage about people of color, and aggressively challenging its organizations at all levels to reflect the nation's diversity." It represents the Asian-American Journalists Association, National Lesbian & Gay Journalists Association, National Association of Hispanic Journalists, and the Native American Journalists Association.

www.nlgja.org—The National Lesbian & Gay Journalists Association site has resources that include a stylebook to terminology and tip sheets for coverage.

www.nabj.org—The National Association of Black Journalists has a style guide to assist writers in word usage.

www.spj.org/diversity.asp—The Society of Professional Journalists offers a diversity toolbox and a Rainbow Diversity Sourcebook.

20th centuries were subjected to discriminatory treatment resulting from a fear of a 'Yellow Peril' that was touted in the media, which led to legislation such as the Chinese Exclusion Act."

Writers can describe people as individuals, not cast them in broad terms ascribed to a group. Writers can also become circumspect when using language and learn the terminology individuals and groups prefer. Diverse groups should be covered year-round, not just on holidays or in certain months.

Students can become more familiar with groups, their goals, their membership, and current issues by accessing websites for organizations that support those groups, such as the American Association of Retired Persons at www.aarp.org. Professional media organizations are also good sources. The Asian-American Journalists Association can be found at www.aaja.org; Native American Journalists Association at www.naja.com; and the National Association of Hispanic Journalists at www.nahj.org. Most sites have links to related organizations. Other helpful websites are listed in Box 11.1.

Considering Specific Groups

Writers must avoid terminology that perpetuates beliefs that all members of any group look alike, talk alike, think alike, or belong to the same political party. Many words and images applied to specific groups have historically negative and derogatory connotations. Writers must be aware of them and avoid them.

Racial and Ethnic Groups

Having the first black candidate for U.S. president in 2008 brought attention to race, culture, and language. Some discussions proved positive and others negative, as evidenced in the fallout from the Rev. Jeremiah Wright's comments and Barack Obama distancing himself from his former pastor.

Race or ethnicity often has relevance for stories but should be used only when pertinent. Writers should avoid racial identifiers that imprecisely identify someone as black, Latino, or Asian-American, particularly in crime stories. Keith Woods, vice president of diversity in news and operations at NPR and former dean of faculty at the Poynter Institute, in using the example of describing a man solely as Hispanic, once wrote:

> *Think about it this way: In order for everyone reading, watching, or listening to the story to conjure up the same image in their mind's eye, they must all share a common understanding of what a Latino person looks like. In other words, people who are Latino would have to look alike.*
>
> *What does a Hispanic man look like? Is his skin dark brown? Reddish brown? Pale? Is his hair straight? Curly? Coarse? Fine? Does he have a flat, curved nose or is it narrow and straight?*

Woods advises journalists to "challenge the presence of racial identifiers" and to "demand more from the people who give vague, meaningless descriptions, just as you do whenever a politician gives you vague or meaningless information."

Writers should also avoid descriptive words that strengthen stereotypes, such as "oil-rich" and "nomadic" to characterize Arab-Americans, says former newspaper editor Fernando Dovalina. He notes the problems surrounding the terms "illegal alien" and "illegal immigrant," which for many have become synonymous with Hispanic and particularly Mexican-Americans. Dovalina writes:

> *Do you use the phrase "illegal alien" or "illegal immigrant"? If so, do you recall using it for Germans or Canadians who are illegally here? Would "suspected undocumented immigrant" work just as well?*

Some language, although it may seem biased, can be appropriate when used in a historical context or with cultural sensitivity, noted Pale Moon Rose, president of the American Indian Heritage Foundation. Terms such as "redskin" and "brave" are acceptable if used appropriately and in a historical context. But the use of Native American names as sports team mascots, such as the Florida State Seminoles and the Washington Redskins, has generated criticism.

How certain groups are portrayed in the mass media is the subject of research and review. *The American Indian and the Mass Media*, published in 2012, is a historical and current look at how portrayals of American Indians have evolved and the resulting stereotypes. It includes the observations of American Indian leaders.

In another article, Keith Woods wrote,

> *The harm here is not that all Native American nicknames are insults on the order of Washington's Redskins. It's that nearly all of them freeze Native Americans in an all-encompassing, one-dimensional pose: the raging, spear-wielding, bareback-riding, cowboy-killing, woo-woo-wooing warriors this country has caricatured, demonized, and tried mightily to exterminate.*

Dovalina, retired assistant managing editor for international coverage of the *Houston Chronicle*, developed a list of diversity questions for a national copy editors' workshop. The questions came from his 37-year career and the experiences of other journalist colleagues. The following were among Dovalina's questions and are still good today:

- Do you absolutely have to say that a black person or Hispanic or Asian or Native-American is the first of his or her race to have attained the distinction in question?… Sometimes the news is that it took so long for a black female or a Hispanic male to be named the first head of a city or college department.
- Do you assume that all blacks are African-Americans or Africans? Remember that culturally some blacks are Jamaicans and Haitians and Brazilians…. Some Latin Americans are more German and Italian than Spanish…. To people south of the Rio Grande, the term "America" does not refer to the United States alone. It refers to the hemisphere, and they too are Americans.

Use of the term "minority" is problematic in an international sense because people of color make up the majority of the world's population, and population changes in the United States mean that some ethnic groups are the majority in certain locations. Remember also that "minority" always refers to a group rather than to certain individuals; it is best to use the term "members of minority groups" rather than "minorities." Always look for a diversity of sources when writing.

A Native American might be interviewed about political struggles instead of the meaning of a ceremonial dance. Dovalina reminds us, "Just as there are no Anglo leaders who speak for all Anglos, there are no black leaders or Hispanic leaders who speak for all blacks or all Hispanics." Keith Woods of Poynter has guidelines for racial identification in the form of five questions (Box 11.2). He notes that delicate material can be handled better "if we flag every racial reference and ask these questions." His questions should be considered when writing about any underrepresented group in society; just substitute the name of the group for "race."

Box 11.2   Guidelines for Racial Identification

1. **Is it relevant?** Race is relevant when the story is about race. Just because people in conflict are of different races does not mean that race is the source of their dispute. A story about interracial dating, however, is a story about race.

2. **Have I explained the relevance?** Journalists too frequently assume that readers will know the significance of race in stories. The result is often radically different interpretations. This is imprecise journalism, and its harm may be magnified by the lens of race.

3. **Is it free of codes?** Be careful not to use "welfare," "inner-city," "underprivileged," "blue collar," "conservative," "suburban," "exotic," "middle-class" "Uptown," "South Side," or "wealthy" as euphemisms for racial groups. By definition, the White House is in the inner city. Say what you mean.

4. **Are racial identifiers used evenly?** If the race of a person charging discrimination is important, then so is the race of the person being charged.

5. **Should I consult someone of another race/ethnicity?** Consider another question: Do I have expertise on other races/cultures? If not, broaden your perspective by asking someone who knows something more about your subject. Why should we treat reporting on racial issues any differently from reporting on an area of science or religion that we do not know well?

Reprinted with permission of the Poynter Institute.

Sexism

Women have risen to powerful jobs in both the public and private sectors, but they have not gained enough power to transform their image fully in the media. Despite attention to sexism in many aspects of society, many writers thoughtlessly still use language that treats women as inferior or that is demeaning or insulting. They are sometimes referred to as girls or mothers and are described by their physical attributes, such as "attractive" or "brunette" or "shapely."

Writers should use description when it is complete and adds to the understanding of an individual's personality. Feature writers must be especially careful when creating a mood. Often what looks like interesting detail might come across as sexism in disguise. Writers should guard against describing women in terms of their physical appearance and men in terms of wealth and power.

Issues of sexism in coverage came to the fore in Rep. Michelle Bachmann's bid for the Republican presidential nomination in 2012 just as they did in Sen. Hillary Clinton's bid for the Democratic presidential nomination in 2008. Media ran unflattering photographs and questioned her knowledge when Bachman committed gaffes. She was referred to as "perky." Critics of the coverage said media should be focusing on her political views.

When Clinton sought the Democratic nomination for president, the role of a woman as the nation's leader had not been defined. Clinton supporter Susan Estrich, who had been involved in other presidential campaigns, noted in a National Public Radio report: "I think that's why there's been so much attention to Hillary's clothes and to Hillary's cleavage and to Hillary's husband and to Hillary's marriage and her motherhood and her own daughter." Having the first woman presidential candidate offered new fodder for political writers and plowed new ground in coverage.

In the 2008 presidential campaign, many stories on Cindy McCain, wife of candidate and Sen. John McCain, mentioned the size of her jeans. She was also described as a "blond, blue-eyed former rodeo queen and cheerleader" as opposed to her philanthropy and work in developing countries. Both she and Michelle Obama, a Harvard-educated lawyer, received praise for their fashion style more than for their accomplishments.

More recently, media have shown little restraint in describing Camila Vallejo, the college student turned Chilean revolutionary. A writer for *The Daily Beast* wrote that she "would be a better fit on the catwalks than at the barricades" and noted that as "the dark-haired woman, wearing loose-cut jeans, a diaphanous blouse, and a billboard smile has taken the stage, her followers are in a lather." Even an article in *The New York Times* on the Chilean Spring called her a "glamorous" revolutionary, hardly a label that would have been applied to handsome male revolutionaries.

Words such as "chairman" have a male bias. *The Associated Press Stylebook* says to avoid "chairperson" unless an organization uses it as a formal title. When possible, use "chair," "firefighter," "flight attendant," "postal service worker," or "letter carrier." Writers should also know their publication's policy about courtesy titles. Many organizations have eliminated courtesy titles, such as Mrs., Miss, and Ms., before women's names. Usually, only the last name is used on second reference.

Sexual Orientation

Writers should also avoid perpetuating negative images based on sexual orientation. Gay and lesbian rights movements since the mid-1950s have worked diligently to recast gay and lesbian portrayals in society. Until the mid-1970s, most news stories that referred to gays and lesbians did so only in the context of police reports or mental illness. Gay and lesbian issues have been addressed in schools, in the workplace, and in the military. People who are lesbian, gay, bisexual, and transsexual need to be covered just as heterosexual people are covered. Writers and broadcasters must be careful not to make value judgments when a source is gay or lesbian or when the subject deals with gay, lesbian, bisexual, and transgender (GLBT) issues.

A person's sexual orientation should be ignored in a message unless it is relevant. People's sexual orientation might be part of the fabric of the message but should be woven in as part of who they are, not presented as their complete identity.

Writers should never make assumptions about people's sentiments toward GLBT issues. Many people favor equality for all people. Remember that individuals who are not gay or lesbian support GLBT rights, just as many white people support civil rights for people of color. Writers should also not feel the need to balance every story that initiates from a GLBT source or event. In covering any group, sometimes balance is not appropriate, adds a shallow reporting element, or reduces the impact of the event.

Despite increased coverage, negative stereotypes continue and became prevalent in the recent federal Defense of Marriage Act and subsequent constitutional amendments passed by voters in more than 30 states. These laws recognize marriage as only between a man and a woman, and supporters focused on same-sex partnerships to generate enough votes for passage. In the coverage prior to state votes, some stories showed how same-sex couples were raising their children and dealing with routine and larger issues, such as the effect on their family structure should one parent die.

The National Lesbian & Gay Journalists Association has a stylebook, accessible online (see Box 11.1), that covers acceptable terminology and phrases and supplements other media style guides. For example, the entry on "transgender" notes: "An umbrella term that refers to people whose physical, sexual characteristics may not match their gender identity, usually preoperative, postoperative or nonoperative transsexuals. Some female and male cross-dressers, drag queens or kings, female or male impersonators, and intersex individuals may also identify as transgender. Use the name and personal pronouns that are consistent with how the individual lives publicly. When possible, ask which noun the subject prefers. As a noun, use 'transgender people.'"

In the Journalists Toolbox section, writers give tips. For example, Randy Dotinga noted that Gay Pride celebrations provide an opportunity for stories that look beyond the colorful parades. He wrote: "The drag queens and brigades of lesbian motorcyclists make flashy pictures, and they are easy to find. But dig a little deeper: You'll find plenty of informative stories by spending more time exploring your local lesbian, gay, bisexual and transgender (LGBT) community."

Disabilities

Unless you or someone in your family has a physical or mental disability, as a writer you might tend to forget people with disabilities exist. People with disabilities face discrimination from attitudes and from actual barriers created by society's architectural and communication designs. For some, their disability might be more visible than for someone who has a cognitive or intellectual impairment.

Many people, including writers, forget that people with disabilities constitute a vital and numerous part of our society. After the 1990 Americans with Disabilities Act (ADA), the federal government began steps to remove the barriers that people with disabilities face. The ADA Amendments Act in 2008 expanded the definition of disability making it easier for individuals with disabilities to seek protection under the ADA. A site managed by the U.S. Department of Labor at www.disability.gov links to more than 14,000 resources, including government agencies, local community programs, and nonprofit organizations.

According to the U.S. Census, about 19 percent of the U.S. population not living in an institution reports some type of disability. That's more than 54 million people. Therefore, a significant number of today's media audiences either has a disability or knows someone who does.

Civil rights violations, court cases, new technology, education issues, federal legislation, and changes in business practices are possible story topics that are of interest to these audiences. One major story that affects all states is the Olmstead Supreme Court decision in 1999. In the case from Georgia, the Court confirmed that people with intellectual or physical disabilities or both should live in their local communities, not in institutions. Even though the case was decided years ago, many states are just now closing their institutions and developing community living options for disabled people. In 2009, the U.S. Department of Justice Civil Rights Division began an aggressive effort to enforce Olmstead.

The late John Clogston, a journalism professor at Northern Illinois University, and Beth Haller, a journalism professor at Towson University, say that writers often portray people with disabilities in one of three demeaning ways: They imply that people who have a disability are somehow less human than other people; they present them as medically defective or somehow deviant or different in society; or they go overboard in trying to portray them positively, thus making them superhuman or "supercrips," as Clogston called them. Writers have a tendency to focus stories on the individual rather than the issues surrounding a disability, and they tend to wrap people with disabilities in pity and sympathy.

The Associated Press Stylebook cautions writers not to describe a person as disabled or handicapped "unless it is clearly pertinent to a story.... Avoid such euphemisms as mentally challenged and descriptions that connote pity, such as afflicted with or suffers from multiple sclerosis. Rather, has multiple sclerosis." Such language carries negative connotations and can exclude people with disabilities. Among the derogatory labels applied to disabled people are "crippled," "deformed," and "invalid." The focus should be on the person, not on the physical impairment.

Be careful about writing that someone succeeded "in spite of" a disability— a phrase often viewed by people with disabilities as extremely patronizing. Some writers might contend that a disability implies that individuals are not able, and if they succeed, then the news value of emotional impact and conflict is there to attract readers. Never assume an accomplishment by a person with a disability is unusual.

In general, people specializing in coverage of disability issues recommend two easy rules in writing about people with disabilities. First, avoid clichés and clichéd constructions. Use value-neutral terms—that is, words that do not stereotype. Avoid saying someone is confined. The person gets out of the wheelchair to sleep and to bathe. To that individual, the wheelchair is liberating. It is more accurate to say the individual uses a wheelchair. Second, never inject pity or a condescending tone into copy.

Ageism

Older people may also face stigmatization by society, and the mass media play a role in that process. In some instances, older people are labeled as forgetful, senile, rigid, meddlesome, childlike, feeble, fragile, frail, gray, inactive, withered, or doddering. Such adjectives might describe older people at some point in their lives or might be medically appropriate. But if such words are used indiscriminately, they demean older people and perpetuate inaccurate stereotypes.

The 2010 Census revealed almost 19 percent of the country's population is 60 years of age or older, and the numbers will continue to grow as baby boomers. With the repeal of mandatory retirement, older people work into their 70s and even 80s if they choose. They do most things that younger people do and are much more active than previous generations of older adults. Good writers portray older people in terms of their deeds and accomplishments and not their age.

The Associated Press Stylebook cautions writers to use terms such as "elderly" and "senior citizen" sparingly and carefully. "If the intent is to show that an individual's faculties have deteriorated, cite a graphic example and give attribution for it," the stylebook notes.

Syndicated columnist Lucille deView, who writes on aging, suggests that writers avoid these myths about older people:

- Older people can participate in a variety of activities, so do not adopt a "gee whiz" attitude toward their abilities. Most people over the age of 50 continue the physical activities they enjoyed when younger, whether swimming, hiking, or playing tennis.
- People are continuing to work well into their 60s, 70s, and even 80s. The American Association of Retired Persons produces a list of the Best Employers for Workers over 50.
- Older people should be seen as individuals, not as members of a senior age group in which people are believed to have the same interests and abilities. Older people's interests are just as varied as those of individuals in other groups.

- Older people are not stereotyped in appearance. They dress in numerous fashions, and not all older people have physical problems or even gray hair.

- Age does not mean loneliness or loss of sexual interest. According to a 2005 AARP study, two-thirds of the individuals polled said they lived with a spouse or a partner or that they had a regular sexual partner.

DeView says writers should focus on realistic presentations of older people. Some older people have no financial problems, whereas others struggle financially in later life. Not all older people have ill health or are unable to cope with poor health. Serious medical conditions may not severely limit their participation in society. Only about 5 percent of older people live in nursing homes.

Children also should not be portrayed in an unpleasant light. Not all children are immature, naive, whining, sneaky, dishonest, or lazy. Children mature and develop at different paces. Some are simultaneously responsible, creative, athletically gifted, loving, aggravating, and mean. Each must be considered individually and be allowed to ascribe traits to himself or herself, as did one 5-foot teenager, who described herself as being "vertically challenged."

Poverty

One societal group cuts across all racial, ethnic, and other groups: the people who live at or below the poverty level. In 2012, that level was defined as a family of four earning less than $23,050.

Although the United States is a leading world power, the number of Americans who live in poverty is 46 million, according to the American Community Survey of the 2010 U.S. Census. Even though people living in poverty might be limited media consumers, they still are part of U.S. society. Poverty, often not breaking news, affects every city in the United States. How the less-fortunate subsist should be part of regular, ongoing coverage—not just at holiday times when their plight stirs a need to give or during recessionary times when more people suffer economically.

Poverty overlaps many areas of coverage: health, religion, social services, local government, nonprofit sector, and education. Many school systems provide poor children with free or reduced-cost breakfasts and lunches. Lack of health insurance forces many people to use emergency rooms for medical care. Almost any story touches poorer segments of society. Reporters can find sources among nonprofit organizations, such as poverty assistance programs; community resources, including government officials; and churches that operate shelters and kitchens. When stories of lessfortunate residents appear, they help agencies and the needy get a boost.

When writers describe lower-income people, they must watch their language. The word "poor" implies "disadvantaged" and often is ascribed to people of color, as are the terms "welfare recipient" and "public housing resident." Census data show that a larger percentage of blacks and Hispanics are among the poor, but in actual numbers, most poor people are white.

Religion

Religion news, which has grown in importance and visibility since the terrorist attacks on September 11, 2001, showed U.S. audiences and media how little was known about different forms of Islam. The intricacies and differences among religions can lead to writers unknowingly conveying biased and misleading information.

Maha ElGenaidi, executive director of the Islamic Networks Group, an educational outreach organization, was quoted in the *San Jose Mercury News:*

> *In all religious traditions, people tend to blame the religion for what a few people have done in misapplying the religion or using it for political ends.*

Her quote could apply to Islam and to U.S. politicians who have invoked religion as a basis for their positions or votes on public policy or law.

In covering religion, writers must be aware that religion stories often involve other issues. While some might see birth control as a medical choice, the topic generates strong opinions from religious leaders. Same-sex marriage stories include politics, religion, and sexual-orientation issues and cause people to consider "What is marriage?" Even the Harry Potter children's book series stirred discussions of witchcraft and whether the stories were anti-Christian.

Anyone who covers religion must also examine his or her religious beliefs before developing questions and interviewing sources. Because the United States is dominated by Judeo-Christian traditions, many writers might be unaware of non-Christian faiths. While most of us grew up with some exposure to religion, whether within our families or our communities, that does not automatically make us tolerant of other people's views and beliefs.

Writers can do research to increase their knowledge and understanding of religions and denominations. Many online sites provide information on denominations, beliefs, and practices and even positions on social, political, and ethical issues. One such site—www.beliefnet.com—has easily accessed information on different religions.

Overcoming Bias in Writing

Even after a discussion of bias such as the one in this chapter, traces of insensitivity or stereotypes can still creep into writing You need to be constantly aware of your own background and attitudes to understand when and how bias might surface in writing, to recognize it, and to exorcise it.

Old biases die hard for many; every time a bias is confirmed by a writer, it is strengthened for readers. Writers, reporters, and broadcasters today must be trained to avoid the flaws of their predecessors, who might not have been as careful in framing particular groups without bias and stereotypes. They must question their own beliefs and assumptions to understand better the diverse groups within society. Through distinctive images of people and groups, writers can determine how others view people and groups who are not like themselves.

Even experienced writers sometimes pass along stereotypes, such as the ditzy blonde or dishonest politician, because they think people like and understand such shorthand portrayals, just as they like cartoons. Therein lies the danger. Writers must work responsibly in disseminating information rather than misinformation.

Stereotypes communicate inaccurate information and can undermine the quality of your work. Make sure what you write or broadcast does not perpetuate stereotypes. Use anecdotes rather than adjectives to show people's attitudes and behaviors. Sensing your own biases and avoiding stereotypes are critical steps on the path to better, accurate writing.

Exercises

1. Describe yourself culturally and ethnically. List any physical disabilities or other pertinent differences. Make a list of words or phrases, both negative and positive, that you have seen used in reference to your special traits. Compare your list with those of others in your class, and compile a directory of words you should avoid when writing—and why. Explain the connotation of each word. Make a list of acceptable words or phrases.

2. Based on what you identify as your own biases, find four to five reliable sources that can help you avoid using stereotypes to describe individuals or groups.

3. What is the ethnic makeup of your college or university? The town or city where your school is located? Do a five-day content analysis of your local or student newspaper or the evening newcast. Count the number of stories each day in the news, sports, and features sections. Count the number that focuses on an ethnic group or an issue related to an ethnic group. At the end of the five days, calculate the percentage of newspaper stories related to ethnic groups. Do the percentages match the groups' makeup in the university's or town's population? Was coverage positive, negative, or neutral? What types of stories do you believe are missing?

4. Search online for stories that did not fairly describe individuals. Highlight the language use. How would you change it?

5. Imagine that have the opportunity to interview the incoming student government president, a son of two Uzbek refugees. List five objective questions you could use to begin the interview, then list two effective questions you could ask to determine his experiences with cultural differences in the United States.

References _____

2012 Federal Poverty Guidelines. Federal Register, http://aspe.hhs.gov/poverty/12fedreg
.shtml. Accessed June 2, 2012.
Americans with Disabilities Act Amendments Act of 2008, at ADA Amendments. http://
www.eeoc.gov/laws/statutes/adaaa_info.cfm. Accessed June 17, 2012.
Association of Asian Journalists. http://www.aaja.org/media-advisory-on-jeremy-lin-
news-coverage/. Accessed June 2, 2012.
Carstarphen, Meta G., and Sanchez, John P., eds. *American Indians and the Mass Media.*
Norman:University of Oklahoma Press, 2012.
Christian, Darrell, Jacobsen, Sally, and Minthorn, David, eds. *The Associated Press
Stylebook and Briefing on Media Law.* New York: The Associated Press, 2012.
Crouse, Timothy. *The Boys on the Bus.* New York: Random House, 1993.
deView, Lucille. "Regardless of age: Toward communication sensitive to older people
and children," in *Without Bias: A Guidebook for Nondiscriminatory Communication.*
New York: John Wiley & Sons, 1982.
Disability Characteristics, American Community Survey. http://factfinder2.census
.gov/faces/tableservices/jsf/pages/productview.xhtml?pid=ACS_10_1YR_
S1810&prodType=table. Accessed June 2, 2012.
Dotinga, Randy. "Dig Deeper at Pride Celebrations." http://www.nlgja.org/toolbox/
pride. Accessed June 18, 2012.
Dovalina, Fernando. Presentation for the Institute for Midcareer Copy Editors, Chapel
Hill, North Carolina, Summer 2005. www.ibiblio.org/copyed/diversity.html.
Haller, Beth. *Representing Disability in an Ableist World.* Louisville, Ky.: The Advocado
Press, 2010.
"Hard-Left Heartthrob." The Daily Beast. http://www.thedailybeast.com/newsweek/
2011/10/02/camila-vallejo-chile-s-hard-left-heartthrob.html. Accessed June 2,
2012.
Lippmann, Walter. *Public Opinion.* New York: Harcourt, Brace and Co., 1922.
"The News Media and the Disorders," Chapter 15 of Report of the National Advisory
Commission on Civil Disorders, Kerner Commission Report, 1968.
"Number of Americans with a Disability Reaches 54.4 Million." U.S. Census Bureau.
http://www.census.gov/newsroom/releases/archives/income_wealth/cb08-185
.html. Accessed June 17, 2012.
Patel, Julie. "Countering Stereotypes." *San Jose Mercury News*, May 30, 2005.
Pickens, J., ed., *Without Bias.* New York: John Wiley & Sons, 1982.
Population 60 years of age and older in the United State. American Community
Survey. http://factfinder2.census.gov/faces/tableservices/jsf/pages/productview
.xhtml?pid=ACS_10_1YR_S0102&prodType=table. Accessed June 2, 2012.
Poverty Status in the Last 12 Months, American Community Survey. http://factfinder2
census.gov/faces/tableservices/jsf/pages/productview.xhtml?pid=ACS_10_1YR_
S1701&prodType=table. Accessed June 2, 2012.
Stocking, Holly, and Gross, Paget. *How Do Journalists Think? A Proposal for the Study of
Cognitive Bias in Newsmaking.* Bloomington, Ind.: Eric Clearinghouse on Reading
and Communication Skills, 1989.
"Supreme Court Upholds ADA 'Integration Mandate' in Olmstead decision." The
Center for an Accessible Society. http://www.accessiblesociety.org/topics/ada/
olmsteadoverview.htm. Accessed June 17, 2012.

"Total and minority newsroom employment declines in 2011 but loss continues to stabilize. American Society of News Editors and the RJI Insight and Survey Center at the Missouri School of Journalism, http://www.rjionline.org/news/total-and-minority-newsroom-employment-declines-2011-loss-continues-stabilize. Accessed November 6, 2012.

White, David Manning. "The 'gatekeeper,'" *Journalism Quarterly* 27, no. 3 (Fall 1950): 383.

Window Dressing on the Set: Women and Minorities in Television: A Report of the United States Commission on Civil Rights, 1977.

Woods, Keith M. "The Language of Race." Poynter Online. www.poynter.org/ special/ tipsheets2/diversity.htm. Accessed September 28, 2005.

Woods, Keith M. "Nicknames & Mascots: Complicity in Bigotry," Poynter Institute. www.poynter.org/column.asp?id558&aid587263. Accessed September 4, 2005.

Legal and Ethical Issues

A newspaper intern is fired after editors discover that he has plagiarized parts of several stories from other publications.

A major broadcast network is sued after it airs a story criticizing a grocery store chain's meat packaging. Two reporters who worked in the meat department didn't state on their job applications that they were members of the news media.

An actor sues a tabloid for libel after it reports she was drunk and disorderly in a Washington, D.C., restaurant. The magazine had not a single reliable source for the story.

A reporter writes a story about a company's alleged bad business practices, using information from executives' voice mails he accessed without their permission. The newspaper renounced the articles and removed them from its website, paid a huge out-of-court settlement, and fired its reporter.

These scenarios may sound improbable, but each is true. Each story and the newsgathering methods used to produce it had consequences for the reporter and the media outlet that printed or aired the story. In gathering and using information, writers often face a mix of legal and ethical issues. Decisions are not always easy because laws and ethics constantly change.

In many cases, state and federal laws aid reporters in their quest for information. For example, shield laws protect reporters from revealing their sources in court. Libel laws outline the conditions under which individuals can sue when they feel defamed. Although state laws protect citizens and public figures in regard to privacy, implied consent may protect a reporter who goes on private property to get a story. Many laws have been around for years and have evolved through the courts. Others, such as shield laws, are more recent.

Over the last decade, the media law battlefront has moved from libel cases to disputes over how media gather information. Subjects of news coverage have sued the media for misrepresenting who they are or the type of story they are working on, for trespassing on private property, and for using hidden cameras or hidden tape recorders. Some media observers say the methods represent unethical behavior by reporters, and some courts have begun to rule that such actions violate the law.

Other issues for writers in the digital age have been plagiarism and copyright violations. Information gathering today via the Internet makes it easy to commandeer information—whether unintentionally or purposefully—and claim it as the writer's own work. Sometimes the writer stores information and later inadvertently uses it without attributing the original source. In other cases, the material is stolen outright. In any case, the writer might have plagiarized and possibly infringed on another's copyright.

Copyright violations occur when writers use another's work and don't get permission. It is not sufficient simply to credit the original author, unless the material falls under a category known as fair use. This legal term and others are explained later.

In this chapter, you will learn

- what libel is,
- the issues of privacy and the relationship between sources and writers,
- the dangers of plagiarism and what constitutes copyrighted material,
- how ethics policies guide writers, and
- when writers cross the line in gathering information.

Libel

Writers can unknowingly or carelessly damage an individual's reputation by publishing false and defamatory statements about that individual. Even if a slip is unintentional, if the libel is in print or is aired, the writer can be sued, as can a newspaper, a website, a television station, a church administration, or a nonprofit group.

Libel can occur in any written form: a news article, a news release, a public service announcement, annual reports, a microblog or Facebook post, corporate financial statements, a television talk show, or a student's website. If a news release containing a false and defamatory statement about a person is mailed but not printed by any of the newspapers that receive it, the writer of the news release might still be sued successfully. Mailing the release to others who read it can be considered "publication" under defamation law. A radio or television station that broadcasts slander (oral defamation) can be sued under a state's libel laws.

Libel often occurs when people write about topics they do not really understand. Inexperienced reporters, student writers, and occasional writers are most at risk. They need to evaluate critically information they uncover. They can be held legally responsible for accurately republishing a false and defamatory statement that someone else made. Good data collection, complete identification, and good writing techniques can prevent many libel problems. Mass communication professors advise their students to be accurate, thorough, and scrupulously fair in what they write. The legal system generally will protect writers who do a good job of investigating and who use many sources. Innocent mistakes that are not negligent or malicious are not usually actionable in a defamation lawsuit.

A huge body of law exists on libel. Thousands of libel cases have been filed. Although most editors, writers, and copy editors do not need to be lawyers, they do need to know the basics of libel law. A writer may be the only member of a nonprofit organization's communication staff; he or she needs to know what might cause trouble. Libel laws differ from state to state. For example, the statute of limitations—the time within which a person can file a libel suit—varies; it is usually from one to two years. Writers should be familiar with the libel laws in their states or in the states in which the material will be disseminated. Writers can stay current on freedom of the press issues through the First Amendment Center at Vanderbilt University. Information can be accessed online at www.firstamendmentcenter.org.

Elements of Libel

Writers who know about libel law do not have to be afraid to write negative information. If they know the essential elements of libel, they won't be chilled into self-censorship.

An individual who claims he or she has been libeled usually has to prove six essential elements to win a libel case:

1. **Defamatory content.** The individual has to show the information was defamatory or bad enough to cause him or her to be held up to hatred, ridicule, or contempt.
2. **Identification.** The story clearly identifies the individual by name, in a recognizable photo, or through description from which others can reasonably identify the individual. In rare cases, courts have allowed individuals to recover when a false and defamatory statement has been made about a group to which they belong even though the statement does not single out anyone by name.
3. **Publication.** The memo was circulated, the story printed, the news release received, the report aired, or the message communicated to at least one person other than the person defamed.
4. **Falsity.** The information published was not true. In a few cases, the burden of proof falls on the media, which attempt to prove the information was true.

5. **Harm or injury.** The individual has to show harm to his or her reputation, not just emotional distress or harm. Proof of monetary loss can increase the amount of money the media will have to pay if they lose.

6. **Fault.** The individual has to prove that the media outlet or other party was at fault in presenting the libel.

To win a case, most plaintiffs have to prove all six elements. On the sixth item, court decisions have set different criteria for private citizens and public figures. In most cases, ordinary folks have to prove a standard of fault, called *negligence*, to win a libel suit. They must show that the writer failed to follow professional standards or acted unreasonably in carrying out his or her research and in writing.

Public officials including politicians, public figures including many celebrities and prominent business executives, and otherwise private individuals who prominently involve themselves in public controversies often must prove more than negligence in establishing fault when suing for libel. In most cases, they must prove the writer knew the information was false or showed reckless disregard as to whether the information was true or false. That fault standard is called *actual malice*. Actual malice came about through the 1964 *New York Times v. Sullivan* case, in which the U.S. Supreme Court ruled that a public official cannot recover damages for a defamatory falsehood relating to his or her official conduct unless he or she proves the statement was made with actual malice. Actual malice is extremely difficult to prove and is the major hurdle for most plaintiffs.

Let's say you are writing a story about your town's mayor. During interviews, an unreliable source tells you the mayor leaves town twice a year to meet his childhood sweetheart—not his wife—at a mountain cabin. If you were to write that bit of information without further investigation, you would be setting yourself up for a libel suit. Your reliance on a single, unreliable source would be reckless disregard for whether the information was true.

People are defamed, perhaps falsely, every day. Just think about the hundreds of police reports naming people who have been arrested. They can prove many of the six elements, such as publication, identification, and defamation. But would they win a libel suit? Rarely.

A Writer's Defenses in a Libel Suit

Nothing can prevent someone from filing a libel claim. But, within the legal system are defenses and privileges writers can use to avoid liability or to reduce damages. The major defenses are these:

1. **Truth.** The writer can prove the information was substantially true through reliable witnesses and documentary evidence.

2. **Qualified privilege.** Writers are protected when they report fairly and accurately matters of public concern from official government

proceedings or reports, such as meetings, trials, or an arrest report. This defense is one reason news media rely so heavily on government meetings and sessions. A witness in court can falsely accuse someone of committing murder, and you as a reporter can print the accusation. Your reporting must be accurate, fair, and complete; attributed to the government meeting or record; and not motivated by spite or ill will.

3. **Wire service defense.** Some states have adopted what is known as the wire service defense. Newspapers and other media organizations are protected if they get and reprint a story from the wire services or other reputable news agencies, such as the Associated Press. They would not be protected if they knew or had reason to know the story contained falsities or if they altered the story substantially. It would be impossible for writers to verify every fact in a wire service story. Wire service clients have to trust that the information sent to them is true.

4. **Statute of limitations.** Individuals cannot sue after a specific number of years has passed from the date of publication. The statute of limitations in libel cases varies from state to state. In some rare instances, a plaintiff might be entitled to extend the statute of limitations in his or her case, depending on the circumstances, such as re-publication of a libelous statement that would start the time frame all over again.

5. **Opinion defense.** The opinion defense protects two kinds of statements. Writers are protected if they are critiquing a performance or service as long as they give a general assessment that cannot be proved true or false. For example, a restaurant critic could probably write that the restaurant food did not taste good to her without much fear of losing a libel case. The critic could not say that the chef stole the high-quality meats for his family, leaving lesser meats for the restaurant dishes—unless that were true, of course.

In addition, many courts consider humor, satire, parody, and rhetorical hyperbole to be privileged under defamation law if the statements are so exaggerated and outlandish that reasonable people would not believe they are true. In a case in 2004, the Texas Supreme Court concluded that a satirical and humorous—but totally false—column about a local district attorney and judge could not be the subject of a defamation lawsuit because the content was not reasonably believable.

Writers should know they cannot be sued successfully for libel by the government—state, local, or federal. Writers can say the federal government or some part of it is an overgrown, bumbling bureaucratic mess without fear of being sued. But, they cannot falsely accuse the director of a government agency of misspending public funds without risking a lawsuit by the director individually.

Minimizing the Risk of Being Sued

Writers do not want to be sued for libel—even if they win. Libel suits are costly, time consuming, and emotionally draining. They can go on for years, then be dismissed. People do win libel cases against media. In 2011, a jury in Minnesota awarded $1 million to a naturopathic healer after it determined that a story aired on the local ABC affiliate contained defamatory statements. The jury ruled the station was negligent in not verifying allegations made by the client against the healer. In 1994, an attorney won a $24 million judgment against the *Philadelphia Inquirer*, which had reported he quashed a homicide investigation when he was an assistant district attorney because it involved the son of a police officer. The case took more than 10 years to conclude.

Ninety percent of libel cases filed never make it to trial. Some are dropped or dismissed, and others end up in out-of-court settlements, which cost media actual payouts and attorneys' fees. Libel suits are to be avoided. The following are some recommendations:

- Don't write lies and publish them.
- Use credible, reliable, multiple sources.
- Recognize the importance of fairness.
- Be accurate.
- Be complete.

Also, be polite if someone complains about inaccuracy. One study showed that most people who sued decided to do so after they were treated rudely when they pointed out the mistake.

Corrections

Most publications have a policy on writing corrections when errors have been made and run corrections because they believe they should correct their mistakes and not lie. Lawyers might caution against widespread use of corrections because they could be used as an admission of guilt: The correction states that the media outlet made a mistake. In most cases, the correction includes the correct title, statistic, address, or whatever was wrong and does not repeat the erroneous information. Many states have retraction or correction statutes that specify ways individuals or media can reduce or avoid damages.

Some editors say that any correction should be as prominently displayed as the error; that is, if the error is in a front-page headline, then the correction needs to be large and on the front page, not buried on page 22. Policies might require requests to be referred to editors and even lawyers. Ignoring a request could have legal consequences.

When to Publish or Not

Media often take criticism when they publish too much information. For example, critics charge that the public doesn't have a right to know the name of a crime victim, such as a rape victim. They contend that the public needs to know when and where such crimes occur, but not the victim's name or address.

Most newspapers do not publish names of rape victims. Some states have laws that allow police to withhold the name of any crime victim if the police believe publication will put the person in danger or cause him or her more harm. Some media will publish or broadcast victims' names only with their permission. Others note that the names are part of public record and if a person is charged, the name of the victim or accuser should also be included.

Media also can get into trouble when they publish quotes they believe are relevant but in reality are libelous. For example, a newspaper reporter is covering the trial of a woman charged with involuntary manslaughter in the death of her 6-month-old daughter. The reporter walks a legal tightrope if he or she includes a family member's quote that implies the woman's guilt and that was said outside the courtroom. If the family member makes the comment as part of court testimony, the reporter generally is protected against a libel suit. But if the remark is said in a parking lot while the trial is underway, the reporter and the editor must be careful not to republish any of the libelous statements. If they do, they can be sued for libel.

Most newspapers follow the policy of publishing private information if it relates to or affects public officials' or public figures' civic duties. For example, presidential candidate John Edwards of North Carolina found many aspects of his life discussed in the media after news broke that he had fathered a child with his mistress, despite his claims on national television that he had not. The case became even more emotional with the illness of his wife, Elizabeth, who subsequently died prior to Edwards going on trial for allegedly misappropriating campaign contributions to hide his mistress and child. The media believed they had a responsibility to publish the personal information about this former U.S. senator and vice presidential candidate.

Privacy

Reporters frequently face privacy dilemmas in their quest to gather and report the news. These dilemmas are both legal and ethical and provoke loud protests when the public believes the media are trampling the privacy rights of individuals in the news.

Right of Privacy

The doctrine of the right to privacy has evolved to protect individuals and to give them the right to be left alone, particularly from unwarranted publicity. Decisions from lower courts up to the U.S. Supreme Court have involved individuals' right to privacy.

Privacy law varies considerably from state to state, and writers should know what constitutes invasion of privacy in their states or in the state where articles will be published or stories aired, and whether certain torts or injuries are recognized. Writers sometimes invade individuals' privacy in one of four ways while gathering and writing information.

First, a journalist might go on private property without permission to get a story. The writer then could be sued for intruding on the property owner's privacy. But people could still sue for *intrusion* in a public place, even though people in public places have less expectation of privacy than when they are in private places. For example, some newsgathering techniques, such as secretly recording someone with high-powered audio or video equipment, could be considered highly offensive to reasonable people—even if it occurred in a public venue. A reporter, for example, could be cited for intruding either physically or with electronic equipment. In such cases, the journalist is sued for his or her means of gathering information, not for the content of what he or she wrote. The writer could be sued successfully even if no story resulted.

Second, a writer might run into trouble for *disclosure of private facts* about an individual, who could claim the facts should not have been published. The facts could be embarrassing but true. Winning such suits could be difficult, however, because of the qualified First Amendment privilege to publicize lawfully obtained information that is truthful and involves a legitimate matter of public concern. Also, courts have recognized a common law defense in such cases when information published is considered newsworthy. Also, express or implied consent from an individual allows media to publish *embarrassing or private facts* about him or her and is a defense. But that protection might not extend to people giving their consent for media to publish embarrassing facts about others or, depending on the circumstances, when minors reveal private facts about themselves to reporters.

Third, *The Associated Press Stylebook* notes that the news media "may be liable for invasion of privacy if the facts of a story are changed deliberately or recklessly, or 'fictionalized.'" An individual can sue in such *false-light* privacy cases even if the publicity seems to be positive. The bottom line is that the publicity is considered false and objectionable, even if it is not defamatory. In cases of false-light privacy, plaintiffs have to prove that the language would be highly offensive to a reasonable person and that the writer acted knowingly and in reckless disregard to the falsity and the image it would create. These privacy cases closely resemble defamation cases, and just as with libel considerations, writers must be careful to be accurate and thorough.

Media can be sued for a fourth privacy injury or tort: *appropriation*. The successful types of such cases involve the unauthorized use of a person's image or likeness for commercial purposes, such as advertising a product or service to consumers. Plaintiffs can file an appropriation suit when the content is news-editorial and not commercial, but there are no examples of plaintiffs winning those suits.

In some states, privacy law is so protective of the media that privacy is more of an ethical problem than a legal one. In dealing with the ethics of privacy, media hold politicians and public officials to a higher standard of behavior than they do for private people and are more likely to write about them, as in the Edwards' case.

Media also hold to a high standard public figures who trade on their public image or who are briefly prominent in the news. Reporters may assume a higher standard means such figures have less privacy. Other people, like you and me, garner more privacy from the media.

Public versus Private Property

Some privacy disputes hinge on whether the news took place on public or private property. For example, a holiday parade on city streets is considered a public event in a public place, and reporters—whether print or broadcast—would have access to people viewing or participating in the parade. Furthermore, people in public places should expect their actions to be public—and those actions can be reported in the media legally. In other venues, individuals have a reasonable expectation of privacy. A grandmother who attends the parade and whose photo is printed in the local newspaper probably cannot sue successfully for intrusion, an invasion of privacy. However, if a reporter used a microphone to record secretly the conversation of the woman and her daughter at the parade, that action would probably violate the individual's expectation of privacy.

Courts consider people's homes to be the most private places, so reporters need to be especially cautious when they gather news in people's homes. Places between private homes and the holiday parade sometimes are more difficult to locate on the public/private property continuum. Shopping centers and restaurants are quasi-public places. Working reporters asked to leave shopping centers must do so, no matter what the news event, or face a trespassing charge.

In all court cases concerning privacy violations, consent might be a useful media defense. The best consent defense results when a reporter is invited onto private property or told explicitly that she or he has permission to be there. Next best is implied consent, which occurs when media are on the property and are not asked to leave. The media might not be protected if a property owner says okay but the tenant feels his zone of privacy was invaded, or they might not be protected if a police officer gives the okay for media to be on private property. The Supreme Court has ruled that the Fourth Amendment rights of homeowners, protecting them from illegal searches, are violated when the police give permission.

At the same time, reporters must heed a police officer's order to leave property and can be charged with trespassing if they don't. Consider the Reporters Committee on Freedom of the Press's guidelines on access:

> *Law enforcement investigators often restrict media access to crime scenes. Journalists who defy their orders may be charged with interference, disorderly conduct or criminal trespass. If convicted, they risk fines or imprisonment.*

Copyright and Plagiarism

Copyright and plagiarism become concerns when writers take original work they did not create and use it without permission. A copyright is a right granted to the creator of an original work to control copies and reproductions of his or her work, derivatives of his or her work, and the rights to perform and display his or her work. Others who want to use the creator's work—such as reproducing copyrighted photos on a personal website—must either receive permission in writing (and usually pay for that use) or agree to a license that specifies terms of the use, such as using a computer program.

Plagiarism is an ethical issue; it occurs when a writer takes original material and claims it as his or her own. A writer can violate copyright law without plagiarizing, and a writer can plagiarize without violating laws. In both instances, however, the penalties can be severe.

Copyright: A Definition

Copyright is the legal ownership of a story, publication, book, song, online article—anything produced as original work and fixed in any tangible medium, such as a newspaper or CD-ROM. When a work is copyrighted, the owner has exclusive legal rights to its use for a limited time. Anyone can copyright material by applying to the Copyright Office in the Library of Congress. Anyone can claim a working copyright as soon as a piece is created. But without registration, an individual is limited from seeking certain damages under the federal copyright statute. Generally, an individual has ownership of the work for his or her lifetime plus 70 years for work produced after January 1, 1978. For corporations, the time is longer: 95 years from publication or 120 years from creation, whichever is shorter.

People, such as authors or songwriters, copyright their work so they can benefit solely from royalties or the money it earns. Newspaper companies copyright each issue of the newspaper, a series, or longer articles. Online sites are also copyrighted. Copyright is designed to encourage the creation of more works and to benefit the public. If authors are given exclusive rights to their works for a period of time, the assumption is that they will create more.

In most cases, anyone who wants to use any portion of copyrighted material has to get permission—and often must pay a fee to use the material. For example, a writer who is doing a book on authors of horror stories cannot quote extensively from author Stephen King's work without permission. An advertising copywriter who wants to use the music from an Andrew Lloyd Webber song must get permission. In both cases, the writers would probably pay a fee based on how much is used and in what context.

Some material can be used without permission or payment of fees. Anything produced by the federal government is considered public domain and can be used. If a private organization does a report for the government, however, that material might be copyrighted.

Generally, copyright law does not protect facts, ideas, procedures, processes, or methods of operation that might be protected under patent law. That means the fact that the United States was a British colony or the text of Einstein's theory of relativity can be used. But a historian's analysis of the British impact on the colonies or a researcher's interpretation of Einstein's work might be copyright protected.

The Copyright Act of 1976, Section 107, allows *fair use* of copyrighted material for "criticism, comment, news reporting, teaching, scholarship, or research." Fair use of material is not an infringement of copyright and does not require the permission of the copyright holder. For example, a book reviewer who wants to quote from Stephen King's novel in his review would not have to get permission to use the excerpt so long as the amount excerpted is reasonable. Because a fair or reasonable amount is debatable, a judge or jury might ultimately resolve a specific use. The factors to consider for fair use are:

1. purpose and character of the use, including whether such use is of a commercial nature or is for nonprofit educational purposes;
2. nature of the copyrighted work;
3. amount and substantiality of the portion used in relation to the copyrighted work as a whole; and
4. effect of the use on the potential market for or value of the copyrighted work.

Translated, a writer or any individual cannot use a major portion of the material without permission, particularly if its use could violate the copyright owner's rights. Some people follow a 5 percent rule; that is, no more than 5 percent of the copyrighted work can be used without permission. Some follow a 50-word rule. To avoid any question over how much is acceptable use, get permission or check out a copyright holder's stipulations. For example, some newspapers do not require permission to use 30 words or less of a story. You can find out through their permissions offices.

Getting into Trouble

With the development of the Internet and the proliferation of computers, more and more material, including software, is illegally copied. Copyright holders sue for copyright infringement and hope to collect monetary damages, including an amount for lost royalties.

Writers get into trouble with copyrights when they believe the material they are using is fair use. Sometimes they believe they are not using a substantial part or that their use is somehow exempt for educational reasons. Or they believe the work has been quoted so much that it has become part of the public domain and can be used. Some also erroneously assume that citing the author or source and giving credit protects against copyright suits.

If writers have questions about copyright infringement, they should consult an attorney familiar with copyright law. The discussion here is not to frighten students or media writers away from using material; however, all writers must be aware of laws and penalties for using others' work without proper credit or authorization.

Recent Copyright Conflicts

A major issue in copyright in recent years has been the unauthorized copying of songs and movies. Artists who made money, or royalties, from the sale and use of their CDs, DVDs, or videos began suing to keep from losing income. One issue in this conflict is who owns the rights to a piece: the artist, the company that distributed the work, or the individual who bought a copy. Ownership is important in any litigation and in determining lost revenue.

To address copyright infringement of digital media, Congress passed the Digital Millennium Copyright Act, signed into law in 1998. Among other items, the act amended copyright law to provide limits on the liability of service providers, or sites that stored information online, from the conduct of their users who might violate copyrights. If service providers are aware of violations and do nothing, they, too, can be liable.

In one case, a group of freelancers sued several publishers because they contended that the distribution of their work to online databases such as LexisNexis was not part of the rights they transferred and sold to these publications. The freelancers won. However, after the case, many publishing companies altered their freelance contracts to include these rights specifically.

Copyright will always be an issue for people who want to ensure they receive credit for and earn income from the work they produce. You as a writer must be aware of copyright laws and ensure that whatever material you use falls under fair use. If you are not sure, consult a lawyer—or find out who owns the copyright, secure permission, and pay any requested fees.

If the fee is expensive, then you will have to determine whether the material justifies the cost. Don't try to get around copyright law by paraphrasing—it will not protect you. If the paraphrase can be readily identifiable as the author's words or if the work is substantially similar, you can get into trouble.

Plagiarism: A Definition

Plagiarism occurs when people take information, copyrighted or not, and use it as their own without crediting the original source. Work such as photos, writing, cartoons, graphic art, and videos can be plagiarized. With the growth of the Internet, plagiarism occurs more easily and more often, intentionally and unintentionally. Attribution of sources can help mitigate plagiarism, but it is not always a protection against charges of plagiarism.

A veteran *Washington Post* reporter was suspended in March 2011 for plagiarizing part of a story on wounded U.S. Sen. Gabrielle Giffords.

ESPN suspended a reporter who copied part of a newspaper column into a script without attribution. A sports columnist for a college newspaper was fired after the editor learned that sections of his column were taken from a *Sports Illustrated* columnist's work. The editor wrote an open letter to the newspaper's readers to explain how the plagiarism occurred and the resulting action.

Student and novice reporters often get themselves in trouble by using information and not properly crediting the source. Sometimes the error occurs out of ignorance rather than deliberately stealing material and using it as their own. In other cases, reporters may take material because of pressures of meeting deadlines, the lack of ideas, or inadequate information through their own research.

Whatever the reason, the consequences are dire. The owners of copyrighted material can sue for copyright infringement. In most cases of plagiarism, however, writers who steal will be suspended or fired—and their credibility will be severely impaired.

How to Avoid Plagiarism

The easiest way to avoid plagiarism is to be honest. Honesty covers how writers gather information, store it, and use it. When writers gather material, they need to be meticulous in their note taking and in citations. If they download a story or a photograph from the Internet, they must ensure they have included the source; such as the organization and the URL, and date accessed. If they copy information from a book, newspaper, online site, or magazine, they must include a citation. Noting sources completely is necessary for proper attribution; that is, giving the original source credit. (Attribution is discussed in Chapter 10.) In some cases, writers will need to seek permission because the material is copyrighted, discussed earlier in this chapter.

If writers are working on a project that takes days or even months of investigation, they must be exceedingly careful when they return to notes they have not viewed in a while. When fashioning the story, they must be aware of which notes were their own and which ones came from another source. Remember from the discussion earlier in the chapter that even material that is condensed, summarized, and rewritten from another source should be attributed, as should any material used verbatim.

Of course, you should never take another person's work and claim it as your own, regardless of deadline pressure. A professor in a reporting class became suspicious when a student turned in a final project story that was much better than her other work throughout the semester. A quick check on the Internet pulled up dozens of stories on the student's topic—and blocks of copy pulled from three or four articles. The student had submitted the work as her own and violated the university's honor code in regard to plagiarism, an infraction punishable by suspension or expulsion. The outcome proved more severe than the penalty of not writing the story at all.

Keeping Up With Digital

The legal issues described so far in this chapter also apply to gathering information that will be used online. What writers post in a blog or microblog, upload on a social media site, or air in an online video is subject to copyright violation, libel, or any other legal consideration. Writers who work in a digital world have to be knowledgeable about how laws are being, or have yet to be, created in a constantly evolving environment.

Concern about journalism students who are getting more of their work published, as newsrooms cut staff, promoted the creation of the Carnegie Media Law for Journalism Schools Task Force in 2011. A group of university professors in mass communication programs and in law schools along with professionals are collaborating to develop newsgathering guidelines related to intrusion, libel, privacy, defamation, and other legal issues. The materials will include advice to journalism programs to ensure that they have clear antiplagiarism and antifabrication policies and that faculty are included in workshops on media law and related topics. More information can be accessed at jschoollegal.org.

The best tactic is to stay informed through reputable sites that track the news around freedom of the press issues, whether digital or not, and legal changes. Several organizations have easily accessible information online. They note that material provided is not to be considered as legal advice but rather a resource or guide to gathering and publishing information. In addition to specific tips and links to other pertinent sites, they keep up with news on freedom of the press and freedom of information issues. One such site is The First Amendment Center at Vanderbilt University that can be accessed at http://www.firstamendmentcenter.org/category/press. Writers should explore the site and read topics that pertain to their work, such as legal discussions around blogging.

Another starting point to get a legal overview is The Citizen Media Law Project at Harvard University. Its website notes the information is "intended for use by citizen media creators with or without formal legal training, as well as others with an interest in these issues." Users can reference the legal guide for general information or go state-by-state to find legal rights. Because of the disclaimer that the site is a work in progress, some state information is not available. Most of the advice relates to content gathering and publication regardless of the delivery—traditional or online. The creators are continuing to develop the section on unique content; that is online, and the associated risks. The site can be accessed at http://www.citmedialaw.org/legal-guide.

The Reporters Committee on Freedom of the Press has a guide for digital resources accessible at http://www.rcfp.org/browse-media-law-resources/digital-journalists-legal-guide. Information that fits content gathering in general is related to online communication. For example, in libel cases, courts will allow the unmasking of anonymous sources who post comments online if the person requesting the identity of the source has a credible reason for a libel claim and if the person revealed has the chance to defend himself or herself in court. Because online content is accessible globally, writers must be aware of where they can be sued, not just for what. At the same time that writers must be aware of actionable points, they should be aware of the protections under Section 230 of the Communications Decency Act that addresses liability when third parties post allegedly defamatory statements on the comments section of their sites. The Digital Millennium Copyright Act addresses electronic posting or use of copyrighted materials. Digital writers should monitor cases as well as federal and their states' legislation that could create new laws for this evolving area.

Ethics in Gathering Information

What is ethical in writing? Just as in any profession, ethics in journalism is a set of moral guidelines regarding what writers should and should not do when gathering and disseminating information. Journalists' ethical decisions determine their behavior.

Communicators must behave ethically. In most cases, you can't be sued for ethical violations. States don't have ethics laws, like libel laws. You can't go to jail for revealing the source of your story even after you promised you wouldn't, but you could be sued for breach of contract.

You might not be sued for libel, but you could be sued for the method you used in getting information. You won't get disbarred like a lawyer or lose your license like a physician, but if you violate your code of ethics or that of your media organization, you lose your credibility or your source—and possibly your job. The bottom line is your professional reputation.

When it comes to ethics, mass communicators often are criticized for publishing certain information and for violating individuals' privacy, as discussed earlier in the chapter. They are criticized for failing to remain objective and for stepping over the line from reporting to commenting. They are criticized for libeling by omission or not including all the information they had collected. They are also criticized for the way they collect information, from stealing to deceiving to harassing unwilling sources.

Former newspaper editor and ABC News President Michael Gartner notes that communicators have an ethical responsibility in the age of technology. "Readers don't know what is fact or fiction, what is an enhanced photo, what is slanted or straight, or what is the docu in docudrama," he cautions. "What comes out of a computer can be just as biased as what comes from a pulpit."

A veteran editor at the Portland Oregonian lost her job when she cited a family friend as the source of information on how a fellow journalist at the paper died. She didn't reveal that she was the family friend. The story became more telling when the fired editor revealed that her colleague was not driving when he had the heart attack that killed him. He had died in the apartment of a woman—not his wife—with whom he had been having sex for about a year. The editor lied to protect the man's wife, a close friend.

Online communication has created more situations where writers and media can be seen as less than ethical when they repost stories they have not vetted as to their accuracy or they rush to post or publish before information is confirmed. Communicators also must be just as careful with their language and how it is interpreted as they are with their information-gathering techniques. In some situations, writers have ethics policies to guide them; in other instances, they have to follow their own ethical compasses.

Ethics Policies

Most news organizations, advertising agencies, public relations firms, online sites, and other mass communication businesses have ethics guidelines. Writers depend on the policies from their parent companies or on professional organizations for guidance, particularly if they are freelance writers or bloggers.

Most ethics policies establish an environment in which employees are to work. Some companies use ethics contracts, and employees agree to them when they are hired. Policies outline areas where ethical considerations arise, such as conflicts of interest, confidentiality of sources, impartiality of reporting, attention to accuracy, acceptance of gifts or honoraria, and community or political involvement. Policies may be extensive, or they can be as short as one page. In the digital age, both companies and organizations are updating their guidelines to point out areas for caution. For example, the Radio Television Digital News Association has developed social media and blogging guidelines that cover issues such as truth, fairness, image, and reputation.

In addition to written ethics policies as guides, writers should have their own ethical standards. In some cases, they have to follow their instincts, rather than refer to the company policy. For example, an editor learns that the son of a popular, local minister has become an out-of-wedlock father. The editor wants you—the reporter—to write a story because the minister has attracted a large following based on his views on teen abstinence. What does your ethical compass say about pursuing this story?

Deception. In recent years, the media have been criticized more and more for using deception to get their information. Deception occurs in everything from posing as other people to giving false promises of confidentiality to using hidden cameras or tape recorders to gather news. When is deception acceptable? Most editors would agree to deception if the information cannot be obtained any other way. The information would have to be of such importance that knowingly deceiving sources is acceptable. And editors and lawyers would have to be part of the decision to resort to such newsgathering techniques.

Deceptive newsgathering is not new. One of the most well-known cases occurred in the late 1970s when the *Chicago Sun Times* set up a bar called the Mirage. Reporters posed as bartenders and waiters and used hidden cameras and tape recorders to secure evidence that building inspectors, police officers, and other city officials were soliciting bribes to allow the bar to operate. The series won several awards and was nominated for a Pulitzer Prize, the highest award in journalism. The Pulitzer Prize board rejected the series, however, because it felt that the *Sun Times'* methods were deceptive and unethical.

Students in an advanced reporting class were investigating whether citizens treated homeless people differently from others on downtown streets. As part of the story, students approached residents and asked for directions. Some students were well dressed and neat in appearance; others wore disheveled clothes and had not shaved or combed their hair. The students found significant differences in residents' demeanor and interaction toward students who were neat and those who were not. They incorporated the reactions into their stories.

Such investigation, sometimes called participant observation, can produce information that adds to a story. However, reporters should not inject themselves into a situation in a way that could change the outcome of the story.

Deception was at the heart of the highly visible ABC/Food Lion case in 1992 in which ABC reporters applied for jobs at a Food Lion store to check out complaints about how Food Lion repackaged meats for sale. The reporters used false information on their applications and omitted the fact that they were journalists. They used hidden cameras to film their work that subsequently was aired on ABC's *Prime Time Live.*

The reports alleged that Food Lion workers repackaged outdated meats, bleached meats, and committed other offenses. Food Lion executives sued, not for libel or falsity in the reports themselves, but for fraud, trespassing, and breach of loyalty. Initially, a North Carolina jury awarded Food Lion $5.5 million, but on appeal, the amount was cut to only $2. Despite the ultimate reduction in a monetary settlement, reporters' credibility had been damaged and their behavior hanged in the public eye.

Reporters should always consult their editors when they plan to use deception or any other method to get information. They should determine that they have exhausted all other means and that the benefit of going undercover outweighs any negative impact. When the stories are published, editors should be forthcoming in letting audiences know how the information was gathered and why such methods were used.

The *San Jose Mercury News* fired a reporter who used his status as a graduate student at the University of Iowa to obtain information from the university archives and use it in a story. The article revealed that university researchers had used children from an orphanage in a project on stuttering—actually turning the children into stutterers. The archives are open only to students, staff, and faculty members, and anyone using the archives must sign a form that the use is for research only. The reporter got the information a month before he began his internship at the newspaper—and wrote on the form that he was a graduate student in psychology when he really was a student in journalism.

Such cases show that individuals or companies are shifting from suing for libel to acting on their concerns with methods used to gather information.

Fabrication.   The bottom line: Reporters do not make up information or people or attribute made-up quotes to individuals. Some journalism teachers boil that down even more simply: Don't lie. But in some cases, a tiny alteration in a quote or description that makes it through the editing process can lead writers of any experience level to even greater fabrication.

A *Chicago Sun-Times* critic was fired in 2011 when she fabricated parts of her review of a Glee Live! concert. She had left the concert early when her children became ill and did not see the entire program, but included description anyway.

Taking a supposed shortcut to producing a weekly poll cost two young reporters at *The Reidsville* (N.C.) *Review* their jobs. Rather than finding a citizen and actually asking the question, the reporters used mug shots of college friends posted on Facebook and made up quotes. The fabrication surfaced when a sister publication owned by the same media group reported the story. The two reporters were fired, and the editor resigned.

Any writer who took a journalism ethics course can cite the cases of Jayson Blair of *The New York Times* and Jack Kelley of *USA Today*—and the outcome—after editors discovered parts of their stories had been fabricated. In another case, the U.S. Supreme Court upheld a false light invasion of privacy verdict against a newspaper whose reporter made up portions of a story about a woman whose husband had been killed in a bridge collapse. The court concluded that the evidence was sufficient to establish actual malice in the case.

Fabrication can also relate to information that is not included and makes a story incomplete. A veteran NBC producer in Miami, Florida, was fired for a report that edited out part of the 911 call made by George Zimmerman, who was later charged with shooting Trayvon Martin. The omission in the story meant lack of context that related to Zimmerman's state of mind.

Confidential Sources.   When gathering information, sometimes reporters are asked to protect the identity of a source. Some media do not allow unnamed sources to be quoted in stories; others require editors to know the source's name. Media might have policies regarding anonymous sources, but often reporters have difficulty getting information if sources are identified. *The Washington Post's* ombudsman addressed that issue, noting "anonymity, granted judiciously, can benefit readers. Sources often require confidentiality to disclose corruption or policy blunders ... but by causally agreeing to conceal the identities of those who provide noncritical information, *The Post* erodes its credibility and perpetuates Washington's insidious culture of anonymity."

The Associated Press and the Associated Press Managing Editors Association jointly surveyed U.S. newspapers about their policies on anonymous sources and learned that one in four of the 419 newspapers that responded never allowed reporters to quote anonymous sources. Others had specific policies.

Journalists know that if they promise confidentiality to a source and then break it, they damage their reputation. In one case, the U.S. Supreme Court concluded that the First Amendment did not prevent a source from recovering damages from newspapers that had breached promises of confidentiality. The source had lost his job after the newspapers published articles identifying him as having notified the newspapers about negative court documents regarding a political candidate. This type of action is not available to confidential sources when reporters are compelled by a court to identify their sources in a criminal or civil proceeding, even though many journalists refuse to testify under such circumstances and instead face possible contempt sanctions, including fines and even jail time.

The most visible case in recent years of a journalist going to jail to protect a source occurred when *New York Times* reporter Judith Miller refused to name who revealed to her the identity of a CIA agent. Miller never wrote a story, but she still refused to identify her source. After months of legal sparring, a judge sentenced her to four months in prison. After spending 85 days in jail, Miller was released when her source, I. Lewis "Scooter" Libby, former chief of staff for then Vice President Dick Cheney, signed a waiver of confidentiality. Miller then testified before a grand jury investigating who leaked the identity of the undercover CIA operative, Valerie Plame.

While judges invoke the Sixth Amendment—the right to a speedy trial—as the reason journalists must comply with their orders to testify or to turn over notes and other materials, journalists contend that the free flow of information will be jeopardized if they cannot offer sources anonymity. Forty states and the District of Columbia have shield laws that protect journalists from naming sources in a criminal case or judicial proceeding. Laws also establish who is defined as a journalist, what kinds of information the privilege protects, and when the privilege is waived. These laws offer protection only in the respective state courts. Reporters should always know their state laws and be aware of changes as well as the policy of their publications or employers in protecting sources. No federal shield law exists, although bills have been introduced before Congress.

More recently, writers have been concerned about how to protect sources' confidentiality when they have kept their notes on their computers. The computer notes can be subpoenaed. Even if the notes are deleted, they could be recoverable. Even a writer's phone records could be subpoenaed and checked to determine whom the reporter had called, as were Judith Miller's phone records. The advantages of technology can also affect a writer's ability to get information from confidential sources, who might not feel so protected.

Other Dilemmas.   Other ethical issues arise in information gathering, particularly in reporters' and editors' discussions about whether a story warrants media attention. You suspect a public official is having extramarital relations, so you stake out her house and discover she spent the night in an apartment of a man, not her partner. Do you write the story? You learn an antiabortion rights activist had an abortion as a 15-year-old. Do you include that information in a story when she leads an antiabortion protest?

Public officials' behavior has been the focus of many news stories, such as a congressman sending naked photos via Twitter. Is reporting such behavior unethical? Journalists would cry no; they are reporting the news. The public outcry comes when the stories report and re-report lurid and seemingly minor details. Audiences become saturated. The answers to such publication issues have to be reached case by case, medium by medium. What one publication decides to print, another may refuse to air.

In addition, reporters must use their judgment when gathering information. Their behavior might prove illegal and could generate ethical questions. Such questioning occurred when *The Miami Herald* fired long-time metro columnist Jim DeFede for tape-recording a conversation with Arthur E. Teele Jr., a former city commissioner, shortly before he committed suicide. The local state's attorney charged DeFede with violating the state law making it illegal to tape record individuals without their knowledge. The case was later dismissed.

But DeFede lost his job for breaking the law and because the paper's editors felt the reporter had acted unethically by not telling Teele he was being recorded. Editors said the taping could damage sources' trust in reporters. Despite management's position, DeFede's firing became the topic of other media articles and generated criticism and unhappiness among *Herald* staff. Some might question whether DeFede should have intervened upon hearing the emotion in Teele's voice, which he later said was unusual in a man he had covered for 14 years. Reporters generally are observers rather than participants in events. They should choose not to become part of the story.

In covering any natural disaster or other event that results in property destruction, injuries, or deaths, reporters must take care in showing their sadness at such losses. Reporters are human beings and must be aware that their emotions could influence readers and viewers.

A good policy is to gather news in a manner that allows the public focus to go where it should—to the wrongdoing you are reporting, advises Professor Cathy Packer at the University of North Carolina at Chapel Hill. Unethical and illegal newsgathering techniques shift the public focus to the media, and the bad guys walk away looking like victims, she notes.

In a digital world, especially with 24/7 news cycles or bloggers' need to create content, writers can fall into the trap of repeating or reposting what appears to be unusual and credible information. A number of media got caught when they reported the death of a chimpanzee described as Cheetah, a co-star in Tarzan films with actor Johnny Weismuller. *The Tampa Tribune* first reported the story because the death occurred in a primate center on the Gulf Coast. The Associated Press picked up the story, which was carried in some form by media ranging from MSNBC.com to the *London Telegraph*. When some questioned the "facts" of the story, many were shown to be unlikely. The need to fill a news hole and the emotional appeal of an animal and his tie to a well-known star caused re-publication of a story lacking in credibility.

Writers searching for information also must be circumspect about using social media sites to find content. People who post photos and other information on sites such as Facebook do so with an expectation of privacy. In some cases, material on such sites can provide context, such as conversations on MySpace that tell a teenager's thoughts prior to committing suicide. Writers must determine that such information is reliable and if there is a compelling reason to use it.

Without circumspect decision making and honesty with audiences, any medium—and the writer—will lose credibility. When credibility is lost, so are audiences.

Aspiring reporters and writers should be honest, ethical, and legal in information gathering. Methods of reporting should be unquestionable. Information should be accurate. Editors should always know a writer's source and serve as backup in the event someone has doubts about a source's or the writer's credibility. Despite the haste to repost, retweet, or republish, care must be taken to check the authenticity of the source to avoid spreading inaccuracies or libelous information.

Exercises

1. Can you lawfully use the following information in a story or blog? Explain your reasoning and any defenses you could use if you were sued for libel.

   a. You are doing a story on drug use in the county. A police source tells you that a certain spot on Main Street, a bench outside Walton's restaurant, is a known place for drug deals.

   b. You are covering a case about a man charged with involuntary manslaughter in a car accident that killed two teenagers. You do a search using public records of prior convictions and find he has two for careless and reckless driving in another state.

   c. A state senator running for re-election tells you that her opponent is a tax evader who has not paid any state in come taxes in the last five years.

   d. You are covering the performance of Alice Batar, a local resident who has begun a successful acting career. You have been assigned to write a review of her performance in the community theater's production of *Who's Afraid of Virginia Woolf?* Prior to the performance, you overhear two people next to you talking about Batar's latest divorce and what one called "a really pathetic settlement on her part."

e. You are to write a story about the chancellor of your university. You interview a faculty member who says the chancellor "runs off at the mouth and doesn't pay enough attention to faculty members' needs."

2. Write a two-page report on plagiarism, using at least three sources. Include a fellow classmate's views on plagiarism. Include at least one example other than what is in this chapter. Include your views on plagiarism as an ethical issue and what the consequences should be for a reporter who plagiarizes. Discuss how digital media increase the risk of material being plagiarized.

3. Go online and find the site for your hometown newspaper. See if you can find on the site the newspaper's code of ethics. If not, email the editor and find out if the newspaper has a written code or how ethical behavior is conveyed to the staff. Ask if the code includes any guidelines in regard to social media. Bring in the code or information to share with class members.

4. Look at codes of ethics from professional organizations such as the American Society of News Editors, the American Advertising Federation, Public Relations Society of America, and others. Compare the issues that each covers as ethical considerations, including use of social and other digital media.

5. Consider the following scenarios. Discuss in class how you would behave in each situation and whether you would use the information gathered.

a. You are a state legislative reporter. A number of legislators meet every Thursday night for dinner at a local restaurant. One of the legislators whom you cover on a regular basis invites you to come along one night. Do you go?

b. You are interviewing the director of the local community theater for a story on the upcoming season. You are having lunch together at a local restaurant. At the end of the meal and interview, the director picks up the tab and goes to pay for both of you. Your portion of the bill is $6.50 to $11.50. What do you do?

c. You suspect a local real estate company is discriminating against Hispanic tenants when it comes to rental housing. Your editor suggests that you and another reporter, who is Hispanic, pose as a couple and try to rent a house from the company. What should you do?

d. You cover the financial industry as a business reporter. At the end of an interview on mortgage rates, the banker says to contact him whenever you are ready to buy a house and he'll make sure you get a really good interest rate. Do you call him when you are mortgage hunting?

References _____

"AP Fires Reporter after Source Query," Yahoo! News. http://story.news.yahoo.com/news?tmpl5story2&cid1519&u5ap2002916/ap_on_re_us/reporter_dismis. Accessed September 17, 2002,

"Appeals Court Sides with ABC in Food Lion Lawsuit." ABCNews.com, October 20, 1999. http://abcnews.go.com/sections/us/DailyNews/foodlion 991020.html.

Cantrell v. Forest City Publishing Co., 419 U.S. 245 (1974).

Christian, Darrell, Jacobsen, Sally, and Minthron, David. *The Associated Press Stylebook and Briefing on Media Law*. New York: The Associated Press, 2012.

Cohen v. Cowles Media Co., 501 U.S. 693 (1991).

Copyright Act of 1976, Section 107. http://www.loc.gov/copyright/title17/.

"Ex-commissioner kills self in newspaper lobby." CNN.com. www.cnn.com/2005/US/07/28/miami.teele.ap/index.html. Accessed July 28, 2005.

Fost, Don. "Mercury News Case Stirs Debate over Ethics of Deception." *San Francisco Chronicle*, August 8, 2001. Ethics: Social Media and Blogging Guidelines, Radio Television Digital News Association, http://www.rtdna.org/pages/media_items/social-media-and-blogging-guidelines1915.php?g=37?id=1915.

Freedom of the Press Research Articles, The First Amendment Center. http://www.firstamendmentcenter.org/category/press. Accessed June 8, 2012.

Friedman, Barbara, and Goldman, Meredith. "When reporters go into MySpace." *The News & Observer*, Dec. 31, 2007.

Gartner, Michael. Keynote address, Association for Education in Journalism and Mass Communication. Washington, DC, August 5, 2001. Legal Guide, Citizen Media Project. http://www.citmedialaw.org/legal-guide. Accessed June 8, 2012.

Legal Guide for Digital Journalists, Reporters Committee for Freedom of the Press. http://www.rcfp.org/browse-media-law-resources/digital-journalists-legal-guide. Accessed June 8, 2012.

"Minn. Station Liable for $1 million in defamation suit." Reporters Committee for Freedom of the Press. http://www.rcfp.org/browse-media-law-resources/news/minn-tv-station-liable-1-million-defamation-suit. Accessed June 8, 2012.

"Police press guidelines." The First Amendment Handbook, Reporters Committee for Freedom of the Press. http://www.rcfp.org/first-amendment-handbook/police-press-guidelines-access-public-buildings-and-schools.

New Times, Inc. v. Isaaks, 146. W. 3d 144 (Texas 2004).

New York Times Co. v. Tasini, 535 U.S. 483 (2001).

"The Oregonian Fires Editor Who Provided False Information about the Death of Bob Caldwell, the Paper's Editorial Page Editor." *Willamette Week*, March 15, 2012.

Packer, Cathy. Interview, School of Journalism and Mass Communication, September 4, 2008.

"Poll finds many newspapers bar anonymous sourcing." The Associated Press, as reported on the website of The First Amendment Center. http://www.firstamendmentcenter.org/poll-finds-many-newspapers-bar-anonymous-sourcing. Accessed June 8, 2012.

Romensko, Jim. "Sun-Times critic fired after leaving Glee Live! early, mentioning song that wasn't performed." June 10, 2011. http://www.poynter.org/latest-news/mediawire/135477/sun-times-reporter-fired-after-leaving-glee-live-show-early-mentioning-song-that-wasnt-performed/. Accessed June 8, 2012.

Shafer, Jack. "Jungle fever clouds chimp obituary." Reuters, December. 28, 2011.

Strouse, Chuck. "The Agony of DeFede." Newtimes.com. www.newtimesbpb.com/Issues/2005-09-15/ news/news2.html. Accessed September 18, 2005. news/news2.html. Accessed September 18, 2005.

Tenore, Mallory Jean. "Roundup of plagiarism & fabrication cases." http://www.poynter.org/latest-news/everyday-ethics/136280/roundup-of-plagiarism-fabrication-cases-in-journalism/. Accessed June 8, 2012.

13

Broadcast Media

Broadcast writing requires requires the basic writing skills discussed in earlier chapters. Broadcast messages must be concise, clear, and simple so that audiences can understand the information.

Broadcast writing differs in some respects from writing for print. First, it differs in what it requires of the audience. Tuning in to radio, for example, audiences have to rely on careful listening. Radio writing has to be simple and specific.

Writing for television news must also capture attention quickly because TV messages can breeze by passive audiences who do not rewind or re-read items of interest. That has changed for more and more Americans who are watching video either online or with DVR devices, where they can replay segments they missed or need to see again for context. While watching the saved broadcasts later, viewers can also bypass ads. Typically still have only one chance to get audience attention.

While broadcast writers must use good writing skills, they must also look beyond the written word. They must find audio and video content that will attract audiences and enhance the message.

In this chapter, you will learn

- how print and broadcast writing are alike and how they differ,
- the essential qualities of effective broadcast writing, and
- basic writing techniques for broadcast media.

The Medium Changes the Style

Broadcast journalists learn early that just reading stories aloud can be dull. They realize that broadcast media require sound, voices, or visuals. While print media use photographs to enhance their stories, broadcast messages are best when voices accompany sounds and images from real life. For example, a radio reporter on the campaign trail can use actual comments from politicians along with the sounds of a cheering crowd. The sounds serve two purposes: They attract audience attention, and they add depth to the report. Audio and visual content complement writing and make any report come alive by appealing to the audience's senses, as online writers have discovered.

Behind every print and online writer are editors and production staff to get the story from the computer to the printed page or online site. In broadcast, the supporting cast is more visible. For a newscast, a central anchorperson or anchor group moderates the newscast, introducing the work of individual reporters. A producer determines the story order, edits the writing, and puts the show together.

Also, broadcast reporters create a message with a careful mix of recordings: interviews with experts or bystanders, background or scenic information (usually with a "voiceover" of the reporter relating information), and a reporter standing and relaying information. The reporter's identity and location close out the piece. For TV reporters, their story might become a package of several interviews and scenes; in radio, the equivalent is a wrap, short for "wraparound."

In today's media environment, many people expect to see declining interest in radio and television. But 2012 statistics from Forbes.com show that television reaches 88 percent of Americans every day, making television the largest audience for media today. The Internet reaches 73 percent of Americans daily (defined as at least 15 minutes of being online), while radio reaches 58 percent. Newspapers daily reach some 38 percent of people in the United States. In-car listening to radio of all kinds, including listening to podcasts of broadcasts, is on the rise, particularly in the morning and evening commute time and when people exercise.

This increase reflects what Forbes.com calls "…the reality of American workers' gradually longer commutes, increasing media options, and more mobile lifestyle."

Television's broad audiences, wide-ranging content, and access to visuals contrast sharply with radio's focus on news, weather, traffic, and sports. Radio also is set apart by the tendency of its audiences to tune in while they are busy with some other primary activity, most common. Writing for both television and radio must take into account preoccupied and even passive audiences.

Anyone writing for radio or television also has to be aware that audio or video can be live streamed on websites; picked up and repurposed, such as part of a YouTube video; or rebroadcast at a later date, particularly via digital recording equipment. The life of any piece will be much longer than the first 30 seconds in which it was aired.

Print versus Broadcast Copy

A well-written broadcast story has much in common with any good print or online story. In all three types, writers work to focus the audience's attention on news values. All insist on accuracy and clarity; however, differences in technologies and audiences result in different formats and approaches.

Similarities

The Writing Process.   The skills learned in the writing process discussed in Chapter 1 apply to broadcast writers. Broadcast reporters start with an idea for a news package, then work with a producer. They do research and interviews, then produce copy that is well written and relevant to their audiences. Outlining is critical for broadcast writers, who must write then shoot or record package materials before they leave the scene of an event. They must collect a variety of sounds or images to illustrate the news as well as quotes. Once editing begins, they usually don't have time to go back and catch additional sources or visuals before deadline.

News Values.   All media writing must include some news values from among those discussed in Chapter 5: prominence, timeliness, proximity, impact, magnitude, conflict, oddity, and emotional impact. Broadcast writing is no exception. Timeliness is the defining news value for broadcast media, which makes broadcast more similar to online than print in this regard. Radio and television, because of their ability to broadcast live, can get information out to audiences in real time as news events actually occur. Online news coverage can also be done in real time and continually updated. Immediacy is a key factor in the success of broadcast news. In radio and television, news that happened in the morning might be revised, refreshed, or even replaced in the afternoon, just as online sites can update stories as events unfold. Consider how immediate and new information, such as the approach of a hurricane, can be updated by the minute on broadcast media, while print outlets are limited to overall summaries of the previous day's events. In weather disasters, print, broadcast, and online coverage would focus on the news values of impact, magnitude, and emotion.

Clear, Concise Writing.   Particularly critical in broadcast writing are the rules of using short sentences, active voice, and short words; avoiding jargon and technical language; cutting wordiness; and getting to the point quickly. Broadcast stories generally are shorter than those in print. A print story may use 250 to 500 words to tell about an event. A broadcast report might have 15 to 30 seconds or 30 to 75 words. Every word takes time away from other reports. In addition, listeners and viewers who don't understand jargon or complicated language usually don't have the chance to go back and replay the words. Broadcast stories must be clear to the entire audience on the first pass.

Research. Like print writers, broadcast writers develop sources and do research and interviews. Research can be difficult when time is limited. Broadcast reporters must be generalists and cover a variety of topics even within a single day. Many have multiple beats. They might attend the governor's news conference in the morning and cover a hotel fire that same afternoon. In trying to stay informed, broadcast reporters use the same library and online resources as their print colleagues. Some broadcast reporters have the opportunity for in-depth research when they specialize in a particular area or beat, such as medicine or business.

Differences

Deadlines. Broadcast reporters often work under multiple, tight deadlines. Traditionally, print reporters had one or two deadlines each day, but today's print writers also post versions of their stories online, meeting many deadlines every day. For broadcasts, deadlines come early and often. Newscasts appear at morning, noon, evening, and late night, with updates in between. A single reporter might be developing several stories for any single broadcast. Once a story is aired, it might need to be reviewed and refreshed prior to the next news show. In addition, deadlines might be more frequent if reporters are also writing news for the company's online site.

Writing Structure. Because radio and television stories are shorter than print or online versions, they must be understood immediately. Most broadcast messages have only one chance to be heard, so they must make it through the clutter to reach audiences immediately. Effective communicators know that radio and television audiences are doing other things: driving, working, exercising, caring for kids, cooking, cleaning, and commuting.

To meet their special challenges with active audiences, broadcast writers use a slight variation of the inverted pyramid style. They typically begin any news item with a hook or headline that will grab listeners or viewers. Then they give the actual lead to the story, setting up some context and giving essential information. Next comes a more detailed explanation, followed by a wrap-up that may mention impact or future possibilities.

Broadcast writers also use a *diamond structure*, in which they start with a specific person or example, then broaden the story to explore the bigger picture. Then they return to the original person or example to close out the story. The example is similar to the use of anecdotal leads discussed in Chapter 5.

Style. Broadcast writers, like many online writers, use a more conversational style. Often the style is narrative, focusing on people and events—more like telling a story to a friend. Words and phrases are less formal and more colloquial, similar to the style found in many blogs. A reporter might use contractions or colloquialisms in sentences or follow specific style, such as writing out numbers smaller than two digits or larger than three, as explained later in this chapter.

Format.   Because broadcast media require sounds and images, they use a specific writing format that differs from how print reporters type their stories. All journalists, both print and broadcast, double-space their copy, but broadcast reporters must leave space for cues and instructions indicating when audio and visual elements are to be added.

Radio reports are typed across the page, just as print stories are, but they include notes on what prerecorded elements are to be inserted between blocks of copy that will be read aloud. In television reports, copy that will be heard fills the right side of the page; cues for the technical members of the crew appear in the left column. Some broadcast writers type their copy all in capital letters, but others prefer uppercase and lowercase. In broadcast writing, paragraphs are not split between pages, and each new story begins on a new page. Specific broadcast style rules on how to use abbreviations, numbers, and attributions are explained later in this chapter.

The Differences in Practice

A radio reporter and a print journalist are rewriting wire service copy for their respective media. How would their leads look, based on the differences between broadcast and print writing? Let's see. The print journalist writes:

> GREENSBORO, N.C.—Jurors continued to deliberate in the campaign finance trial of former presidential candidate John Edwards, asking to review evidence but giving no indication of how close they might be to a verdict.

The broadcast journalist writes:

> Jurors in Greensboro, North Carolina, have yet to reach a verdict in the John Edwards campaign finance trial.

The broadcast writer needs no dateline and names the location—Greensboro—as context for listeners and viewers.

Consider two other examples:

> A SURVEY REPORTS THAT ALL WOMEN HAVE SIMILAR CONCERNS.

> WOMEN ARE MOST CONCERNED ABOUT BALANCING HOME AND JOB, HEALTH INSURANCE, AND STRESS, ACCORDING TO A SURVEY RELEASED TODAY.

Which is the broadcast lead? The first one is. It is short and uses attribution at the beginning to establish the source immediately. It also establishes a context for the story to follow.

Leads and Structure

No matter where an electronic journalist works, the need for clear, concise writing is essential. Writing for broadcast means writing for the ear by using short sentences, conversational speech, subject–verb–object sentence order, clear and understandable copy, and smooth, clear transitions between thoughts. Let's look at producing broadcast copy, following these guidelines.

Broadcast Leads

A broadcast lead is short and gives basic information. It should be written in present or future tense to set the tone of breaking news. The lead may be catchy and even entertaining. It causes the audience to stop and listen to the story. As noted earlier in the chapter, the lead generally establishes a context for the story. Such leads ensure specific information will follow:

THIRTEEN PEOPLE GET RICH IN INDIANA.

TOMORROW THE MAYOR WILL ANNOUNCE THAT NEW JOBS ARE COMING TO THE AREA.

The context is clear in each example. The first story will be about Powerball lottery winners. The second lead sets up audiences for a story on economics, with information about how many and what kinds of jobs and the name of the company. In both instances, the leads are much shorter than in print.

Broadcast writers who cover continuing or recurring stories try to find leads that will pique audience attention and interest in just a few words:

A SUCCESSFUL ROCKET LAUNCH COULD MEAN A NEW ERA IN SPACE FLIGHT.

A SURPRISE WITNESS MAY TESTIFY BEFORE CONGRESS TODAY IN THE PLANNED PARENTHOOD INVESTIGATION.

WHAT'S UP IN THE STOCK MARKET TODAY?

Broadcast Structure in the Message

Again, the structure of any electronic message must appeal to the audience's ear. The message must be clear and direct. Sentences are short and written primarily in subject–verb–object order. Language must be simple. The writer develops the story using the three-part format: context, explanation, and effect. This format sets out the context or the reason the story is being written. It might focus on a particular news value or the latest information—that is, timeliness. The second part is explanation, in which listeners or viewers get more information, whether it is background, a historical perspective, or more details of the current situation. Then the writer wraps up with the effect, generally with a look to the future or the impact of the event. Specific examples are shown under Broadcast Formats later in this chapter.

Writing Guidelines

Basic writing principles apply for broadcast stories. Because timeliness is crucial to electronic media, writers should open their stories in the present tense, explaining the latest developments. Even if they have to shift to past tense later in the story, present tense is preferable in the lead.

Avoid:

A CONVICTED RAPIST WAS EXECUTED TODAY AFTER MONTHS OF APPEALS FAILED.

Prefer:

A CONVICTED RAPIST DIES AFTER MONTHS OF APPEALS.

Avoid:

SIXTEEN WINNERS WERE DECLARED IN THE LONG-AWAITED STATE LOTTERY.

Prefer:

SIXTEEN PEOPLE ARE WINNERS IN THE LONG-AWAITED STATE LOTTERY.

Some other writing rules to follow:

▪ Introduce unfamiliar people before using their names. Describe people in terms of employment, life's work, or relevance to the story. Then name them, as in "sprinter John Jones" or "angry ticketholder Billy Cupp." Only the instantly recognizable names of widely known people should be used without prior explanation.

A ROCKLAND SECOND-GRADE TEACHER IS THE NATION'S TEACHER OF THE YEAR

RONNIE MILLER, ...

Or

ROCKLAND MAYOR JOAN TILLIS IS IN GOOD CONDITION AFTER BACK SURGERY.

■ Avoid tongue twisters that can cause problems when reports are read on air. Always read copy aloud before it is broadcast. "The clandestine clan committed continual crimes" or "the player's black plastic pants" may look clever on paper, but it may be difficult for an announcer to enunciate.

■ Use action verbs. Remember that verbs can paint pictures, an especially important aspect of radio reports. "Race car driver Rusty Wallace roars to victory" has more life than "Race car driver Rusty Wallace wins."

■ Use quotes sparingly. Paraphrased statements are more easily understood. If a quote is particularly good, use it live from the source. Make sure the writing does not imply the statement is from the reporter or newscaster. Direct quotes that use "I" or "we" can cause such confusion. Consider this quote: "Chamber of Commerce president David Fall says, 'I have doubts about the town's development practices.'" Listeners who miss the attribution may infer the reporter is doubtful. Instead, write: "Chamber of Commerce President David Fall says he has doubts about the town's development practices."

■ Put attribution at the beginning of a quotation: "Medical experts say the new treatment may cause cancer cells to die." If you must use a direct quote, try "Johnson said in his own words, 'The new treatment may cause cancer cells to die.'"

■ Avoid writing that uses a lot of punctuation. Punctuation—even a question mark—cannot be heard. Listeners may miss the inflection.

■ Avoid long introductory clauses, like this one: "While doing a routine maintenance check at the school, a plumber found...." Instead write: "A plumber found the defect while doing a routine maintenance check at the school".

■ Avoid separating subjects and verbs, particularly with phrases. "Marian Johnson, a director for the Rockland Little Theater, will leave her job in two weeks" becomes "Rockland's Little Theater director will leave her job within two weeks. Marian Johnson...." Don't leave verbs at the end of the sentence. Follow subject–verb–object order as much as possible.

■ Break up lengthy series of modifiers and adjectives, such as this one: "Police described the man as blond, long-haired, blue-eyed, and five-feet, six-inches tall." Rather, write: "Police say the suspect has long blond hair and blue eyes. They also say he is about five feet, six inches tall."

■ Avoid negatives. A listener might miss the negative words "no" and "not" in a broadcast and thereby be misinformed. Use alternatives: "Police could find no motive for the shootings" can be translated "Police say the motive for the shootings is unknown."

■ If your report runs long, say more than 30 seconds, look for ways to unify the story. Repetition of key words is one way to help listeners and viewers follow along.

Style in Copy

In Chapter 3, we looked at copyediting style. Broadcast writers also follow style rules for preparing copy:

- In the case of a word that might be mispronounced, spell it phonetically, just as you would with complicated names. For example, if you are reporting about house paint containing lead, write it "led." Even though it is misspelled, you won't have to worry about an anchor reading "lead" as "leed" paint.

- If a name is difficult, write it out phonetically. Anchors and reporters can stumble in stating people's names. Sound it out. For example, names with "ei" or "ie" can be confusing, such as Janice Weinberger. Write out "Wine Burger" so the anchor will use a long "i" pronunciation. For Barack Obama's middle name, Hussein, the pronunciation spelling is "Who Sayn." The same applies to city and state names. For example, Waukesha, Wisconsin, is pronounced WAH (accent on this syllable)-keh-shaw. An inexperienced broadcast reporter referred to the city as Wau-KEE-shaw.

- Put titles before names and keep them short. Use "former Florida Governor Jeb Bush" rather than "Jeb Bush, the former governor of Florida." A university vice chancellor for institutional research services becomes "a university administrator." You can use a descriptive title if audiences easily identify a person that way, such as "evangelist Billy Graham" or "singer Katy Perry."

- Use people's names the way they are commonly cited. Former President Clinton is known as Bill Clinton, not William Clinton. Former Vice President Al Gore is rarely called Albert Gore, Jr.

- Write out single-digit numbers. Use numerals for two- and three-digit numbers. Return to words for thousand, million, and so forth; write out numbers between zero and nine. Use numerals for 10 through 999. Above 999, you can combine numerals and words. For example, write "nine thousand 45," "10 thousand 200," and "22 billion."

- Round off numbers. Say "more than 10 thousand" rather than "10 thousand 232 subscribers."

- Write out amounts for dollars and cents, percent, and fractions:

GASOLINE PRICES ARE THREE TO FOUR CENTS A GALLON HIGHER.

THREE-FOURTHS OF TOWN RESIDENTS SAY THEY ARE PLEASED WITH THE MAYOR'S PERFORMANCE.

ABOUT FIFTY-FIVE PERCENT OF WHAT YOU READ, YOU REMEMBER.

- Use numerals for phone numbers and years: 919-555-1212, 1999, or 1865.
- Keep statistics to a minimum. Put them in a format people will understand. If a poll says 67 percent of the state's residents support the legislature's plan to increase tourism, report that "two out of three state residents say they favor the legislature's plan to increase tourism."
- Write out Roman numerals. Write out "Harry Holland the third," rather than "Harry Holland III," or "Queen Elizabeth the second," not "Queen Elizabeth II."
- Avoid acronyms on first reference unless an organization is better known by its initials than by its full name, such as E-S-P-N, F-B-I, and N-C-A-A. Insert hyphens between letters if they are to be read individually. Omit hyphens if the acronym is to be read as a word, such as in FEMA. For local or state law enforcement, it is better just to say police or law officials on subsequent references.

Broadcast Formats

A major difference between print and broadcast media is the format for the final message, as noted earlier in the chapter. Broadcast media use a script format that indicates the text along with the sound bites or visuals. Time is critical in broadcast writing. Scripts indicate how long the total story runs plus the length of specific segments within the story. Radio reports are typed across the page, much like a print story, with audio cues.

In television reports, the cues on the left side of the page give information to the director or editor, such as the length, points where interview quotes would be used, or a voiceover that is read by the anchor to begin or end the piece.

When the story text is typed, sometimes all capital letters are used. That helps clarify writing where a lowercase "l" might resemble a capital "I" and create problems for announcers. Capital letters are also easier to read from a distance. But some broadcaster are moving to using uppercase and lowercase letters.

When students study broadcast journalism, they learn the codes and copy preparation style early on. A complete radio piece might seem longer than a story typed for print or online because cues take up space on the left side of the page. The goal is to make the copy legible for the anchor and the reporter who read from the copy.

You can see the difference in format in the radio and television scripts for the same story below. Professor Jim Hefner at the University of North Carolina at Chapel Hill uses the examples in an audio-video reporting course. The subject of the story appears at the top left along with the reporter's name and date. In both examples, the cues are evident. "TRT" refers to the total run time or length of the story. "Track" refers to the reporter's voice recorded, and "bite" is a sound bite or short audio or video piece. "On Cam" indicates where the anchor is reading in front of the camera. First is the radio script.

Tuition to Increase
Joe Smith
Date:
TRT: 1:07

Lead:

UNC undergraduates facing a jump in tuition and fees next year.
Not much doubt about it.
The only question?
How much?
Joe Smith talked with one student who says she can't take much more.

<<Track One: 12>>

Mary Miller's a sophomore from Lenoir.
Her parents are laid-off furniture workers.
They're on unemployment.
Mary *has* student loans.
And she *works* part time.
Still, she struggles.
And things are about to get tougher.

<<Miller Bite: 04>>

"This is death by a thousand cuts."

<<Track Two: 10>>

Mary Miller has company.
Tuition is going up for UNC's some 18 thousand
undergraduate students.
At least, that's what it sounds like.
University Board of Trustees Chairman Roger Perry.

<<Perry Bite: 08>>

**"The cost of education is getting higher and higher. If we're going to continue
to give our students the quality of education they deserve, tuition is going to have
to go up."**

<<Track Three: 22>>

Tuition remained flat this year for in-state students.
That, thanks to the state general assembly, which gave the university a 15 percent
budget increase.
But cuts are predicted for the coming year.

Tuition increases are capped at six-and-a-half percent for in-state students.
Not so for out-of-state students.
No cap.
Chairman Perry.

<<Perry Two: 05>>

"It's easy to sit on the sidelines and say, 'I want a high-quality education but I don't want to pay for it.'"

<<Track Four: 06>>

Sitting on the sidelines is exactly what worries Mary Miller.
For Carolina Connection, I'm Joe Smith.

Anchor Tag:

It's unclear just when a decision will be made.
A task force will make a recommendation to the chancellor and the board of trustees.
The university system board of governors must approve any tuition increase.

For the television script, the cues are on the left-hand side of the page and the content on the right. Instructions at the end tell the director where to insert the audio and video bites.

Tuition to Increase On Cam	UNC undergraduates facing a jump in tuition and fees next year. Not much doubt about it. The only question? How much? Reporter Joe Smith talked with one student who says she can't take much more.
PKG	

<<Track One: 12>>

	Mary Miller's a sophomore from Lenoir. Her parents are laid-off furniture workers. They're on unemployment. Mary *has* student loans. And she *works* part time. Still, she struggles. And things are about to get tougher.
Miller Bite: 03	**"This is death by a thousand cuts."**

<<Track Two: 10>>

> Mary Miller has company.
> Tuition is going up for UNC's 18
> thousand undergraduate students.
> At least, that's what it sounds like.
> University Board of Trustees Chairman Roger Perry.

Perry Bite: 08

"The cost of education is getting higher and higher. If we're going to continue to give our students the quality of education they deserve, tuition is going to have to go up."

<<Track Three: 22>>

> Tuition remained flat this year for in-state students.
> That, thanks to the state general assembly, which gave the university a 15 percent budget increase.
> But cuts are looming now.
> Tuition hikes are capped at six- and- a- half percent for in-state students.
> Not so for out-of-state students.
> No cap.

Perry Bite: 05

"It's easy to sit on the sidelines and say, 'I want a high-quality education but I don't want to pay for it.'"

<<Track Four: 06>>

> Sitting on the sidelines is exactly what worries Mary Miller.
> For Carolina Week, I'm Joe Smith.

(Instructions)

Supers:
:05-:08 Joe Smith/reporting
:26-:29 Roger Perry/Chairman
:35-:38 Chapel Hill
1:07   tape out   Outcue: standard

On Cam

> Tuition, room and board are around 14 thousand dollars for in-state students; more than 30 thousand for out-of-state.
> It's unclear just when a decision will be made.
> A task force will make a recommendation to the chancellor and the board of trustees.
> The university system board of governors must approve any tuition increase.

Effects of Technology

Television is a regulated and competitive medium that depends heavily on technology. And in the past decade, it has been on a roller coaster of change.

In the last quarter of the 20th century, the television industry went from a handful of networks and few cable or satellite services to hundreds of channels that offer 24/7 news about lifestyle topics. In this century, audiences increasingly use television as an entertainment medium, relying more on online sites and social media for breaking news.

The television industry has moved to HDTV, or high-definition television, that changes the way television signals are transmitted. The picture viewers see on HDTV screens is much crisper and more detailed, giving the feeling of seeing images in a three-dimensional form. While HDTV has changed the visual aspect of television programming, writing styles and structures remain the same, and news videographers have learned that their pictures air on a wider format with greater clarity.

Social and online media are extending the reach of television, just as with other traditional media. Owners and managers are experimenting with new options to reach and retain their audiences. As handheld devices get smaller but more capable of streaming video, the competition is increasing to deliver news and programming in a way that reaches audiences—and entices advertisers.

Harold Wright, general manger of WVIR-TV in Charlottesville, Virginia, has witnessed the evolution of the television news business in the last 30 years. He notes the pressure for stations to interact more with viewers, to reach viewers through Twitter and Facebook, and to generate revenue. The station has 20,000 Facebook friends, and Wright admits he follows certain Twitter sites daily to get information.

"When the Internet was in its earlier stages, we used to hold news stories so we could present them first on TV," he recalled. "Now we immediately post content related to stories as they develop, then we put them on TV and post the video of our broadcast news stories on our website. We also stream our newscasts live on our NBC29.com website."

Many newspapers and television stations within communities are sharing the reporting of their staffs so that they can cover more of what's happening, particularly as newsrooms have endured budget cuts and employee layoffs. Some newspapers have broadcast desks where reporters can be interviewed by the television station anchor about an event or issue.

In addition to reporting on social media trends, some television reporters have Facebook accounts where they post what they consider to be interesting links and even report on them on air. This effort extends the recognition of the reporter and the station within the viewing area. Many reporters also use Twitter to share late-breaking developments in news.

Wright noted that the market and ways to deliver news continue to evolve as technology charges ahead. "New media are changing our industry, but we don't know how to profitably adapt to the change. Nobody really knows yet how all of this is going to sort out. I feel our primary obligation is to report news professionally."

Exercises

1. Write a broadcast lead for each of the following stories:

    ■ The Federal Reserve Board raised interest rates one-quarter percent, which means consumers will be paying higher rates on their adjustable-rate home mortgages.
    ■ David Parkinson of Waverly County won first place at the county fair yesterday for the largest squash. It weighed 6 and 1/2 pounds. David is 6 years old.
    ■ Competition begins Thursday for the National Collegiate Athletic Association title. The tough competition in basketball has been dubbed March Madness.

2. Using the formula that a 60-space typed line equals 4 seconds of air time, write a 20-second radio script for the following information:

    A masked man robbed the university dining hall of $3,000 and escaped after locking the dining hall manager in a closet.

    Tony Jones, the manager, escaped unharmed. Police are looking for a heavyset white man about 5-feet, 5 inches, and weighing about 175 pounds. He has a round face and broad shoulders. Jones could give no description of the man's facial features because he had a stocking pulled over his face.

    Jones was preparing the payroll when he heard a noise in the kitchen. When he went to investigate, he said, the man came charging at him. The man ordered him to open the safe and put money in a blue sack. Jones complied, and the robber locked him in a closet before leaving.

3. Write a 20-second radio script for the following information and indicate an audio you could use to illustrate the spot:

    The legal age for minors to buy cigarettes in most states is 18. Studies show that underage youth or minors still buy up to 500 million packs of cigarettes a year, despite the states' laws. About 25 states have agreed there should be stricter laws on tobacco products, and even tobacco industry officials claim their advertising is not geared to teenagers.

4. Write a 30-second television script for the following information. Type the copy in the right column and indicate on the left what visuals you would use.

> A coalition of child-care advocates marched on the state legislature today. They distributed flyers encouraging legislators to approve monies during the current session that would subsidize the cost of day care for families earning below $16,000 a year. They claim that day-care costs in the state have skyrocketed, and even working families are finding it hard to pay for quality day care out of their salaries. The coalition estimated 15 percent of the state's population fell below the federal poverty level guidelines last year. The coalition officials said that last year it had to turn away almost 400 families who needed financial assistance because funds just were not available.

5. Interview the manager of your local television station. Find out what he or she thinks about the future of television in regard to information delivery. What changes have been made in the last year to use social media to extend the station's reach to audiences? How is breaking news handled?

6. Based on the information in Exercise 5, follow the television station's Twitter feed or Facebook page. Keep a log for a week on what types of news, features, or other stories the station chose to post. Did you link to the full story? What motivated you to do that? Did you find yourself more informed about local events and issues?

References

Finn, Seth. *Broadcast Writing as a Liberal Art.* Englewood Cliffs, N.J.: Prentice-Hall, 1991.

Friend, Cecilia, Challenger, Don, and McAdams, Katherine C. *Contemporary Editing.* Chicago: NTC/Contemporary Publishing Group, 2000.

Radio-Television Digital News Association Web site. www.rtdna.org.

Tuggle, C. A., Carr, Forrest, and Hoffman, Suzanne. *Broadcast News Handbook: Writing, Reporting, and Producing in a Converged Media World.* New York: McGraw-Hill, 2006.

Wright, Harold. "New Media—A Work in Progress." Email summary per author request. June 1, 2012.

14

Strategic Communication

The president of a national company that operates health clubs and sells exercise equipment wants to improve its corporate image. In addition, he wants to increase the company's name recognition in the fitness market. He needs to develop a plan for integrated advertising, including online and social media, with public relations efforts in the community around each health club. But he doesn't know how.

That's when he seeks the talents of professionals who can develop a strategic plan to target specific audiences and develop the communications tools to reach them. The plan will use PR and advertising in an integrated marketing program that might include news releases, pop-up Internet ads, mention by niche bloggers, a Twitter presence, sponsorship in a community bike race, and local appearances of well-known athletes at company gyms.

This book has focused on producing factual content for audiences. Many writers, editors, multimedia producers, and others in advertising and public relations jobs perform the same tasks. But in addition to factual information, they usually have a specific, persuasive message to share. The goal is to influence people to buy their products and services or to take some other sort of action, such as writing a legislator or donating money. Whether the purpose is persuasive or not, these writers have to consider audiences, content, message style and format, mode of delivery, and cost.

Most journalism and mass communication programs separate public relations and advertising as courses of study, but many students take one or two courses in the other subject. Some jobs specifically require PR skills, others just advertising, and others knowledge of both.

In today's world, students need some knowledge of social media strategies and resources so that organizations and companies can extend their reach in ways that audiences adopt. They also need to know how companies collect demographic information to target advertising specifically to an individual.

As the PR director for your town's historical society, you might write the news release to promote the society's annual Christmas tour of homes. You might keep the website updated, blog once a week about historical spots worth visiting, and solicit a local company to underwrite the cost of anniversary events marking the town's founding.

As the marketing manager for a retail company, you might use data collection software to design pop-up ads for high-income consumers who have a history of using your products. To reach all the company's audiences, you would need to be versatile in a variety of communications methods.

Many advertising and PR professionals are joined in what the industry is calling integrated marketing communications—and what we will refer to in this chapter as strategic communication. While all communication is strategic, this concept is more so for advertising and public relations. It requires input and planning for all aspects of message delivery from advertising to direct marketing to news releases—whatever is necessary to get a client's message to the audience. It also requires knowledge of the company's business strategy and the organization's mission. Technology has changed the way advertising and public relations messages are delivered, and professionals must stay current as even more media products develop and others fade.

All aspects of strategic communication cannot be covered completely in one chapter in a media writing text. The aim here is an introduction to concepts and communication tools that would be explored more fully in specific courses. Strategic communication is also in great flux. Where it once focused marketing materials primarily to the traditional media of newspapers, television, and radio, the reach today is much broader and requires consideration and adoption of new technologies. What is in vogue today might not be tomorrow.

This chapter looks at the importance of

- good writing in strategic communication,
- the practice of public relations,
- public relations communications tools,
- advertising strategies, including branding and product placement,
- guidelines for effective ad writing, and
- strategic communication in an online, social media world.

The Importance of Good Writing

Within strategic communication, good writing is at the heart of every successful and effective campaign and event. Strategic communicators must send news releases and buy ad space so audiences, including media, know that their organizations or businesses exist and what they do. The reporter must receive the media advisory or see the microblog before becoming interested enough to write a story. The mother must read the brochure on a community's child-care offerings before calling for more details. The college student must peruse the company's home page to learn about its internship program.

Practitioners of strategic communication must identify audiences to determine the best methods to reach them, then conduct research, plan and carry out communication strategy, develop specific tools, and evaluate plans. Writing is crucial at each stage, but particularly in crafting the messages to important audiences.

As writers, strategic communicators must be able to adopt different styles and tones because they have many more audiences than the writer for a newspaper, TV or radio station, website, or specialized publication. They might also have to learn a specific style, such as in microblogging. In the morning, they might write a general-interest news release and in the afternoon a speech in the language style of the company president. Or they might write an article for the employee newsletter, proofread ads in a statewide magazine, and later consult with a production company on a video script for an upcoming stockholders' meeting.

PR and advertising students often take mediawriting courses to learn the inverted pyramid and other formats. The courses also teach the fundamentals of grammar, punctuation, and style, and they stress the need for clear, concise, and accurate writing that interests and attracts targeted audiences. Students are also trained in building and maintaining websites for specific audiences. These courses are essential because content is crucial, regardless of the way it is delivered.

Strategic communicators generally divide writing into two categories: informational and persuasive. The organization's or company's objective for the particular message will determine the type and tone of the writing.

Informational writing is just what it says: It presents materials in a straightforward, factual manner—just as in journalistic writing. A brochure can be informational, simply listing an organization's history, services, address, and telephone number. It might give specifics about an upcoming program or new service.

A brochure can also be persuasive. Persuasive writing clearly pitches a particular point of view and reflects a specific attitude and behavior. Some types of communication are deliberately persuasive. A direct mail letter to university alumni will try to persuade them to donate to endowed professorships. A public service announcement on radio will encourage listeners to donate canned goods to the local food bank.

The best persuasive writing makes use of two-way communication. The writer sends out a message, and the recipient responds by acting on it—by sending a donation, signing a petition, casting a vote, or running a 5K charity race. Much two-way communication builds the relationship between the communicator and the individual and prepares the way for future contact.

Persuasive writing follows the tenets of good writing: accuracy, clarity, and conciseness. A brochure can be persuasive and still be informational, using facts and graphics to portray positively the company's position.

Such writing adheres to journalistic standards of fairness and impartiality. Experienced practitioners know that arguments explained factually will have more impact than those that are biased and long-winded.

Public Relations in Practice

Professor emeritus James Grunig at the University of Maryland defines public relations as the management of communication between an organization and its publics, or audiences: employees, clients, customers, investors, and alumni. Grunig emphasizes the importance of strategy and analysis in approaching those relationships.

Successful public relations builds and maintains good relationships between an organization and its publics through balanced, open communication. Public relations might be as simple as an announcement by the local literacy council about its success rate for the past year. Or it might be a complicated integrated marketing program that incorporates public relations with advertising, investor relations, and market research.

A wide variety of organizations use public relations: local, state, and national nonprofit organizations, such as the American Heart Association; schools and universities; small companies; multinational corporations; and local, state, and federal government, including the president and the armed services. Public relations practitioners share information with the public to help the organization achieve its objectives to announce new products or to show how a company works as a good corporate citizen or as a leader in its field. The objective might be public service, as in broadcast messages to reduce teenage pregnancy or to warn smokers about the risks of heart attacks.

Some people erroneously think of public relations as free publicity, believing there is no cost. But real public relations—ongoing, two-way programs of communication with various publics—is expensive. Organizations must pay salaries and production costs, buy supplies and equipment, and cover additional overhead expenses, such as office space, computer support, and utilities. Even keeping up with publics through electronic means, which might seem to be low-cost, is not cheap, requiring at the very least equipment and continual training for staff. Most are hidden costs the public does not see or consider.

Public Relations Stages

In the late 1960s, Scott Cutlip and Allen Center identified four stages of a PR campaign: research, planning, communication, and evaluation. Despite time and technology, public relations practitioners still follow those stages today.

For example, a bank plans to change its checking account service in three months. The PR department is charged with informing the bank's publics of the change. Look at how the PR practitioner would use each stage.

Research. Research is essential to allow the bank to state public relations goals, identify relevant publics, describe the service, and identify its strengths and weaknesses. For example, the bank's reputation would be a strength; competition from other banks' services would be a weakness. Research could use focus groups or surveys to determine what the bank's customers would like in a checking account and how they get information.

Planning.   In planning, the practitioner devises a communications plan or strategy. The practitioner determines what communications tools will be used during the next three months and sets deadlines for each one. For example, the best dates for sending news releases to trade publications differ from those for statewide media. Magazines usually need copy several months before publication dates; broadcast media, online sites, and newspapers can publish information within 24 hours of receiving it. There might also be strategies for communicating directly with publics, through the company website, blogs, Twitter, and even direct mail letters that can be strategically targeted to certain publics.

Communication.   In the communication stage, the practitioner carries out the plan. Information is written and distributed via the communications tools: news releases, microblogging, brochures, fact sheets, annual reports, other publications, websites, social media sites, and speeches, just to name a few. Although writing is important in developing the plan, good skills are crucial in the communication stage.

Evaluation.   In evaluation, the practitioner uses qualitative and quantitative ways to evaluate the success of the communications plan and strategy and any change in audience attitudes or behavior. After each news release is emailed, the public relations staff could count the number of hits to the company's website for the new product details. Staff could survey customers to determine how well they understood communication about the service. And branch managers could count the number of new accounts opened as a result of the campaign.

Public Relations Tools

Public relations practitioners often use the term *public relations tools* or *communications tools* to describe the techniques or methods they use to reach audiences. All require solid writing skills. What follows is a list of the more common communications tools and a definition of each. Courses in public relations writing teach students how to research, write, and distribute each type of tool. In today's environment, most of these tools would also be kept online in a company's or organization's online media kit on its website. Media could access these tools prior to face-to-face contact, such as an interview with a company official. Such information should always be current; users will be frustrated if pages or documents are months or even years out of date.

News releases.   Articles that describe newsworthy events and are distributed to specific editors at media outlets usually by email or online. They are written in a style that follows media style so that they are ready to be used.

Feature releases.   More in-depth, less timely articles about organization employees, projects, services, issues, or observances. These releases generally are targeted to a specific publication and can be sent via email.

Media kits.   Folders or online locations that contain relevant information on the organization or company or a special event. These materials provide background to media or interested individuals and can be packaged to target specific groups. Included are fact sheets, photographs, reprints, biographies, audio, and other material.

Direct mail letters.   Letters written to targeted publics, generally to solicit support for a project or event. Many direct mail pieces are still sent via the U.S. mail to homes, while others use special-interest, email listservs that individuals have joined.

Brochures.   Booklets or folders that include general information or targeted information about an organization or one of its services or products. These pieces are designed to be easily mailed, distributed at events, posted online, or attached to email.

Websites.   Full-service websites that give information about an organization, invite the public to interact in a multitude of ways from email to games, and link to other sites. Websites should have a clear, visible path so users can find contacts and ask questions via email.

Multimedia presentations.   Productions that incorporate text, audio, photography, graphics, and video to supplement information and to depict more visually an organization or its services. Such presentations can be posted online or distributed on CDs.

Specialized publications.   Newsletters, annual reports, and magazines produced for internal audiences, such as employees, or for external audiences, such as customers and the general public. In some corporate settings, annual reports are produced by the investor relations department, and the PR practitioner might help with some writing and coordinate with financial and legal departments to produce the final document. Many specialized publications are online and linked to websites.

Video and audio news releases.   Actual video footage with or without sound, such as voiceover, to give radio and television stations ready-to-use material. The video is referred to as "B roll." Some organizations have broadcast footage or other images that can be downloaded from their websites.

Public service announcements (PSAs).   Short announcements, generally sent ready-to-read to radio stations or in video format for television use or posted on websites to be downloaded.

Blogs.   Short for Web logs. These online diaries are managed usually by one person, but companies are also using them for conversations among internal and external audiences and to share product or service information.

Social Media. Electronic communication, such as networking sites or microblogs, to share content, information, opinions, or other messages with online communities and to create dialogue with these publics.

Communications tools are incorporated into strategic plans that serve as guides for PR activities or campaigns. Corporate communications departments, for example, begin work in the fall on the next year's plan to support business goals, specific actions that might occur in a certain cycle or season, and target dates for all communication.

Of course, not all public relations is planned. A reporter might call the corporate communications department requesting information to support her story idea. The PR practitioner will respond or arrange for a company executive to reply. The practitioner might email the reporter a media kit that contains a mix of communications tools, often called *collateral materials*, such as a news release, a fact sheet, a CD with a multimedia program, and a brochure.

Considering Audiences or Publics

Just as in any other mass communication field, PR practitioners must consider their audiences, or what they call *publics*. The publics are the people who will be visiting websites, accessing microblogs, reading news releases, or viewing video news releases. They might be employees, customers, other business-people, town residents, lawmakers, reporters, or officials in local, state, or federal government agencies. Public relations practitioners must identify and know which publics are important to their organizations.

Imagine you are the public information director for a university system that is planning a capital campaign to raise funds for new buildings. The university administration has set a goal of $500 million. In planning a strategic campaign, you would have to consider the university's publics: alumni, faculty members, staff members, students, students' parents, potential students, donors, legislators (if the university is public or state supported), the general public, and the media. From that list, you might identify and prioritize five key or important publics.

Practitioners use research, such as informal surveys or focus groups, to learn about their publics and how their publics get information. Then practitioners can decide which communications tools, are most effective in reaching publics and the tone and style of the messages.

As part of targeting publics, PR practitioners must be aware of the growing diversity of U.S. society and how to reach specific audiences. Specialized publications, social media, and websites can be geared to particular interests. Some PR materials are translated into other languages, such as Spanish. PR professionals monitor media and other resources to stay up to date. For example, a range of news pertinent to African-American audiences can be found on Black PR Wire at www.blackprwire.com and for Hispanics on Hispanic PR Wire at www.hispanicprwire.com. More on considering diverse audiences is discussed in Chapter 11.

How Media Reach Publics

An important public for any public relations practitioner is the media. The media learn about an organization through standard communications tools, such as news releases and media advisories, and through social media, such as Facebook or microblogs. Media writers also use annual reports, websites, investor publications, executive speeches, brochures, federally required filings, and other means to find information about companies.

In turn, practitioners must know the media and their audiences, formats, and content, just as they know about other targeted publics. Media are essential audiences because through newspapers, magazines, radio and television, specialty publications, online sites, and other locations, the practitioner reaches many other publics. Among the primary tools PR practitioners use to reach their publics through media are news releases, fact sheets, brochures, public service announcements, websites, and microblogs.

News Releases

News releases provide timely information to media. They might announce a promotion or staff change; a service or product; new information, such as the effects of legislation or the results of a survey; financial earnings; an upcoming event; or community service, such as a scholarship program. Some news releases, especially those concerning events, are presented in the form of media advisories, or short notices that tell media in advance about an event or issues and that focus on *who, what, when, where, how*, and *why*.

News releases must contain some of the news values discussed in Chapter 5: prominence, timeliness, proximity, impact, and magnitude. They might also include conflict, oddity, or emotional impact. The lead should summarize the relevant information. The rest of the release should be organized in the inverted pyramid style of writing discussed in Chapter 6 and follow Associated Press style, which most news outlets use.

The practitioner's goal in sending a news release is to get the message out through media. But the practitioner must remember that news releases are uncontrolled; the final story is up to the reporter's and editor's discretion. Reporters might use the release as a basis for an expanded story, or they might take the news release as is and even give the PR writer a byline. Reporters, editors, and producers need news releases that are complete, accurate, newsworthy, and appropriate for their audiences. They will favor news releases in a ready-to-use format.

News releases should contain the PR contact name, organization, organization address, organization phone number, fax number, email address, and even the PR contact's home or mobile phone number. The information goes above the headline. (If the organization's address is readily visible on letterhead, it can be omitted.) The date and the headline follow, setting up the contents of the news release.

Often PR practitioners will include a contact name and telephone number within the text of the news release, usually at the end, to ensure that further information is available to interested publics if the news release is run verbatim. Online news releases, such as those posted on PR Newswire or other online news services, often contain a link so readers can give feedback on whether the information was useful and understandable. Examples of news release formats can be readily found on company and government websites.

Fact Sheets

Fact sheets generally are one page long—or the front and back of one sheet—and are designed to be read quickly. Information about the organization, a service, a product, or a special activity is highlighted in short segments.

An easy way to develop a fact sheet is to follow the news elements discussed in Chapter 5: *who, what, when, where, how,* and *why.* A statewide children's forum is planning its annual fund-raiser. The fact sheet about the upcoming event would be organized:

Who:	The Children's Forum
What:	Annual fund-raiser—a black-tie dinner and dance
When:	June 14
Where:	Downtowner Hotel
How:	Ticket prices $75 per individual for the dance and $150 for dinner and dance through the institute offices at 444-1234
Why:	To raise money for administrative and program costs

A separate historical fact sheet could be developed to provide background information, such as how long the event has been held, how much money it has raised over the years, how many children have benefited, and so on. Both fact sheets would be included in a media kit.

Fact sheets should also contain the contact name, organization, and phone numbers if reporters and others want additional information. When fact sheets are produced or updated, the date should be placed at the bottom of the fact sheet to indicate how current the information is. Fact sheets are also uncontrolled. Media can use the information any way they wish.

Brochures

In writing and designing brochures, PR practitioners are limited only by their talent, creativity, and budget. With desktop publishing and multimedia technology, many more organizations can produce high-quality, good-looking brochures for little cost. They can also publish brochure content online. The more work that is done in-house, the more money saved. Here are some questions to answer when writing a brochure:

- Is the brochure persuasive or informative? If the brochure's primary role is to persuade, it will be written with emotional language, comparisons, and familiar concepts. If informative, material will be to the point and language straightforward.

- Who is the audience? Whether the audience is specialized or general will determine the level of language used.
- Will the brochure be saved or read and then thrown away? Deciding how it will be used will affect the cost and design.
- Will the brochure be a stand-alone piece, such as those in a display rack at a state's welcome center, or a collateral piece in a media kit or with a related website? A stand-alone brochure must be complete because it cannot rely on information in other pieces or online links.
- What is the appropriate format? If the brochure is a self-mailer, it will need to have an address space. Information has to be arranged logically. Decisions have to be made on artwork, such as photographs, and on graphic elements and white space, the size, the number of folds or pages, and how the brochure will open. Also important to consider is how the brochure copy will be formatted for a website.

Brochure copy should be short. People are looking for a quick read. Each panel should stand alone, and copy shouldn't jump from one panel to the next.

Brochures, whether printed or online, are appealing to PR practitioners because they are controlled messages. The practitioner has the final say on copy and design. No one can change the content or wording; the only uncontrolled aspect is placement. Brochures left at a doctor's office depend on the visibility of the display rack to reach a target audience. Brochures given to volunteers to hand out might not be widely distributed.

Public Service Announcements

Public service announcements, or PSAs, are generally short pieces that give information of value to a specific audience. Traditionally, media have accepted brief PSAs from nonprofit organizations or government agencies and run them for free. Most PSAs range from 30 to 60 seconds in length, though some produced by individuals and posted on YouTube can run as long as the creator thinks people will watch.

Public service announcements must get basic information into as few words as possible. When they include audio, writers must grab listener attention and write clearly so that the message is understood. Increasingly, the audio and transcripts of PSAs can be downloaded off websites. Running PSAs is part of broadcast outlets' community service programming.

Any online search can uncover hundreds of PSAs on any topic, produced by anyone from individuals to government agencies and on topics ranging from healthy behaviors to public services. For example, PSAs on drinking and driving use images from simulated accidents to the bar scene from *Star Wars Episode IV: A New Hope* to catch attention and ensure that the message gets through to audiences. PSAs are free for the taking because the creators want the message widely distributed.

Social Media Outreach

Media writers often will follow microblogging accounts, such as Twitter, to find out what individuals as well as organizations are saying about themselves. That information could give them ideas or names of potential sources for stories. Many writers have their own microblogging accounts that readers or viewers follow for breaking or feature news. A practitioner who has a Twitter account and wants to reach specific publics could tweet data that would be of interest to those publics and also to a media writer, who in turn might repost the information.

Many details of world events have been broadcast via social media, especially from the interior of countries such as Syria, where journalists have trouble accessing information. The first photos of earthquakes or other natural disasters now are posted via social media before ever reaching a media outlet.

The world of social media is in flux, and practitioners must stay current on the latest site or forum that is attracting audiences. College students who become experts in social media marketing are increasingly in demand by companies and organizations that recognize the need to reach clients and consumers in new, faster, and popular ways of communicating.

Companies are developing policies governing employee use of social media applications to protect intellectual property and confidential material. More on social media can be found in Chapter 8.

A Case Study in Public Relations

Any practitioner whose client is launching a new product or service must bring into play traditional and new media to reach as many potential buyers as possible. Take the case of a writer who decided to self-publish a book and, therefore, did not have access to a publishing house's public relations machinery. Because the book combines historical events in Chicago, starting in the 1940s, as told through the experiences of a major newspaper's operations, she knows she must reach a diverse audience that includes World War II buffs, celebrity watchers, journalism historians, people interested in media history, and those who follow politicians.

The public relations plan around the launch of the book combined traditional news releases within the local community where the author lives, an article in a journalism history publication, and fact sheets about the book and the author with outreach to microbloggers on topics, such as World War II, history, or classic movie stars.

Prior to the publication date, the author produced the fact sheets and the news release and had headshots taken to create a media kit. A freelance writer contacted the history publication editor to get information about length and content of the story, interviewed the author, and wrote the piece. A social media marketer researched and identified relevant blogs, then grouped them by topic of interest, prioritizing them based on their influence, as gleaned from such information as the number of Twitter followers.

When the publication date became known, the social media marketer went to work a week in advance, emailing a short, customized message to each blogger along with a password-protected link to the manuscript. The hope was that these niche bloggers would review the book and share an online link where the book could be purchased. The media kits were emailed to the targeted list, and the freelance writer sent the article to the editor.

The public relations plan for the book was carried out on a minimal budget and with no advertising. The upfront research and preparation allowed the plan to go into effect in conjunction with the publication date. The strategy required knowing audiences, finding the ways they accessed information, and presenting a hook that would entice them to learn about the book—and possibly buy it.

Advertising's Role in Strategic Communication

Advertising is probably the first form of media writing that children notice. Kids respond to ads, often before they can talk. Toddlers excitedly point at Ronald McDonald and "read" the golden arches as a sign for food even before they know their ABCs. The Nike swoosh and the Target red bull's-eye are easily recognizable. By combining color, sound, movement, symbols, and language, advertising creates some of the most powerful messages in our world today.

Like all media writing, successful advertising depends on good writing. "Good advertising writers are writers first. They are personal writers—people who bring their own feelings and reactions to the product," observes Professor John Sweeney, former creative director for a major U.S. advertising agency. "Good advertising slogans are some of the most effective communication available today. They have a concise, pithy, sensory quality that other writers would do well to study and adopt."

Volney Palmer is generally credited with being the first advertising "agent." In 1841, he began selling newspaper advertising space for a profit. Advertisers prepared their ads; Palmer and other agents placed the ads for them. Such advertising agents became concerned with copy and artwork for the ads several years later. In 1869, F. W. Ayer started N. W. Ayer & Son, an advertising agency that provided writing, art, and media placement to its clients.

Advertising agencies have changed throughout the years, but the seeds of the modern agency planted with N. W. Ayer & Son and other early agencies still exist today. Today's advertisers have myriad ways to reach consumers, not just traditional newspapers or billboards. A company might create a "like" page on Facebook or target ads to electronic listservs to start conversations with customers.

New technology and the changing media habits of audiences require advertisers to stay current on the most direct ways to funnel product information directly to specific and special audiences. They can do that through software that tracks consumers each time they go online and make a purchase. Details such as type of computer or Internet connection can give retailers information on a consumer's possible income bracket and purchasing power.

Despite almost two decades of exploration and development, the advertising-technology world is still in its toddler stage, while maturing giants such as Google are creating ad-tech platforms that cross-market products. Others are watching their experience to determine their behavior and business decisions.

In any delivery mode, the goals of ad writers, across media, have remained constant over the years:

- To communicate availability of products to audiences
- To communicate product benefits to audiences
- To provide accessible information about products in a few words
- To communicate reasons the product can deliver benefits

Other goals might include corporate image building, as in cases when a company wants consumers to view it as a good corporate citizen; response to a disaster, such as a utility company telling customers how soon power will be restored after massive hurricane damage; or public service messages, such as alerting audiences to the dangers of unprotected sex or the benefits of low-fat diets.

Some people think of advertising as propaganda—distorted information designed to lead, or mislead, its audience. Propaganda is manipulative, and so is advertising, some people say.

Unlike most other forms of published writing, advertising is one-sided by its very nature. No one wants to spend his or her advertising budget extolling the benefits of a competitor's product. But the absence or inclusion of other products does not have to mean that an ad is biased if the information presented is accurate.

Presenting your best to the public, Sweeney explains, is a core value of advertising culture. Advertising that is less than ethical is not advertising; it is propaganda or huckstering or manipulation. Professional advertising writing is an accepted form of argument—a fair argument—and it abides by an ethical code.

Advertisers are subject to many government rules and regulations. The Capital Council of Better Business Bureaus advises that all advertisers stay abreast of regulations through subscription services, such as *Do's and Don'ts in Advertising* or the *National Advertising Case Reports*. Such subscription services are quite expensive and typically are used by large agencies or companies. The industry has self-regulators, such as the National Advertising Review Council (NARC). The Federal Trade Commission has information on how advertisers should behave, whether advertising in print or electronically.

Skechers agreed to make a $40 million settlement in 2012, the largest ever in money refunded to customers, according to the Federal Trade Commission.

The FTC said its advertising hyped benefits of its Shape-ups shoe line and noted that a chiropractor in one of the ads is married to a Skechers marketing executive. The previous year Reebok agreed to a $25 million settlement in regard to deceptive advertising for several of its shoe lines. Both companies disagreed with the FTC's charges but agreed to the settlements to avoid expensive, protracted legal battles.

Advertising and Today's Audiences

The environment for advertising has changed tremendously in the past decade. New media and new products compete for audience attention, and advertisers no longer assume that mere publicity will lead to success or consumers using services and buying products. Advertising on mobile devices is still in early development, and some observers say its use will increase as electronic devices allow the tracking of consumers' locations and buying patterns.

In conjunction with technology, today's advertisers must continue to understand how audiences think, feel, and behave, plus they must know what devices they are using to search for products and services. Only through knowing those audiences' preferences can those advertisers reach consumers.

Ad production is seldom the work of just the writer. In most cases, the copywriter is part of a team. For an advertising agency, the team could include account planners, who determine audience interest and product competition; an account executive, who oversees the account and serves as the liaison with the client; the copywriter, who takes the research and theme and creates text; the art director, who designs ads and other collateral pieces for the client; the creative director, who oversees the concept and production; media planners, who develop strategy for placing ads; social media marketers, who determine outreach; and the media buyer, who places ads.

All members of the team must know the others' roles. The copywriter often works most closely with the art designer on aspects such as typeface, length of copy, size of the ad, and graphic elements. While much advertising is moving online, many advertisements are still full-page, full-color ads in print media.

Advertising Strategy

When a copywriter and an art director sit down to design an ad, they are guided by a creative brief that presents the advertising strategy. The advertising strategy is made up of the media strategy (where the ads should be placed and when to place them) plus the creative strategy (what should be in the ads and how they should look). Generally, the ad strategy lists marketing or business goals, such as more sales or improved corporate image; target audience; positioning, or how consumers perceive the service or product vis-à-vis competitors; benefits; creative approach, such as tone of the advertising message; and appropriate media to reach audiences.

The plan will help the copywriter to know what structure will have the greatest appeal to the target audience. The creative approach is affected by the goals—selling a product, providing general information about a company, positioning a product as superior among its competitors, or boosting a corporate image. Target audiences will determine the tone of language and whether the ad must be serious or can have humor. Even corporate image will affect how a copywriter pitches an ad.

Targeting Audiences

The process of identifying and communicating with specific audiences is often called *targeting*. A skateboard company might target teens 12–15 years of age about a new material that makes the boards strong but more flexible. With the target group in mind, the ad writer designs messages that will appeal to teens, and ads are placed in locations where teens go, such as malls, or online publications on skateboarding.

Targeting is a necessity in an era of budget consciousness, increased media channels, and audience fragmentation. These trends have limited advertisers' ability to reach mass audiences. To get maximum benefit from advertising dollars, advertisers select target audiences for specific products. Beer, tires, and trucks are advertised in sports sections and game broadcasts; toys and sweet cereals are advertised with children's programming; and pain relievers, laxatives, and investments are sold with financial news.

Professional market research is used by major corporations to identify the best possible markets for particular ads. Cluster marketing attempts to impose some order on the new media-and-audience mix, dividing Americans into subgroups and predicting specific media behaviors, as well as products and services that each group is likely to use. Companies, such as Nielsen, offer their clients detailed information about consumers, helping them identify appropriate segments of shoppers, and then target advertising among radio, online, mobile, or television options.

Companies can gather consumer behavior information from when, where, and how people go online. Software tracks anyone who chooses to shop online, including what is purchased, when, and how much. Armed with such information, advertisers can target to an individual consumer online ads offering special deals from companies that the consumer visits regularly online. While some might object to having unknown marketers know that much about them, others counter that people make a choice to go online.

Product Placement

You are watching a sitcom on television, and the scene moves to the kitchen. On the counter are cereal boxes, diet soda, and cans of spaghetti. All the product names are clearly visible. Having real products in movies and on TV shows is called *product placement*. The benefits of product placement seem obvious: product reinforcement and possible recall when consumers shop.

Product placement has been around for years and is a fairly well-accepted advertising tool. When product placement first came into vogue in movies, skeptical viewers wondered about the effects of certain products on younger viewers. For example, the war on tobacco and on smoking among teens included criticism of tobacco product use in movies.

Most product placements are the result of a business deal, and some companies make product placement their business. Popular television game shows, such as "The Price Is Right" or "Wheel of Fortune," award specific products or trips to participants. The product names and logos are repeated during each broadcast. Companies also sponsor events, such as bicycle races, and have their products and logos included with promotional materials, such as T-shirts.

Advertisers use the word "integration" to describe incorporating specific products into movies, television shows, and other places. Most agree that integration needs to make sense, that the product needs to fit with the show's theme or message. Product placement is less common in magazines or newspapers.

Whether product placement actually works is still debated. Research has shown that in some instances, cross-cultural differences prevent audiences from connecting with the products they see. As more and more products are included within television programming, some observers are concerned about consumers' reactions to their top picks becoming more commercial-laden. Most companies, however, like the idea of product placement as yet another way to create brand recognition.

Branding

Branding has become a primary factor in advertising strategies. Consumers are part of the branding process every day as they walk around with the apple on their MacBooks, Lexus logos on cars, Gap on baby overalls, Starbucks on coffee cups, and L.L.Bean on backpacks. Meaningful branding can inspire depths of customer loyalty, and companies rely on such loyalty to maintain sales and market share.

When a product is branded, it has a brand identity immediately recognizable to consumers. Part of the immediate recognition is an icon, a slogan, a jingle, and even colors that can trigger in consumers' minds the product—the distinctive theme music used by NBC with the Olympic games, the mermaid in the green circle on a Starbucks cup, or Ben & Jerry's black-and-white cows. Once consumers recognize the product, they ascribe certain feelings or values that create brand loyalty.

Companies have determined that brand loyalty is a combination of overall satisfaction and confidence or trust. Another component is emotional attachment. Think about brands you use and why you use them. You may use a certain deodorant soap because that's the one you always found in the shower's soap dish at home. Whoever did the grocery shopping in your family had a loyalty to that particular brand. Perhaps you prefer a certain type of fast-food pizza because of the crust, the toppings, the service, or the group of friends you usually eat pizza with. People develop a familiarity with a product, and they may oppose any changes to it. Companies bank on consumers and their ties to certain products.

More and more in the last two decades, companies have considered branding as a key to retaining customers and profits. Research has shown that the cost of attracting new customers is five times the cost of keeping current ones. As a result, companies are investing more research dollars into understanding what makes customers stick with certain products or brands.

Businesses have adopted practices so they can determine which products and services customers buy and why. With technology, they can even track individual customers' visits to websites or geographic locations via their cell phones to find out more about their habits and needs. Such information is invaluable in focusing advertising—and in developing other areas that provide customer service.

Branding is important for anyone writing or designing ads. Choosing the right representative to represent the product can be critical. When golfer Tiger Woods's infidelities became public, sponsors AT&T and Accenture dropped him, and others such as Procter & Gamble scaled back their relationships. Nike, however, stood by him. In another example, Salma Hayek joined the ranks of other celebrities in the well-known "Got Milk" ad campaign. Swimmer Michael Phelps took on endorsements after his seven gold medals in the 2008 Olympics, showing qualities of determination, stamina, and just an average American who won big.

Tips for Ad Copy That Sells

No matter how an ad is produced and distributed, its strategic messages must motivate consumers to at least consider, then buy, products and services. In some cases, copywriters can include photos, video, games, or other ways to attract audiences. Even in today's digital advertising world of shorter messages via electronic delivery, writers should consider advertising Professor Jim Plumb's broad tips:

1. **Identify selling points.**   Focus on concrete reasons for purchase. An abstract reason to buy a Subaru wagon is safety, but a concrete selling point is that buying a Subaru keeps the driver from shoveling snow or paying a tow truck because of the car's all-wheel drive.
2. **List the benefits.**   Find and list the benefits of your product that are important to your audience. Build your ad content around these benefits. Make sure they are unique from competitors' products. List them in the ad if you can, but be sure to mention them in some way. Don't forget to look for intangible benefits. Sometimes the most powerful benefits are intangibles, such as the mood a perfume creates or a feeling of belonging that comes from a health club.

3. **Identify the single greatest benefit of your product.** Research should identify the quality of your product that is most meaningful to your intended audience. Then create a headline or slogan that will convey this benefit. With "Just Do It," Nike sells discipline, an intangible benefit, as its star quality. By communicating benefits in a few words, ad content has the power to modify attitudes and behaviors.

Some contend that if such rules are followed, the result will be well-produced but boring ads. Other techniques might be needed to go beyond just noting the functional aspects of products. The touch points of a brand could be accented through fun or zany advertisements to attract attention, particularly in products with seemingly few differences from their competitors, notes Professor Sweeney. Examples of unusual packaging are the man playing Mayhem for Allstate and even the Gecko for Geico.

Other experts in the field offer practical reminders for better advertising content. In their book, *The New How to Advertise*, advertising executives Kenneth Roman and Jane Maas note that a good ad will show solutions to a problem; that effective ads will aim for target audiences; and that every good ad projects the tone, manner, and personality of the product. Other experts recommend that ad copy should note details; use well-chosen language; have strong, clear words; have one unifying idea or theme; contain a beginning, a middle, and an end; and, for the most part, use correct grammar.

Strategic Communication in a Digital Environment

Since the mid-1990s, any organization that wants to reach audiences quickly and provide in-depth information has moved internal and external communications online and to digital outlets. Corporate newsrooms use their websites to post the latest news releases as well as archives of past releases and visuals that can be downloaded. In-house websites, email lists, social media, and electronic message boards help employees and investors stay in touch, whether they are in the same building or scattered across the world.

Strategic communicators use online software to track how many people access information on a website or incorporate GPS tracking via smartphones to know users' geographic locations when the user clicks "allow" on the location pop-up. Instead of sorting through clips of print stories, a media manager can count clicks to digital sites and find out how long the visitors stayed on the site, what information they accessed, and what they bought. Software can also help build electronic listservs.

Companies that once relied on blinking banner or pop-up ads on websites are moving to more innovative ways to reach customers. Such innovation has been necessary to catch a visual audience with a short attention span. While some companies still buy space next to editorial content on Web or social media sites and use animation and video to attract attention, others have moved into creating social media communities that revolve around particular interests, such as sports.

Many companies have developed apps for smartphones so that customers can be a touch away from product information or services. Convenience sells products, and any communicator must be creative and proactive in thinking about digital ways to increase an organization's reach and relationship with its audience.

Nike is an example of a company that continues to use traditional media, although it has cut spending on TV and print advertising in the United States by 40 percent, according to a *Fortune* article. Instead, in 2010, the company spent almost $800 million on nontraditional advertising. Nike has used new technology and gadgets to interact almost one on one with some of its various customer bases. Where Nike has reached an audience of 200 million on Super Bowl Sunday, it can now do so via its digital sites, including those on social media.

Nike made advertising history during the 2010 World Cup when it debuted on its Nike Football Facebook page—which had 1 million fans—an ad called "Write the Future." Within a week, it had 8 million views, thanks to a viral explosion via blogs and social media posts.

In a move to generate business from advertisers, Google rolled out its DoubleClick Digital Marketing to enable advertisers to reach consumers who move among digital platforms. It noted in a DoubleClick Advertiser Blog: "It's hard to reach the right audience at the right momentum with the right message when every channel requires its own system." Google is proposing solutions to the problem of reaching customers and selling that service.

Other professionals are watching the leaders and examining case studies to rethink advertising and public relations strategy and what will be cost-effective and reach as many people as possible.

Case Studies in Strategic Communication, an online journal, launched in 2012 to publish cases as a useful resource for practitioners and teachers. Cases relevant to public relations, marketing, advertising, and strategic communication will be included. In the first year, several cases showed how organizations and corporations had used social media, such as the Centers for Disease Control's posting to You Tube to provide health messages about swine flu.

For college students, the specifics that make up digital strategic communication could be wildly different at graduation day from what they see in today's landscape. Those students who are comfortable and knowledgeable in a social media, digital environment will find more kinds of career opportunities. Students must also have the skills to use words effectively and correctly and to add visually rich elements to any message.

Exercises

1. You are the public relations officer for the Campus Literacy Program. You want to recruit more volunteers to serve as readers to children in the community.

   a. Identify the audience(s) you are trying to reach as potential volunteers.

   b. Knowing your audience interests and media usage, identify three communications tools you would use to reach each audience.

   c. What information would your audience(s) need to make a decision whether to volunteer? Make a list.

   d. How could you evaluate the success of your communications effort?

2. You are the public relations director for Bicycle World Equipment Co. You are to write a news release for the local newspaper based on the following information.

   Also write a tweet that you would post on your Twitter site to drive followers to more information in the news release.

   > Bicycle World is planning to sponsor bicycle safety clinics in the public schools located in Wayne County, the company headquarters. The clinics will be held on two consecutive Saturdays from 10 a.m. to noon. Each of the county's six elementary schools will house the clinics. People who want to attend must call 555-3456 to register. The clinic is open to children 6–12 years of age. Each child must have a helmet.
   >
   > Bicycle World staff members will check each child's bicycle for safe operation and indicate on a check-off list any equipment that needs repair. Children will be advised of good bicycle safety, such as wearing helmets, riding in bike lanes, and using proper hand signals. Then each will be allowed to enter an obstacle course, which will test their riding proficiency. For example, as they ride down a "road," a "dog" may run out from between two cars. Children's reactions and reaction times will be monitored. After the road test, they will be briefed on what they did well and what they need to improve. At the end of the course, they will receive a certificate of accomplishment.
   >
   > "We believe bicycle safety is crucial for children," said company president Dennis Lester. "With just a little guidance, children can learn habits and rules that could save their lives. Those of us in the bicycle business want to ensure that children who use our products do so competently and safely. We want them to enjoy bicycling as a sport they can continue into adulthood."
   >
   > The clinics are free.

> Bicycle World is a three-year-old company that produces bike frames, components, bike helmets, clothing, and road guides to bicycle routes. Company President Dennis Lester is a master rider and formed the company to provide quality equipment to bicycle enthusiasts.

3. From the above information, write a one-page fact sheet based on the bicycle clinics sponsored by Bicycle World Equipment Co. You would be the contact, 555-3456. The company's address is 67 W. Lane Blvd., Your town, Your zip code.

4. President Dennis Lester at Bicycle World wants to implement a comprehensive advertising and public relations plan that will help sell more bicycles in your community. Develop a strategy that identifies three target audiences and then include at least three types of advertising and PR activities, including social media, to reach each target audience.

5. Based on Exercise 4, you are to create an advertisement for Bicycle World to reach parents of children who ride bicycles. Make a list of the words that would appeal to parents looking for children's bikes, focusing on the prominent characteristics of bikes. Write at least three possible headlines for your ad, focusing on a characteristic in each.

6. Invite a professional who specializes in strategic communication to visit your class. Ask this person to talk briefly about advertising and public relations as part of strategic communication in today's competitive media environment. Have him or her talk about the importance of good writing and the influence of the Internet in strategic planning.

References

American Advertising Federation Web Site. www.aaf.com.

"Auto Giants Push Harder for Magazine Product Placement." www.adage.com/news. cms? newsId545807. Accessed August 19, 2005.

American Society of News Editors. www.magazine.org/Editorial/Guidelines/Editorial_ and_Advertising_Pages/. Accessed September 3, 2005.

Bendiger, Bruce, et al. *Advertising: The Business of Brands.* Chicago: The Copy Workshop, 1999.

Burton, Philip Ward. *Advertising Copywriting,* Sixth Edition. Lincolnwood, IL: NTC Business Books, 1990.

Cutlip, Scott M., Center, Allen H., and Broom, Glen H. *Effective Public Relations,* Seventh Edition. Englewood Cliffs, N.J.: Prentice-Hall, 1994.

ElBoghdady, Dina. "Skechers agrees to $40 million settlement for claims about shoes' benefits," *Washington Post,* May 17, 2012.

Felton, George. *Advertising Concepts and Copy.* Englewood Cliffs, N.J.: Prentice-Hall, 1994.

"Marketing beyond the Pop-Up." *Advertising Age,* March 10, 2003.

Medialink Web Site. www.medialink.com.

Nielsen, "MyBestSegments." http://www.claritas.com/MyBestSegments/Default.jsp?
    ID=0&SubID=&pageName=Home. Accessed June 20, 2012.

Plumb, James. "Writing Advertising Copy, " Lecture, University of Maryland College
    of Journalism, College Park, MD, 1990.

PR Newswire Web Site. www.prnewswire.com.

Public Relations Society of America Web Site. http://www.prsa.org.

Roman, Kenneth, and Maas, Jane. *The New How to Advertise*. New York: St. Martin's
    Press, 1992.

Wilcox, Dennis L., and Nolte, Lawrence W. *Public Relations Writing and Media
    Techniques*, Second Edition. New York: HarperCollins College Publishers, 1995.

Appendix A

Keys to Grammar Quizzes

After years of working with these exercises, we recognize that no single answer exists for any exercise item. Each answer we provide is what we consider to be the best or preferred answer, rather than the only answer.

Grammar Slammer Diagnostic Quiz
(pages 23–24)

1. Punctuation error. A comma replaces the semicolon because clauses on either side of a semicolon must be independent.
2. Subject-verb agreement error. The subject of the sentence is list, so the verb must agree. It is the LIST that HAS BEEN TRIMMED.
3. Punctuation error. A period or semicolon replaces the comma because commas may not separate independent clauses. Some would label this a comma splice; others, a run-on sentence.
4. Punctuation error. A comma is needed after OCTOBER 25 because commas follow all elements in a complete date and the phrase OCTOBER 25 is nonessential.
5. Sentence structure error. The modifying phrase, TRADITIONALLY EXPECTED TO BE IN CONTROL OF THEIR SURROUNDINGS is misplaced and needs to follow the word STUDENTS. In its present position, the phrase modifies THE INSECURITY.
6. Word use error. LIE instead of LAY when no action is taken.
7. Agreement error. HIS or HER books.
8. Punctuation error. Semicolons are used to separate all punctuated items in a list. A semicolon is needed after EASTERN.
9. Word use error. Use NEITHER and NOR as a matched pair. The same goes for either and or.

10. Pronoun error. Use the pronoun IT to agree with the noun COMPANY, a singular thing.
11. Punctuation error. Phrases that rename subjects (appositives) are nonessential and therefore set off by commas. Place a comma after COMMITTEE.
12. Subject-verb agreement error. LIVES is the verb that agrees with the true subject of the sentence, which is ONE.
13. Punctuation error. Commas follow both elements of a city and state (N.C.) combination that occurs in mid-sentence, even if the state abbreviation ends in a period.
14. The past tense, USED, is correct usage in this idiom. Agreement: Children used to believe THEY could acquire.
15. Sentence structure error. Including WILL PLAY in this list of parade items makes for faulty parallelism. Delete WILL PLAY.
16. Sentence structure error. This sentence is incomplete. It is a sentence fragment. Even though it is lengthy, it has no verb. Add the word CAME after SEVERAL PEOPLE.
17. Comma error. Semicolon or period needed after COOKIES.
18. The coordinate conjunction AND is used here when a subordinate conjunction, such as BECAUSE or THAT, is needed; also delete the comma after COMPLAINED.
19. Modifier problem. His muscles are not being a weight lifter.
20. Agreement. ITS SKIN.

1. Correct. Your princiPAL is your PAL. PrincipLES are LESSONS.
2. Correct. A waiver is a document of permission; a waver is a person who waves.
3. Incorrect. A bore is a dull person or event. A boar is a wild pig.
4. Incorrect. A navel is a belly button. Naval means pertaining to the navy.
5. Correct. StationERy is sold by stationERs.
6. Incorrect. A role is a part in a play. A roll is something rolled up, even a class list.
7. Correct.
8. Incorrect. Canvas is cloth. To canvaSS is to cover thoroughly, as in a canvass of the neighborhood.
9. Incorrect. Complement is a verb that means to complete. A compliment is a flattering statement.
10. Correct. Cite is correct in this case, short for citation.

Slammer for Commas, Semicolons, and Colons (pages 28 and 29) (Rule numbers are noted before each answer.)

1. Rule 4, comma after Bowl.
2. Rule 7, commas after Blimpo and man.
3. Rule 10, semicolon after strings; Rule 9, comma after basses.
4. Rule 2, comma after tall, after dark, after reading, and after fishing.
5. Rule 5, colon after concern; Rule 2, comma after 2 and 4; Rule 5, comma after 2009 and after yours.
6. Rule 8, comma after Dad.
7. Rule 10, semicolon after halftime; Rule 4, comma after however.
8. Rule 1, comma after bill.
9. Rule 7, comma after well.
10. Rule 10, semicolon after disappointment.
11. Rule 6, comma after 4, after 2008, after Baltimore, and after Md.
12. Rule 12, colon after semester; Rule 2, comma after journalism, after English, and after political science.

Slammer for Subject-Verb Agreement (pages 31 and 32)

1. include	9. exhibits	17. are
2. appear	10. are	18. are
3. gives	11. constitute	19. is
4. results	12. was	20. is
5. have	13. believes	21. teach
6. do	14. is	22. is
7. is	15. decides	23. consider
8. are	16. typifies	24. disagree

Slammer for Pronouns (page 34)

1. his or her	6. is	11. its
2. its	7. was	12. it
3. himself	8. was	13. are
4. its	9. their	14. himself or herself
5. its	10. is	15. his or her

Slammer for Who/Whom and That/Which
(page 36)

1. whom (everyone adored whom/him, the object of the sentence)
2. who (who/she was, the subject)
3. whom (Alvin avoided whom/them, the object)
4. who (who/she needed, the subject)
5. whose (not who's or who is health)

1. which, commas after gun and sale (the fact that the gun was on sale is additional, nonessential information)
2. which, comma after car (the mileage is additional, nonessential information)
3. that, no commas (the Jersey plates helped police identify the car, so essential information)
4. who, commas after Texans and drawl (Texans are people, so who or whom; who is subject of spoke; how they spoke is nonessential information)
5. which, commas after gun and compartment (where she kept the gun is nonessential information)
6. who, no commas (again, person takes who or whom; who/he is subject of was; phrase tells which officer was shot, so it is essential)
7. that, no commas (the lack of bullets allowed the officers to get the gun, so the phrase is essential)
8. which, comma after jail (the view from the jail cell is nonessential)

Slammer for Modifiers (page 38)

1. The waiter served ice cream, which started melting immediately, in glass bowls.
2. Correct.
3. On the way to our hotel, we saw a herd of sheep.
4. Correct.
5. The house where Mrs. Rooks taught ballet is one of the oldest in Rockville.
6. Correct.
7. Without yelling, I could not convince the child to stop running into the street.

8. The critic said that after the first act of the play, Brooke's performance improves.
9. While we were watching the ball game, Sue's horse ran away.
10. Correct.
11. The bank approves loans of any size to reliable individuals.
12. Running on the beach, I saw the sun rise before my eyes.
13. Correct.
14. Aunt Helen asked us to call on her before we left.

Slammer for Troublesome Words (page 39)

1. The most Effective writing follows good writing principLEs.
2. The pROspective budget for the coming year will include raises for the city's firefighters.
3. An incoming ice storm will Affect whether we can drive to work tomorrow.
4. The state historical society will re-enact signing the state constitution in the CapitOl.
5. The country's navAl force has been reduced.
6. His desire for money is his principAL guiding force in business.
7. The coach said the team ignored his adviCe to make it a passing game.
8. Jiminy Cricket said Pinocchio should let his consciENCE be his guide.
9. The engineer eliminated the High Road siTE because it sloped toO much.
10. Returning the stolen car to ITS owner is the best decision.

Appendix B

Key to Math Test

Slammer for Math (pages 43–45)

1. **a.** The ratio of men to women is 9:4. Subtract the number of women from the total to get the number of men.
    b. To get percentage, divide the difference by the base. In this case, 4 (the number of women) is divided by 13 for a percentage of 30.8 percent (the actual number is .3076 but is to be rounded to the nearest tenth for 30.8).
    c. The same process is used to figure the percentage of Hispanic men on the jury: Divide 1 by 13 for an answer of 7.7 percent.
    d. Again, divide the number of African-American men (1) by the base of 13 and you get the same answer as 1c: 7.7 percent.

2. **a.** To get the cost for the center alone, multiply the number of square feet by the cost per square foot, or 15,000 by $85 for a cost of $1,275,000.
    b. The cost follows the same formula: Multiply 15,000 square feet by $25 for a cost of $375,000.
    c. To get the total cost, add the cost of the building to the cost of the furnishings for a total of $1,650,000.
    d. To round off, remember that you round up after 5, 50, 500, 5,000, and so on. Rounded to the nearest 100,000 would be $1.7 million.

3. **a.** To get the size, multiply 12 by 8 to get the size of one booth (96 square feet); then double it because each booth is two parking spaces. The answer is 192 square feet. Note: You can't double both measurements then multiply because the booth will grow only in width, not in depth. The booth measures 16 by 12, which is 192 square feet.
    b. The company can rent 120 booths. Divide the number of spaces in the parking lot by 2 because each booth is two spaces.
    c. Multiply the number of booths (120) by $30 to get $3,600.
    d. Go back to 3a. One booth is 192 square feet. If you get two booths, you get 384 square feet.

4. **a.** First, you have to calculate how many units per $100. Divide the house value of $175,000 by 100 and you get $1,750. Then multiply by the tax rate of 85 cents (.85) to get a tax bill of $1,487.50.

   b. Under the new tax rate of 88 cents, Sarah will pay 1,750 times .88 or $1,540.

   c. To calculate the increase in her tax bill, you need the difference between the old bill and the new bill. Subtract $1,487.50 from $1,540 to get $52.50. To find the percentage increase, remember difference divided by base or $52.50 divided by $1,487.50, or a 3.5 percent increase.

   d. To find out how much her property would increase, multiply $175,000 by 5 percent (0.05) to get $8,750. Add that amount to $175,000 to get the new value of $183,500. To find the tax bill, follow the steps in 4a. Remember to use the new tax rate of 88 cents per $100 to get the answer: $1,617.

5. **a.** The total female respondents was 275. Add the female counts of 107, 137, and 31.

   b. Total respondents is 627. (Add all the individual counts for male and female.) Divide the total number of women respondents, 275, by 627 and the percentage is 44.

   c. You cannot add rows of percentages to get this answer. You have to go back to your counts. Fifty-four respondents (male and female) supported Tucker. Divide by the total of 627 and the percentage is 8.6.

   d. The same rule for 5c applies here. A total of 274 supported Small, divided by the total respondents of 627, and you get 43.7 percent.

6. The key here is that if she has a 75 percent chance of band practice, she has only a 25 percent chance of going to the fair (100 percent −75 percent band practice = 25 percent no band practice). Multiply the two prob-abilities, 50 percent (.5) her mother will take her and 25 percent (.25) no band prac-tice. The likelihood she will get to the fair is 12.5 percent.

7. The answer is C: $310. If he earns $7.50 an hour, 25 cents more means $7.75 an hour. Multiply by the number of hours, 40.

8. The answer is 61.29. You multiply the number of pounds by 0.454 to get the number of kilograms.

Appendix C

A Gillette Teacher Finds His American Dream After Fleeing a Country Where He was Forced into Battle as a Child

By Nathan Payne,
City/Living Editor Gillette News-Record

Bertine Bahige leaned back against the wall outside his classroom and looked at the ceiling as he tried to regain his composure.

It was his second class of the day and he already had been in a conversation with a student, trying to keep her in school long enough to graduate in a few weeks.

"I try to give them hope," he said, looking upward.

He wouldn't turn to face his class until he could regain his normal smiling demeanor.

Only minutes before, the 32-year-old math teacher had been greeting each of his students, as he does before every class. He asked them about their most recent performances in track or soccer or sometimes he ribs them about not keeping their grades up in English class.

"I don't understand that because I thought you all spoke English," said the teacher, whose native language is French.

Then came along the one he'd been looking for, the one whose future could hinge on his effort.

He knows she's looking ahead at life hoping to survive, not considering the idea of thriving. It's a fate he once faced himself, a fate he wants to help her overcome.

The countdown

Bahige caught her as she approached his classroom a few minutes before the bell rang.

Like an elementary school pupil might, the high school senior scuffed her feet a little on the polished terrazzo floors as she stepped to within a couple of feet of her teacher. The girl, a pre-calculus student, looked down and kicked at a line with the toe of her retro sneakers while the last few of her classmates walked past and took their seats.

They both knew what was coming. She is a good student, but she had missed several classes.

"Where have you been?" Bahige asked with concern in his voice.

She looked up with the forced smile of someone who has given up, the kind of smile that is betrayed by the pain in her eyes.

"My dad has been in jail, Mr. B," she said. "We're about to lose our house. I have to work."

She quietly told Bahige that her mother wasn't around, her uncle was moving across the state and she had nowhere to live. She had been working as many hours as possible to simply feed herself, and told him that by the end of the week, she could be sleeping in her car.

"I think I'm going to have to drop," she said, shaking her head.

"It's only 15 days," he pleaded with the senior, hoping she wouldn't lose the past 13 years of hard work, hoping she would see the value in a high school diploma.

She explained that administrators told her that they had limited options for a student like her who has missed so many days of school. How could she worry about coming to the last weeks of school, taking her last exams and wearing a cap and gown if she were homeless?

"I'll talk to some people," he said. "We will figure something out. Just come back to class Wednesday."

She uttered a less-than-reassuring "I'll try," and took her seat between a pair of classmates.

Bahige gazed at the ceiling as though he might find answers there.

He had only a few moments to compose himself before going into his classroom to try to make vectors, parametric equations and matrices relevant to his students' lives.

"I would let her stay in the spare bedroom in my house if it was appropriate," he said, trying to suppress his frustration with the system in which he works.

As he walked through the doorway, he smiled, said "good morning" and pointed to the chalkboard on the west side of his classroom.

On it was a calendar with a white "X" through each of the days past — a countdown to graduation.

"You only have 30 days left until graduation, that's only 15 days in each class," he said. "Make sure you get your work done. You're almost there."

As Bahige began to diagram a math equation for his students, he was as far from his past as he could be.

A chance at life

Bahige doesn't like to sit around with nothing to do. That's when the memories get the best of him.

The place where his journey began, in his hometown on the eastern border of the Democratic Republic of Congo, still occupies his mind during quiet moments.

It is the place where he was snatched from his home at age 13. It was the last time he saw anyone in his family.

More than 500,000 refugees from Rwanda had spilled over the border into the country after the genocide in that country in 1994. Infighting between ethnic militias and the government continued to widen the divide that began in the neighboring country.

Rebel militia leaders were in need of soldiers for their battles over the mineral-rich land that lies under the country's jungles. They went from house to house looking for boys like Bahige who were old enough to hold a gun, old enough to kill for their cause.

Bahige, the oldest boy in his family, was taken along with his older sister. Today, out of 10 children, he knows of only four who survived.

"It's something I wish I could lose, but it's become part of me," he said. Bahige spent a year in a rebel camp, forced to fight for a rebel leader, watching other children die.

Boys were forcefully conscripted into the militias where they were used as soldiers and porters. But girls often were treated as "soldiers' wives," suffering a much worse fate than death.

Life was about survival. Trusting anyone but yourself could get you killed.

Militia leaders were quick to sacrifice their child warriors because they were easy to replace and train. As many as 30,000 child soldiers had been pulled into battle by a variety of militias, as well as the country's central government by 2006, according to numbers reported by the BBC.

The children often were told to make a choice between joining or death.

Once in the force, commanders indoctrinated the boys and encouraged them to become hardened warriors. They were snatched from the relative comfort of childhood and forced into a world that scars even battle-hardened professional soldiers.

It was a place that he knew would mean certain death if he wasn't able to get away. About a year after he was abducted, Bahige decided that he must escape.

In the dark of night, sneaking away from camp through the thick jungle, he encountered a group of rebel soldiers. Thinking quickly, he made excuses for why he was away from camp at night. If they didn't believe him, he would surely be executed.

For days, he waited to be summoned when someone realized he had lied. But it never happened.

A short time later, he again snuck away from the camp in the night.

With silent steps, he crept away, tiptoeing through the jungle. The snap of a twig or the rustling of leaves could have meant the end of his life.

"I knew I didn't have a choice for failure," he said. "Death was not an issue. There was no prison. You have to overcome fear."

It wasn't long before he made his way to a river. He didn't know where it led, but knew it couldn't be as bad as where he had come.

For three days, he hid on a hilltop near the waterway watching for other refugees to jump into large canoes made from hollowed trees and head downstream. When his chance came, Bahige made a dash, and jumped into a boat.

The trip lasted two or three weeks, he's not sure. It was marked by silently floating down the river under the cover of night and hiding on small islands during the day.

"I didn't care where I was going," he said.

When he hit Tanzania, Bahige split from the group and jumped on the back of a cargo truck. But when the driver of the truck realized that he had an unwelcome passenger, he dropped the dirty boy on the side of a road.

"I walked for five straight days," he said. "The person that tells you an uncooked meal will kill you is lying to you."

He ate raw vegetables stolen from gardens, trying to survive. But after days of walking, and a raging malaria infection, Bahige had hit his limit.

He crawled to the shade of a tree and passed out. He was dying.

"People can tell you what they want, because I know God exists," he said. "I was at peace with whatever was going to happen."

What he didn't know was that he had made it all the way to Mozambique and had collapsed next to a trail between a small village and its garden plots.

That morning under that tree, he awoke to people standing over him speaking a language he didn't know.

The language was Portuguese. It was the start of what would become his American dream.

His American dream

When Bahige was plucked out of a refugee camp in Mozambique, where he landed after escaping the militia, he was dropped in Maryland with a missionary couple. The opportunity to break free from the camp and come to the United States was offered to him only after five years of living in limbo, in a country not his own. It is a chance that few got.

He didn't know English and had to work three jobs to pay for school, but he was happy.

He rode a bicycle everywhere and taught himself English by listening to tapes at a nearby library. He took community college classes to catch up on the education that he had missed while struggling for his life.

Bahige was 23 years old, and unlike most of his classmates, had spent the past five years of his life learning to survive on his own. He took on new languages, adding Portuguese and English to the French and Swahili he grew up speaking. Years later he would expand that to six languages.

It wasn't an easy road, but Bahige didn't complain.

"That was the American dream to me," he said with a bright grin. "Bad for us here is sleeping in the homeless shelter and eating in the Soup Kitchen."

In 2006, opportunity came calling again. All the hard work mopping floors, flipping burgers at Burger King had paid off. He was offered a scholarship to the University of Wyoming where he would study to become a teacher.

That's where he met Amanda Hays, a young woman who had spent her entire life in Gillette, growing up in the relative safety of small-town America.

He graduated from UW and married Amanda. The couple recently had their second child, a baby boy named Marcus.

They moved to Gillette, where her roots are set deep and, with the help of a large surrogate family, Bahige planted his own roots.

Outside the window of the three-bedroom house he and his wife bought a few years ago is a green sod lawn that he laid himself. Downstairs is the meticulously constructed basement he finished with his own hands.

He refuses to pay someone to do a job he knows he can do himself. He has realized his American dream. His goal now is to use his skills to help those left behind find their way to their own dreams.

His past has made it easy for Bahige to connect with students who feel the dream slipping away before their lives have really begun.

"If you show them that you care enough, you'll be surprised at how much kids are willing to open up," he said. "It's not only about teaching them math." That encouragement is something he didn't have for a long time, but he knows it can make the difference.

It made the difference when he met Amanda.

Her family, the Hays and Rothleutener clans from Gillette, quickly absorbed the transplant. They even produced an 11-member cheering section for Bahige's naturalization ceremony Feb. 22.

The milestone is what Bahige characterized as a little thing, no big deal.

But it is nothing for the large Catholic family to gather dozens of people to help support one another or to celebrate a holiday.

"To end up in a family that knows what family is all about is a blessing," he said. "It was a big challenge for me to let people in." Sometimes, a little hope can make all the difference in the world.

"I know through the whole process, God had a plan for me," he said. "I think I'm not doing this for myself. I have to fight for the others, the ones who didn't make it." Today, he continues to fight, albeit not for himself.

He fights for the students who need a chance. He fights for his two sisters and two brothers who remain in a Ugandan refugee camp. He fights so that his children might grow up in a world without the struggles he has known.

All it takes is hope

Two days after pleading with his student to stay in school, Bahige got what he had hoped for. When class began that Wednesday in April, she was there, in her chair, waiting to learn math.

Each day as Bahige crossed off another box on his countdown to graduation, she was there.

In a week when she and a few hundred of her classmates walk across the graduation stage, it doesn't matter that no one else in the Wyoming Center knows the significance of her accomplishment. Bahige will clap a little louder. She will smile a little wider.

They both know what it took to get there.

Hope.

June 1, 2012
Reprinted with permission from the *Gillette News-Record*

Index